The Autobiography

HENRY SHEFFLIN

D1493398

PENGUIN
IRELAND

PENGUIN IRELAND

UK | USA | Canada | Ireland | Australia
India | New Zealand | South Africa

Penguin Ireland is part of the Penguin Random House group of companies
whose addresses can be found at global.penguinrandomhouse.com.

First published 2015
001

Copyright © Henry Shefflin, 2015

The moral right of the author has been asserted

Set in 12/14.75 pt Bembo Book MT Std
Typeset by Jouve (UK), Milton Keynes
Printed in Great Britain by Clays Ltd, St Ives plc

A CIP catalogue record for this book is available from the British Library

ISBN: 978-1-844-88288-5

To my wife, Deirdre; my daughters, Sadhbh and Siún;
and my sons, Henry Junior and Freddie

Contents

Prologue

Isn't it human to want the Hollywood ending? I did.

In the dream, I'd play a blinder on my last big day for Kilkenny, securing that tenth All-Ireland medal through some heroic personal deed. The perfect sign-off, a hurling fairytale.

It didn't quite happen that way, of course. I didn't start a Championship game in 2014: management seemed to have lost faith in my ability to last seventy minutes. This challenged me in a way that I hadn't been challenged before.

I still believed absolutely that I could do it. But thirty-five-year-old inter-county men aren't exactly commonplace these days and I suspect that my age became factored into the story of my last year in a Kilkenny jersey.

I can honestly say it didn't diminish my joy at the final whistle in Croke Park on 27 September. True, I'd only played a small amount of time in the two All-Ireland finals against Tipperary, but it was a really tight, united Kilkenny group. Young and old bonded in a seamless way, despite it being a year in which individual status in the dressing room altered pretty fundamentally for quite a few of us.

Still, I left Croke Park that evening with one consuming ambition.

I wanted to get back there. I wanted to play one last full game in the great stadium, if only to prove to myself that I could still do it. And I knew now there was probably just a single way that could be achieved.

I had to get back there with Ballyhale.

To put it mildly, the road to fulfilling that ambition was heavily mined. Within Kilkenny, the view would have been that Shamrocks were a team with our best days behind us. Maybe the perception was we had gone soft.

But something quite powerful flowered in the group as we won our sixth Kilkenny title in nine years, beating the defending champions, Clara, in the county final. Personally, I felt a great sense of freedom in my hurling now. Released from the pressures of trying to prove myself all over again within the Kilkenny set-up, it was as if some kind of simplicity had been restored to my game.

On one of the foulest days of the year, we then won the Leinster title, beating the Offaly champions, Kilcormac-Killoughey, after extra time. The longer that game went on, the stronger I became. In the All-Ireland semi-final against Gort, I scored 0-5 from play.

With Shamrocks, I had re-discovered my love for the game. The sheer, uncomplicated joy of playing.

It's true, I didn't pull up any trees in the final against Kilmallock but, God, the feeling of victory was truly special. Just looking around the group, thinking of all the stories shared, all the friendships carried from childhood, gave it a really personal resonance.

I didn't get overly emotional at the finish and I can't say I was looking around Croker thinking, 'This is my last time on this field . . .' I suppose I just felt very eager at that moment to be with my family, given they knew better than anyone what this all meant to me.

As a child, my overwhelming ambition had always been to wear the Ballyhale colours in Croke Park. Now, this victory had a special meaning for me. Because I'd made it back and, in doing so, maybe proved something fundamental to myself. Against all odds, I'd got the fairytale.

The thought of retirement always frightened me, given the sheer size of the door it would mean closing in my life.

But the question didn't have to be answered until after the All-Ireland club final. That was a blessing. Ballyhale's story allowed me to put up a shield against the endless inquiries about my future intentions with Kilkenny. That shield only came down with the final whistle in Croke Park on St Patrick's Day.

We all met up in Carrolls Hotel in Knocktopher the following day to celebrate Shamrocks' sixth All-Ireland title. I remember particularly wanting to go for a pint with Paul, my brother, that morning and he collected me from the house. Soon enough, the banter was flying.

The Fennellys and TJ Reid were knocking good craic out of my situation, wondering aloud if I'd be at Kilkenny training in Nowlan Park that Friday. Colin Fennelly joked that he, personally, couldn't see the attraction of retirement.

'When you retire, you become old,' he grinned. 'So you needn't think you're going to be hanging around with us young lads any more!' That night, the celebrations in full flow, Joey Holden and Colin got the band to play the Clash's 'Should I Stay or Should I Go'.

I laughed as loud as everyone else, but my mind was racing. I had a sense that this was decision time and, if I'm honest, that thought trip-wired a little panic. Having the first drink, I remember thinking, 'I don't really want to be here . . .' I just wasn't settled. I knew I had something that needed to be sorted.

That Friday, I went to Brian Cody's house for our first chat on the subject and, as I always knew he would, he left the decision entirely to me. Looking back, I think my mind was already settled. I just wanted the comfort of time.

In the GAA, your other life keeps taking hold in any case. You may be defined in the national psyche simply as a hurler, but you are a family man too, you work for a living. That Saturday, we had thirty children up to the house for my daughter Sadhbh's birthday party and, later that evening, there was a function in the club for the presentation of Ballyhale's county championship medals.

I was presented with a beautiful watch in recognition of winning my tenth All-Ireland, but the formalities were clipped and undramatic. Cyril Farrell and the county secretary, Ned Quinn, both said a few kind words without there being any question of me ever taking the microphone.

I gathered subsequently that some people thought the function might have been organized simply to facilitate a formal announcement of my retirement. The clock, clearly, was still ticking in that regard.

The following afternoon, Kilkenny played Clare in a televised

National League game. I watched it from the comfort of home and, for the first time in a small eternity, felt that I was a Kilkenny supporter again. Somehow, it was as if a point of separation had already been passed; there was just a sense that the team I was watching now had different ownership.

That evening, I pucked a ball against the gable of the house, something I'd often do just to clear baggage from my head. And, going to bed that night, my mind was made up.

It was just after five when I returned from work in Dublin that Monday, ready to end the uncertainty. As I took the phone towards the living room, I remember turning to Deirdre and saying, 'Once I make this call, that's it . . .'

Then I closed the door behind me, took a deep breath and dialled.

1. King Henry? Not Here I'm Not!

I come from a part of the world where kids dream uncomplicated dreams.

If you are a boy, you hurl. A girl? You most probably play camogie. Those who grow up yearning to be airline pilots, racing drivers or heads of state probably feel a little eccentric in our midst. Maybe, in some eyes, that makes us one-dimensional, but the sky never seems unreachable in Kilkenny.

Childhood becomes a covenant with our history, because no house is far from the home of an All-Ireland medal winner or, in my case, a number of them. Ballyhale had a national profile long before I was remotely accomplished with a hurl.

It sits deep in the south of the county, pressing hard towards the Waterford border, a parish of no more than 300 houses. Throughout my childhood, we owned a pub in the middle of the village and my earliest memories are of it being almost routinely thronged for triumphant homecomings, celebrating a team that came to dominate Kilkenny hurling in the late 1970s and early '80s. That Shamrocks side, backboned by the Fennelly brothers, also won three All-Irelands.

When I'm asked if I had heroes when I was growing up, though, I struggle to summon an honest answer. These men weren't superstars in my eyes. They were just neighbours who hurled for the village. A couple of my brothers, Tommy and John, were part of the 1990 All-Ireland club championship team. To me, hurling and winning trophies was simply a tradition that Ballyhale families honoured.

Manhood put some manners on me in that regard. I came to understand the privilege of those days when I was trying desperately to win a county medal long after I'd started winning All-Irelands with Kilkenny.

That's probably why the 'King Henry' tag has never sat easy with me. There is no hurling royalty in a village like Ballyhale or, for that matter, in a county like Kilkenny. Certainly not among those still playing. Ego is best parked at the dressing-room door if you don't want to be met by a fairly rude awakening. There's no 'King Henry' in that environment. Rightly so, too.

Shamrocks' dominion stretched far at the time, and all of the great team would have been in and out of the pub. The Fennellys, Dick Walsh, Jimmy Lawlor, Wattie and Paul Phelan. Kevin Kennedy, the groundsman. Hurling seemed to tether everything and everybody together. I remember a sixtieth-birthday party for Big Tommy Walsh, now club President, one night and, because Tommy idolized Frank Cummins, Frank drove all the way up from Cork to make a guest appearance. That was the beat of life in the pub. The beat of hurling people.

The idea of one single house giving seven sons to an All-Ireland winning team seems almost ludicrous now, but back then the Fennelly brothers would have been seen as just part of the club furniture. Liam and Ger were the best known and, when Liam was Kilkenny captain in '92, RTÉ turned up with a camera crew down on the Shamrocks' pitch. They wanted a back-drop of a couple of young lads pucking the ball while Liam chatted about the final, and so I got my big TV break, a red-haired urchin doing his damnedest to get noticed on the evening news.

When I wasn't hurling, I was watching my older brothers hurl. Somebody would be detailed for pub duty while we piled into the family Toyota and headed away to Nowlan Park, Walsh Park, Semple Stadium or – on the really big days – Croke Park.

Henry and Mai had seven children in total: Aileen, Helena, Tommy, John, Cecilia, myself and Paul. As a family, I suppose we've never been overly tactile or expressive. Maybe we're old-fashioned in that regard. My wife Deirdre's family tends to be the opposite, always affectionate and animated towards one another. The Shefflins are more private about their feelings. That said, if I have a few pints with my brothers, the barriers often come crashing down and, by the end of the night, we'd have no problem exchanging soppy hugs.

The pub had been in my father's family since his grandfather bought it in 1917, and it would remain so until it was sold in '97. My mother, Mai, ran the pub while my father, Henry senior, looked after the farm. The work was hard on her. Paul arrived in June of '81, and it was only then that we got a girl in for three days a week to take some of the pressure off her. Pub hours were long and unpredictable. Fellas full of drink could lose the head with one another very easily. One of the more frightening images of my childhood would be of rows spilling out of the pub at two or three in the morning and my parents wading in to the middle to act as peacekeepers. I hated those nights. To this day, I feel literally nauseous at the sight of people swinging punches at one another.

But, for a child, the pub had its consolations. I adored the hurling talk, the endless cycle of preview and analysis. There was always a match to be dissected, a row or a selection issue to be discussed. In Ballyhale, the exchange of hurling gossip felt as natural as breathing.

If I loved the talk in the place, I hated the chores. We all did. The glass collecting, the changing of kegs, the cleaning of tables became little penances we found ourselves exposed to from the moment we were old enough to be trusted. We'd be particularly busy coming up to Christmas with card schools and the general air of giddiness that sets in at that time of year. To be fair, my sisters took up most of the slack as John and Tommy were usually needed on the farm. I recall doing my bit too, though they'd probably beg to differ. I didn't really warm to anything that couldn't be done without the accompanying fashion statement of a hurl. One of my earliest memories is of going down the fields, checking cattle with my brothers and always dragging this piece of ash behind me, like a surplus limb.

My father had built a squash court behind the pub in '76, hoping to turn it into a steady stream of income. He would have been playing a lot of squash himself at the time – there was a bit of a craze for the game in Ireland. I think he managed to break even on the court for a couple of years, but maintenance costs were high and he eventually came to regret the investment. For a time, though, the court was a real social hub, league matches drawing decent crowds, and I have a memory of Noel Skehan arriving one evening.

That squash court was a godsend to myself and Paul especially. I've no doubt that that's where some of my hurling skill came from. In the wintertime particularly, when most other kids were probably watching TV, we'd be heading out to the court with hurls, a tennis ball and a fifty-pence coin to put in the meter for the lights. We'd spend hours just beating a pattern into the back wall, taking shots at one another into makeshift goals or tussling for possession under a dropping ball. Thirty years on, that last drill was still the one I hated most in Kilkenny training: Brian Cody positioning two players in the middle of the field and landing high balls in on top of them. It calls for real physical contact that you just can't simulate.

Back then, Paul and I would go at it hammer and tongs, all the time oblivious to the outside world until one of us might get an accidental belt and run in, screaming blue murder. We were also drawn to the gable wall of Walsh's, the shop next door. Any surface, really, that could promise an even bounce of a ball.

In the springtime, the squash court drew friends like a jam jar drawing wasps, and it would become the focal point of our evenings. At a given time, you could have anything up to twenty kids playing hurling at the back of the house.

Then, in summer, we'd be drawn down to the field behind Knocktopher church. The 'Friary Field' we called it and, at the time, it was where Ballyhale played their games. It was primitive enough, a big, plain meadow essentially, devoid of dressing rooms or any such luxuries. Lads would have to tog off in cars right up until the new ground was opened in '91. Looking back, it belongs to another world.

I remember Cork were reigning All-Ireland champions when they came to play a challenge against Kilkenny for the formal opening of our new ground. Almost all of the kids in Ballyhale would have been deployed to pick stones off the field at some point, so there was a real sense of community pride afterwards as we converged on the players for autographs.

Every act of our young lives seemed somehow geared towards the passing of tests in a hurling ground. Tommy, my eldest brother, would go on to win All-Ireland Colleges (with St Kieran's) and under-21 medals, while John won an All-Ireland minor medal in 1990, scoring 0-3 off Brian Corcoran in the final replay against Cork. At the time, John was considered an exceptional talent, probably the best of us all. But then the Celtic Tiger took over and, for a man working in and making good money from the building game, priorities simply changed.

Initially, genetics didn't seem to have dealt me the kindest of hands. In my under-age days, one of the gentlest observations coming my way on the matter of pace would have been 'not especially quick'. The more candid deemed me 'chubby and slow'.

Still, a love of the game rolled in from every corner. Having gone to work in Birmingham at the age of twenty, my father hurled with Warwickshire for three years, reaching (and losing) an All-Ireland junior final against Roscommon. He worked as a machine operator for the British Motor Corporation. Mai, apparently, got permission to follow him over, on condition that they lived separately and she joined the Legion of Mary. This she did and, to this day, she winces at the memory of knocking on doors and inquiring of total strangers if, by chance, they might happen to be Catholic?

My father's own father had died suddenly at the age of forty-nine, his body discovered lifeless on the kitchen floor early on Christmas morning of '54. Heartbreak revisited in August of '63 when one of his sisters, Cecilia, was knocked down by a car and fatally injured while walking home from Knocktopher one evening with friends. To this day, we use Cecilia's First Communion dress for family christenings.

Henry and Mai got engaged in '64 and came home in the summer of '65. Shortly after they married in '67, my father took over the family pub and farm. He had hurled for a couple of years with Knocktopher before being diagnosed with a common farmers' curse at the time, tuberculosis. This effectively finished him as a player. It was a turbulent period for the game in the parish, Knocktopher and Ballyhale at loggerheads until they amalgamated under the Shamrocks banner in '72.

The next few years would reap a remarkable harvest. Shamrocks became county junior champions in '73, intermediate champions in '74 and would take The Village (James Stephens) to two replays before losing a senior semi-final in '75. By '78 the Fennellys had arrived, and Shamrocks won their first county senior title with my father's brother, Denis, as captain.

But all of the success that followed bore the copyright of one remarkable man.

Joe Dunphy was a national school teacher in Ballyhale for thirty-eight years and, throughout that time, he became the founder of a true faith. The seven Fennelly brothers would all pass through Joe's academy, as would Michael Fennelly, James 'Cha' Fitzpatrick, TJ Reid and myself.

If he was determined to get the best out of Ballyhale children academically, Joe was positively evangelical in his passion to develop them as hurlers. He was principal by the time I arrived, a small, slight man, firm but always fair.

As kids, we were in awe of him and I have an abiding memory of a group of us running around after our very own Pied Piper during an under-12 match, pleading to be given game-time. 'Sir, sir, sir,' we screeched, a pack of hungry gulls, not one of us older than eight!

In some respects, I was arriving at the end of the cycle. During my time at school, we played largely Roinn B or Roinn C competitions. The club, similarly, was struggling for a new harvest. Having been All-Ireland senior champions in 1990, Shamrocks were relegated just four years later. That's the nature of the GAA in small villages, I suppose. You get what you can from a decent crop, then you wait in hope that another might follow.

We did enjoy the good times. I have the fondest memories of the '89 county final against Glenmore. My mother is a Glenmore woman and I would have had plenty of cousins at the game just waiting to sow it into me if the Shamrocks were beaten. Tommy started that final and John would have been on the bench against a serious

Glenmore team that had the likes of Christy Heffernan and the O'Connors, Eddie and Willie, to call upon.

The final was played in Nowlan Park and, in those days, any number of people could take up residence inside the wire. That day, I was among them. With the game entering injury-time, Glenmore led by two points and I suddenly became uncomfortably conscious of how visible I'd be to my cousins. I just wasn't in the mood for what I knew they'd have in store.

I remember sidling as discreetly as I could towards the Shamrocks' dugout and the protection of my father when Paul Phelan, a great club hurler, made a wonderful break upfield, before striking the ball low and hard to the Glenmore net. I jumped as high as my scrawny legs could lift me and remember being tempted, momentarily, to go back over to where Mai's people were gathered.

Ten years old and already tribal.

The following day, the pub was thronged, everyone leafing through the newspapers, chuckling at the mad drama of it all. That Shamrocks team would keep winning right through to the following St Patrick's Day, and they were Kilkenny champions again in '91, their ninth crown in fourteen years. But they were an old team by then. Shamrocks didn't win another senior county title until 2006, by which time I had begun to wonder if maybe our village was cursed.

For me, the pub could be a real source of frustration on county final days. All of my friends used to hang around Nowlan Park afterwards, having the craic. I still see it happening today with my own nephews. It's just part of the big-day ritual, door-stepping players in the hope they might toss a sliotar or some gear in your direction. That was never possible for the Shefflins, though. The pub wouldn't allow it. We'd be hightailing it straight home to Ballyhale to make sure everything was ready for an inevitably busy Sunday night.

When John had his day in the sun against Cork in that replayed minor final of 1990, I never even made it to Thurles. Sean Walsh, a next-door neighbour and great clubman, was buried that same day and all hands were needed on deck at home for the impending funeral business.

I'd been to the drawn game a week before, sitting on my father's lap in the Cusack Stand, blown away by the sheer power of Kevin Hennessy for Cork in a cracking senior final against Galway.

Pub-life, to be fair, wasn't all hardship. Whenever Shamrocks hurled outside the county in either the Leinster club or All-Ireland, we'd run a bus from the pub, something that always made me feel at the very heart of operations. I specifically remember heading to Ballinasloe for the 1990 All-Ireland semi-final against Sarsfields of Galway. Myself and Bob Aylward, a friend and Shamrocks team-mate up to my very last match, wandered off down the town on arrival, carrying ourselves as real men of the world. Bob was fond of some girl at the time and decided to buy her a Valentine's card. It all felt very adult, though neither of us would yet have reached our twelfth birthday.

At school, Joe Dunphy focused not so much on what a hurler was, but on what he might become. I always felt that he saw things in kids that would have been hidden from general view. And he took an interest in anyone who put in the effort, never tolerating any sense of hierarchy in a dressing room.

To us, he was simply Mr Hurling. He wasn't slow to give out, but there was never a sense that he was shouting for the sake of it. Some days we'd have been hammered out the gate and Joe would just stick his head in the door afterwards to tell us we'd been unlucky.

It would be fair to say I knew, even then, I was a half-decent hurler. I remember in first class being put under pressure to play in the school leagues even though, technically, you weren't supposed to until second class.

Joe made it clear that he saw me (as Brian Cody subsequently would too) primarily as a corner-forward. I've always begged to differ, I suppose, but when I was in third class we won a Roinn C Kilkenny title and, the following year, a Roinn B. I was definitely becoming a key player at corner-forward. My role was different with the club, where I have pretty much always been seen as a centre-forward.

Still, the shirt-number was incidental. Whether with school or club, I already took my hurling seriously. Sometimes, maybe, too seriously.

Once we played a match in Muckalee, which is in the north of the county, and I can remember seething with my mother as she got lost on the way. One of the lads in the back wasn't playing and he thought it hilarious that we seemed to be going around in circles. I threw the head a bit. For me, the possibility of missing the game had me in a cold sweat. Needless to say, we got there in plenty of time. I just didn't appreciate the uncertainty.

As a family, we'd always back one another, but in an understated way. My father rarely missed a game, but he wasn't a man to be splashing easy compliments. He'd always encourage and offer advice, but would make it clear there was never any room for a 'Big Time Charlie' in his car on the way home.

Looking back, I now recognize the scale of his influence. I see a lot of parents trying to build their kids into something they'll never be. Maybe it's just the fashion to keep telling them that they're brilliant, but it ends up too extreme.

When things went well for me, Henry was more inclined to focus on what I might have done better, how I could improve. The back of our farm used to stretch up to a small apron of land, maybe a quarter of an acre in size, directly behind the school. That apron was where we played our school league matches and, if I looked out through the ditch, I could see my father standing there in his wellingtons, still on the farm, but watching.

I remember once captaining my team to one of those school league finals, and Paul happened to be on the opposition team. He ended up marking me, and Paul's style is, shall we say, tenacious. That day, he pretty much got stuck into me.

The field was so small I was inclined to go for goals from supposed '65s' and, on the day, ended up with three, plus another from play. I suppose I came away feeling I'd held my end up. But we'd lost and, that evening, my father pretty much gave it to me between the eyes.

While congratulating Paul in the house, he took me aside later out in the yard for a private chat. His opinion was that I hadn't worked hard enough for my team. The message, basically, was: don't try to hide behind your scoring total from frees. If you're not contributing from play, you're not doing your job.

To be honest, he was rarely wrong. Years later, I played an under-18 league match against The Village and the grass was a bit long, clearly unsuitable for ground hurling. But I didn't have much stomach for battle that day and so I kept just trying to jab the ball forward, essentially looking to avoid physical contact.

The Village would have been seen as a 'town team', which I suppose carried certain connotations of not being quite as tough as those of us from the country. Yet I was pretty much dodging physical contact that day. Was I a bit yellow?

Henry saw through it straight away and told me on the way home. 'You were just trying to get the ball away from you, weren't you?' he bristled. Right again.

By the age of fourteen, I was scoring pretty freely at under-age with the club and feeling strong. Aidan Cummins was centre-back and I was centre-forward. Cummins and I go back all the way to play-school, which we started on the same day in Noreen Bookle's house across the road from the pub. He is a nephew of the great Frank Cummins, and we would hurl together at under-14, under-16 and minor level with Kilkenny. I remember us getting to a Roinn B county final against Thomastown in Bennettsbridge and trailing by two points with a minute to go when the referee awarded us a penalty.

Of the three Thomastown players on the goal-line, the goalkeeper was tiny and his corner-back not much bigger. The exception was their centre-back, Niall Nevin. Standing to my right, he looked big as a wardrobe beside his team-mates.

Not exactly rocket science, was it?

Well, it might as well have been. With the smart target to my left, I drove the sliotar sharply right and straight at Nevin. Penalty saved, county final lost. I slumped to the ground after – the Thomastown lads whooping past – and began bawling my eyes out. Henry wasn't slow coming in, telling me brusquely to get up and 'grow up'.

Good advice.

I was big for my age, but not quite big enough to make the Bally-hale under-16s at that juncture. This stung my pride, because it wasn't as if they were working off a huge selection. In such a tiny rural parish, most able-bodied kids would have been confident of a game. Maybe, like my own father, the selectors could see I still had a bit of maturing to do.

I remember a game in Thomastown: although we only had seventeen or eighteen players available, I didn't get a start. They put me on about twenty minutes into the game, but only because we'd already leaked three goals. I went on as a substitute goalkeeper!

True, I did make Kilkenny's team for the Tony Forristal (inter-county under-14) tournament in Waterford, picked at corner-forward. But I did little that was memorable and we didn't make much of an impression.

I was always playing a bit of soccer too and, in national school, would have nursed a whispered dream of making the Community Games team for Mosney. Tommy had competed there as a runner and it just sounded terribly exotic. In fourth class, the opportunity arrived when a trial was held on a Tuesday night in Knocktopher. Invited in to play, I faced an awkward complication.

The school had just reached a Roinn C county hurling final against Urlingford and that game was down for the Wednesday. I wasn't specifically told not to play the soccer, but I think it was pretty clear that Mr Dunphy would have preferred it if I didn't.

I decided as a bit of a compromise to play the soccer match in goal. Word got back, naturally, and though we beat Urlingford the following day, I played poorly and was substituted. To this day, I blame the soccer. Maybe it left me with a guilty conscience.

The plan was always to follow my brothers to St Kieran's for secondary school, but I was happy enough when my mother suggested staying behind a year before sitting the entrance exam.

This meant I was now in the same class as Paul in Ballyhale, which, given I was still under-age for the hurling, suited everyone just fine, not least Joe Dunphy. We actually got to the quarter-finals of the Roinn A Championship in my final year and won an inaugural 'Country Cup' for rural schools in the county.

My father had, by now, done a stint as a selector with the Kilkenny senior team and I'd occasionally accompany him to county training. Looking back, it wasn't something I was massively into. If I felt like it, I travelled. And if I travelled, I'd invariably end up pucking a ball around Nowlan Park with Podge Delaney, whose famous father – Pat – was also serving as a selector.

My preference, though, was to hang around with the lads at home, playing out our own All-Irelands against the squash-court wall or down on the new Shamrocks field. I was hurling a lot with the club now and, with the shoots of a new crop coming through, we had begun contesting a lot of under-age county finals.

The step up to secondary school, I knew, would ask very different questions of me. We had always travelled as a family to the colleges matches and I was hugely aware of St Kieran's stature in the game. I particularly remembered the excitement of seeing Tommy win that All-Ireland in a team that included the great under-age stars in Kilkenny of that time, DJ Carey and Adrian Ronan. Those two were already household names, men who had featured on the county senior panel before they even sat their Leaving Cert.

Tommy and John both boarded in St Kieran's, but Paul and I were going in as day pupils. This probably made the transition that bit less daunting, as I'd often watched John literally cry into his breakfast on a Monday morning at the thought of heading back in for another week.

There was – and still is – an aura to the college that could very easily intimidate a newcomer. The corridors are lined with photographs of teams from the past, almost all with the seemingly compulsory silverware positioned in front of them. You get a compelling sense of history in the place. And, I suppose, of duty.

In my first year, I made the under-14 panel, but we lost a Leinster final down in New Ross to a Good Counsel team whose goalkeeper, Niall Mackey, was almost unbeatable. Niall was from Glenmore and, years later, I would end up sharing a house with him in Waterford. To be perfectly honest, there wouldn't have been too many falling over themselves with excitement at my early impact in St Kieran's.

A local man who worked in Glanbia, Willie Darmody, would give us a lift to Kilkenny in the mornings. But often we'd have to thumb our way home as Mai and Henry were too busy with bar and farm work to collect us. I have a particularly vivid memory of those black evenings coming up to Christmas in my first year. The under-14s trained after school and I'd be absolutely starving afterwards, walking down to the Springhill ring road to begin what could often become a bit of a safari home.

Some nights I'd be so hungry getting in the door, I'd all but eat the plate Mai put down in front of me. At night, all four boys slept up in the loft where, in the depths of winter, it could feel colder than the North Pole. I shared a double bed with Paul, and there was always an argument about who'd turn off the light. The modern indulgence of central heating had not reached us up there and it felt like we were sleeping on the slates. You could say we grew up with a lot of love, but little sense of privilege.

Homework would be done in the bar. You'd be clearing glasses or pulling pints between subjects, Mai overseeing everything.

By our second year at St Kieran's, we no longer needed to hitch lifts home. A local man – JJ Houlihan – started running a bus service to Kilkenny from Knocktopher twice a day (and he still does) and that took a lot of the randomness out of our arrangement.

It's been pretty well documented that I barely made the under-16 panel at St Kieran's. Going into the final trial match, I had a sense that I wasn't going to make it. In fact, I'm pretty certain that I'd already been written out of the equation. But Adrian Finan decided to play me at full-forward, and I suppose some days you'll just hit a game when everything runs your way.

I scored something like 4-7, then waited an excruciating few days for the panel to be put up on the noticeboard. When it was, I frantically began reading from the top down. Goalkeepers first, then corner-backs . . . There were maybe twenty-six names and there, rock bottom, I finally found 'H Shefflin'.

In by the skin of my teeth.

Though I eventually made the starting fifteen, my form wasn't exactly sending shock waves across the county. I was a strong player, essentially, in the lower grades. I captained Shamrocks to an under-16 'B' county title and I was now getting my game with South Kilkenny. But whenever I stepped up to full inter-county grade, it just felt a step too far for me.

There was also the odd little experience that made me wonder about my mental strength. Playing in the Nenagh Co-Op under-16 series one year, I took a fairly high belt that frightened me a bit. I hadn't been going well at corner-forward and I took this as a gilt-edged invitation to escape. So I feigned concussion.

At the time, I wasn't sure I really fitted in and I suppose I just wanted to be free of the pressure. Even on the bus journey home I pretended I had a pain in my head when I had nothing of the sort. That would haunt me for a long time afterwards because, basically, I knew I'd bottled it. There was nothing physically wrong with me that day. The problem was in my mind.

I skipped 'Transition' in Kieran's, moving straight into Fifth Year and immediately making the senior team. This was massive for me. If I was going to fulfil my ambition of becoming a Kilkenny hurler, making the starting fifteen with Kieran's was pretty much obligatory. Not much was expected of a predominantly young side that year (1996), but we went all the way to an improbable All-Ireland win. My own involvement, mind, wasn't maybe what I'd dreamed it would be.

I was picked at corner-forward for our opening match in Leinster against St Peter's College, Wexford. The game was barely two minutes old when the ball came skittering towards me and, pulling first time, my marker managed to break a bone in my foot. That was that. Two minutes into my senior career, bye-bye Henry, almost certainly for the season.

I had two pins inserted and was on crutches the day we surprised

Good Counsel of New Ross in the Leinster final. We then beat Antrim opposition in Navan to make the All-Ireland final, at which point I just couldn't bear being sidelined any longer. Maybe two weeks before the final against St Colman's of Fermoy, I begged our manager, the late Denis Philpott, to let me get the pins out early.

He consulted my parents and I was duly booked into the Ardkeen hospital in Waterford for a procedure that would turn into something of an ordeal. The surgeon managed to get one pin out, but couldn't extract the other. I was in a fair bit of pain during the process and the foot became quite swollen through all the pulling and dragging.

Did I care? Not when agreement was reached that, even with one of the pins still in my foot, I now had a fighting chance of playing in the final.

Timmy McCarthy, the future Cork inter-county player, was an absolute superstar of that Colman's team, but then they were a team of stars. We had a lot of guys who would become high-profile hurlers subsequently, men like Tipp's Donnacha Fahy and Willie Maher or Kilkenny's Michael Kavanagh, Sean Dowling and Podge Delaney. Our centre-back was David Carroll, son of the late, great Ted. But, at the time, we were given little chance. The consensus had been that Good Counsel were the strongest team in Leinster that year, but they just happened to get taken out. We were greenhorns. St Colman's were strong favourites.

For the next two weeks, I virtually ran myself into the ground to prove my fitness, and eventually I was given the green light to start at corner-forward. I scored a point within seconds of the throw-in and, while I wasn't exactly pulling up trees after, I did OK in what turned into a magnificent team performance. They moved me to full-forward eventually, where I managed to throw my weight around to reasonable effect!

The final whistle triggered extraordinary scenes. I'm not sure any of us could quite believe we were champions of Ireland. Champions of the world.

★

It wouldn't have been all hurling in my life at this time. I continued playing soccer for a good few years with a local club, Southend, more for fitness purposes than anything else. In my final year at St Kieran's, the college soccer team got to a provincial final and the manager asked me to play. There was no conflict with the hurling as, sadly, we'd had the misfortune of running into Good Counsel and Niall Mackey again in the Leinster final. It was played in New Ross and we thought we had an even stronger team than the one that won the All-Ireland. But Good Counsel just hurled better than us and Niall produced another goalkeeping performance straight out of Lourdes. I'll never forget the sense of silent dejection that hung over our post-match meal that evening in the Hotel Kilkenny.

The defeat meant that my last sporting engagement with St Kieran's was with the soccer team. The Leinster final was played at Buckley Park and I was picked up front alongside a certain Martin Comerford, who, back then, played a lot more soccer than hurling. 'Gorta' was seen locally as a pretty accomplished striker and he actually set me up for a goal that day. The game was drawn and we then lost the replay in Dublin, yours truly squandering a couple of chances.

It being my last year at Kieran's, I took immense pride subsequently in being presented with the 'Sports Star of the Year' award at the post-Leaving Cert prize-giving. Put it this way, I wasn't walking away with any academic prizes, so the sports award gave me a sense of having made an impact in the college. I knew too that the brief soccer experience had contributed to the award and I had every intention of continuing to play locally with Southend.

To me, it was a perfect fit. I could enjoy my few beers on a Saturday night, then sweat it out of me with a game (or two) of soccer on the Sunday. Once, I played for Southend's A team in the morning, scoring three, then lined out with the Bs that afternoon, scoring four. Heaven.

Could I have made it at a higher level? No chance. I was asked to play in the Oscar Traynor once – I can't actually remember why I declined – but there was never any question of being invited over to

England for trials. Deep down, I knew I wasn't quick enough and, once I began to experience a recurring groin injury, my soccer career had to be sacrificed.

To this day, I retain a mild fondness for Arsenal FC. I've been over a few times and have a couple of signed jerseys that were organized by an acquaintance through their former long-time assistant manager, Pat Rice. My brother Tommy is a Liverpool fan and, given a lot of the lads who drank in the pub had similar affiliations, they'd happily spend a night throwing money into the jukebox for another fifty renditions of 'You'll Never Walk Alone'. One of my best childhood friends, David 'Brunch' Kennedy, was an Arsenal fan too and we went to town with the slagging the night of Michael Thomas's famous last-minute winner at Anfield in '89 that took the title off Liverpool.

If a single year could change just about everything in someone's life, my year was 1997.

I didn't leave St Kieran's as a colleges star. I wasn't signposted for greatness the way Eddie Keher or DJ might have been, slipping out the college gates, a whole county giddy with expectation about your future.

Ballyhale, meanwhile, had been relegated, the old lads having finished up and retired with pride. A new brigade was coming in. I had come through the ranks alongside Aylward and Cummins and Tom Coogan and Liam Grant. It was rough at first – we didn't know anything. But we learned a lot pretty quickly when thrown into that environment as teenagers. You were playing against guys sometimes old enough to be your father, marking fellas of thirty-eight or thirty-nine. You had to learn on your feet.

I'd been playing in goal for our intermediates in '96, and Liam Fennelly, being a county minor selector, came out to have a look at me one day in Hugginstown. Our opponents were Thomastown, and the first two balls I had to deal with spilled to the net for easy goals.

My father was standing behind the posts and the Thomastown

full-forward said something to him along the lines of 'The young fella's not having a great day.' My ears were burning. A third ball came in and hopped out of my hand, but I somehow managed to retrieve it and got in the clearance.

After that, my nerves began to settle and I actually played a decent game that we recovered to win. But those two early bloopers had clearly sealed my fate. I went home that evening knowing I wouldn't be first choice to guard the Kilkenny goal in that minor championship. This wouldn't have been long after winning the colleges All-Ireland with Kieran's and, being honest, I had little interest in being the next Noel Skehan anyway. The marquee forwards, the likes of DJ or – in previous years – Nicky English, were the people who caught my eye. I wanted to be getting scores, not stopping them.

As sub goalie with the county minors, I was low enough down the food-chain to be allowed play away with Shamrocks in the minor league. They still used me in the forwards, and one Sunday morning, feeling a little the worse for wear from the night before, I managed to hit 3-7 against Gowran.

This was picked up on by a neighbour, Carmel Harrington, who happened to write the parish notes for the _Kilkenny People_, and, before I knew it, I was starting as a forward in the Leinster minor final against Dublin. Unfortunately, all this succeeded in visiting upon me was the corner-forward's curse. Not a single ball came my way or, indeed, that of my bored marker. We were both withdrawn. Kilkenny won.

Yet, within a year, I was a slightly different animal and the club was at the heart of it. Maybe I just grew up a little, filled out a bit. I was certainly becoming more assertive.

Shamrocks got to the South Kilkenny minor final but were considered rank outsiders. Our opponents, Dunnamaggin, had five Kilkenny panellists to call upon. Cummins and I were Ballyhale's only county men. The game was played in Thomastown and would prove extremely tight and low-scoring.

With ten minutes remaining, I leaped high to catch a ball but, as I landed, Noel Hickey and Conal Herity — two fellow county panellists — came in to crowd me. I reckoned they were fouling but, as I tried to break free, the ref whistled for over-carrying. A red mist descended and, let's just say, my language wasn't what you'd hear in a presbytery. Already on a yellow, I probably said too much.

As the ref reached into his pocket, my good friend David Walsh helpfully decided to intercept the bad news, grabbing the referee's notebook with a Galvin-esque flourish. He saw sense immediately, mind, handing it back so my expulsion could be formalized. Those last ten minutes were agony, everything I owed the club now suddenly pressing down hard on my shoulders. Mercifully, Shamrocks survived, but I was facing a suspension.

It cost me an intermediate county semi-final place, but I was eligible again the Sunday after when we lined up against James Stephens in the minor final. This was massive. The game would be played in a packed Nowlan Park as the curtain-raiser to the Dunnamaggin v. Gowran senior decider. The biggest hurling day of the year in Kilkenny.

We were rank outsiders again, many predicting a double-digit victory for The Village. Some of our players would have been thirteen- and fourteen-year-olds, fast-tracked into minor. We were, essentially, trying to hot-house children into county champions.

A few years ago I watched a video of the game, and it gave me goosebumps. I've been involved in some epic team performances over the years, but I'd find it hard to pinpoint a game that gave me greater satisfaction. Our display was unbelievable. The team didn't take a single backward step from the moment the ball was thrown in, and we won, in the end, pulling up. The victory would secure Paul the captaincy of Kilkenny minors in '98.

One week later, I scored a goal within thirty seconds of the start of the intermediate final, hurling alongside Tommy and John. Again, an easy win followed and, incredibly, we now had two county titles in the bag as well as the club's senior status restored. For about a month after, the village would walk on air. I was grateful that, by then, we'd sold the pub!

The black-and-amber jersey still wasn't fitting perfectly, though, albeit I'd started every championship game for the Kilkenny minors that year. I was taking frees and feeling a central part of a team that included Michael Kavanagh and Noel Hickey. I'd gone well in the Leinster final win over Offaly, scoring a goal and a few points. We were fancied to take care of Clare in the All-Ireland semi-final after they'd come through the back door, beaten by Tipp in the Munster final.

As Leinster champions, we'd had a six-week break and came bounding into Croke Park like stags determined to mark their territory. For a month and a half I'd been thinking about nothing other than getting to an All-Ireland final. I was a main man now. I had to deliver. And I ended up over-hyped, nervous, fragile.

My brother Tommy is an electrician, and I'd spent that summer working with him for Suir Electric. Every single day, I fixated on Croke Park. Ordinarily, I enjoy the buzz of big crowds but, that day against Clare, that same buzz turned into a hand clamped around my throat.

The senior match that day was also Kilkenny v. Clare, and there was a massive crowd from the West. Now Clare's supporters can be a boisterous breed and, as one or two of my frees dropped short, the Banner roars began to get into my head. The longer the game went on, the less I wanted to be out there.

By the finish, I was willing the ground to open up and swallow me whole. Final score: Clare 0-13, Kilkenny 1-7. I was inconsolable.

That night I drank a few beers with Hickey, the two of us talking pretty much from dusk till dawn. The drink did nothing for me. I could have been there for a week and still been stone cold sober.

This had been my last year hurling minor, so the mistakes made could never be corrected.

It was five in the morning when I got home, and I was out the door again two hours later for work in the Stanley factory in Waterford. That night I played an intermediate championship match with

Shamrocks down in the field, which we won. Hurling as detox, you might say.

But, for all the glory that would come Shamrocks' way that autumn, I still had no clearly signposted future with Kilkenny. On the Tuesday after the intermediate county final, I was heading for a new life in Waterford IT.

I went there with a hangover humming in my head.

2. 'Henry, You're Going On!'

My first year in third-level education amounted to a year on the doss. I blame my mother. She blames the career-guidance teacher at St Kieran's. The real culprit was probably my brother.

Electronics, Mai enthused, would be 'right up my street'. She'd seen Tommy do a course in Carlow IT and emerge as a qualified electrician. He was good at it, too. He had a mind for the mathematics and the technical jargon. At the time, I just had a head full of hurling.

I suppose I presented myself to Waterford IT under false pretences. I'd done physics in my Leaving Cert and just about scraped a pass in the subject. In fact, I'd been so immersed in the hunt for another colleges All-Ireland at Kieran's, I even slipped into a mindset that it mightn't be the worst thing in the world if I ended up repeating. While the more studious would bypass training at that time of year, my whole day revolved around the looming session.

I scrambled a reasonable Leaving in the end, but hurling undoubtedly hampered the grades. I didn't care. I was a Kilkenny minor now, heading to Waterford with old friends from Kieran's like Derek Lyng and Michael Kavanagh and Willie Maher from Tipp, looking to play Fitzgibbon Cup. If the opportunity arose, I'd find time to study. If not . . .

Pretty soon, the penny dropped that electronics just wasn't my thing. I'd sit at a lecture, eyes quickly glazing over, ears clamped shut to whatever voice was in the hall. There were seven subjects on the curriculum, one of them German! I might as well have been an alien from outer space.

Before long, I was missing classes and slipping into denial. A Fitzgibbon campaign brewed and the lads in my class would smile knowingly as they passed me in the corridor, inevitably talking hurling with someone, while they headed off to their next '*der Mann*; *die Männer*' recitation.

The hurling team became my family. I travelled up and down from Ballyhale daily that first year and would routinely ring home to say I'd have to stay over for study. I was growing up, essentially, discovering a degree of independence that was available only away from home. Beer and craic and a palpable sense of belonging were available in Waterford. I loved it.

I was one of maybe only two freshers to make the Fitzgibbon team that year, and it was a step up physically from anything I'd known. Tadhg O'Sullivan, the orthopaedic surgeon who today has pretty intimate knowledge of my knees, was manager. Shay Fitzpatrick looked after fitness.

The big achievement that year would be a semi-final win against Garda down in Limerick. There was a bit of an edge to the rivalry between the two colleges, not much love lost, as I recall. They had Jerry O'Connor from Newtownshandrum, one of a fair smattering of county players.

We had Andy Moloney (who was our Mr Fitzgibbon), Eamonn Corcoran and Alan Geoghegan on board, and Enda Everard from Templetuohy, someone I will always remember as the lad with access to butter vouchers (these were introduced by the government in the '90s so that social welfare recipients could purchase butter at a reduced price). Enda would show the vouchers to his landlord, explaining that he was on the dole. It led to his rent being slashed and a surplus of butter in the fridge.

We came up against UCC's 'dream team' in the final, a team with the likes of Joe Deane, Seanie McGrath, Dave Bennett and Eddie Enright, looking to secure their three-in-a-row. And they just had too much for us in the Gaelic Grounds.

I didn't so much waste that year academically as ignore it. By Easter, it was time to come clean. I'd decided not to bother sitting the exams, seeing little point, so breaking the news to my father had to be strategically planned. He'd every right to be furious at the flagrant waste of money, but I reckoned I had one trump card.

You see, if there was anyone who'd enjoyed our Fitzgibbon run more than me, it was probably Henry senior.

We were mending fences down the fields one morning when I said I'd something to tell him. He took the news pretty calmly. 'Sure do the exams anyway,' he said. 'Just see how you get on.'

I did as he said and, incredibly, passed two of the seven subjects. Including German! The lecturer pretty much told us that if we attended every day for the final couple of months, he'd mark us as having passed. His kindness helped rescue a tiny thread of respectability from an academic fiasco.

Once the carnage of the exam hall had been absorbed, we decided that a degree in Business Studies was probably a more practical target to pursue than a degree in electronics.

In the meantime, I hurled. I was on the Kilkenny intermediate panel but, as club training took priority, there wasn't really much that our manager, Noel Skehan, could do when we met up other than get us pucking balls across the field. The only thing that had my undivided attention was the post-training grub. A good dinner could override any sense of agitation.

One of the selectors, Paddy Harney, was from Knocktopher, and as Shamrocks had been intermediate champions in '97 I suppose we were guaranteed a decent representation. So Tommy was wing-forward, Padraig Farrell full-back and captain. Me? Even with rationed numbers, I was on the periphery.

We had sixteen players one midweek night for a challenge against James Stephens. I was working with Suir Electric again that summer and recall eating a bar of chocolate and a packet of Taytos as I waited on the street for my lift. You might gather that I wasn't exactly a coiled spring of pre-match tension or the greatest devotee of sports science at the time. I didn't start.

So in the summer of '98, I was sixteenth man out of sixteen on Kilkenny's intermediates and seemingly two galaxies away from the attention of those picking the county's under-21s. I sat in the dugout that night in Larchfield, messing around on my own with a sliotar, swinging out of the dugout rails like a distracted child.

Then half-time arrived and the magic words, 'Henry, you're going on!' changed everything.

Legend has it that Brian Cody was in the small crowd that evening, and it's certainly feasible because, personally, I doubt he's missed too many home games involving The Village. I hurled well, got a few scores and walked out the gate as the intermediates' free-taker.

Now, suddenly, I was on a carousel, gathering speed. I found myself in Enniscorthy on a filthy evening, hurling a Leinster final against Wexford and picking my brother's teeth out of the grass. Tommy was playing out the field and had the misfortune to lose his footing by a dugout. The Enniscorthy dugouts were sunk below ground level, with tiny stone ledges protruding that – today – would send Health and Safety into paroxysms. Tommy hit one of those ledges face first, leaving six teeth as a deposit.

We won the final, and then a call came through the following Tuesday to join the under-21s. To be honest, the timing was a god-send, because four nights later a voice from Chicago would come on the line, offering a summer job, some dollars and a little sun-splashed hurling in the USA. If the sequence had been reversed, I'd have gone to the States.

A few locals might have bellyached that it took the selectors so long to call me into that under-21 panel, but the noise wouldn't have been thunderous. Now, within a matter of weeks, I had gone from near-invisibility to being the county's under-21 free-taker. We beat Dublin in the Leinster final, then squared up to Galway in an All-Ireland semi-final and got beaten out the gate.

This game was played in Thurles, the curtain-raiser to Offaly's famous third and decisive All-Ireland semi-final with Clare after Jimmy Cooney's unfortunate error in blowing up their second meeting early. A massive stage, a huge crowd. This was the Galway of Eugene Cloonan and Kevin Broderick, a team with a lot of slickness in their wrists.

So we took a heavy shelling, but my name was suddenly beginning to mean something a little different. Two months on from being sixteenth man out of sixteen with the intermediates, I scored 3-4 in that All-Ireland under-21 semi-final. With Kevin Fennelly, my own clubmate, managing the county seniors, brains began to whirr.

They'd already qualified for the senior final so, naturally, Kevin had been in Semple Stadium that day to view their prospective opponents. I went out that evening, stayed with a friend, and it was maybe lunchtime the following day when I got the message that Kevin had been on to home, inviting me to train with the seniors that morning in Thomastown. By the time I got the message it was too late.

This wasn't as big a deal as it might sound. There were just two weeks to go to the All-Ireland final and any new invitations in to training were, essentially, to make up the numbers. I'd already gone in one Saturday earlier that year. The call had come via my father that Thursday while I was sitting in my uncle's pub in Waterford, nursing a large Bulmers. On the phone, my father counselled, 'Look after yourself now,' and I pushed away the cider. I remember thinking this could be my moment. That Saturday I turned up in Danesfort, full of it, hungry for solo runs and 'look at me' tricks. And I was lucky not to end up in A&E.

Once, I took a ball around Liam Keoghan only to find that big oak, Pat O'Neill, waiting for me on the other side. For a split second, Pat considered this open invitation to put manners on the little snipe now looking for attention. Thankfully, the humanitarian in him took over. He stepped aside. I've never forgotten that. Pat could have broken me into tiny pieces, but I knew him from working in Suir Electric and maybe that was a factor in him passing on the opportunity.

The '98 final weekend was a momentous one in our house, as Paul was captaining the minors against Cork. If I'm honest, that was more my focus than the senior final against Offaly. I decided to enjoy the experience, heading down to our old pub to watch *Up for the Match* that Saturday night, then tucking into a big fry-up the following morning and breaking for Dublin early with Dermot Ryan and Paul Phelan.

It's one of the few All-Ireland weekends in my adult life that I've felt completely free of hurling obligations. Put it this way, I was supping a pint in Quinn's of Drumcondra just after midday. Kilkenny, unfortunately, lost both finals and, though I had a ticket for the team banquet, I just settled back in Quinn's for the night.

The defeat of the minors had been more disappointing than watching Brian Whelahan do his Miracle of Fatima thing, one of the greatest defenders of all time stepping from a sickbed to morph into Offaly's match-winning full-forward.

Some years later, hindsight would have Kevin facing spiky questions about not including me on that Kilkenny panel. Ballyhale didn't actually have a representative on the senior team that year and, that winter, Kevin lost his job to a certain Mr Cody.

I didn't share the view that my omission had been some kind of aberration. How could I? Three months earlier, I'd been unable to get a game with the intermediates. If anything, standing on the Canal End that September, my overriding feeling was that the pace of the game was frightening. I honestly wondered if it was a pace that I could ever hope to meet.

Tommy had got a brief call-up to the senior panel the previous October. Back then, the National League started before Christmas; and a letter arrived, inviting him in to training. He would have been twenty-eight at the time and the invitation was seen as reward for our intermediate success.

My father, naturally, was delighted for Tommy. But he felt Kevin could have gone further. 'Where's Henry's letter?' he asked Mai. Tommy, for his part, would get one Walsh Cup game and be gone.

Now, a year on, my season finished with an All-Ireland intermediate final against Limerick that has gone down in history for a remarkable turnaround. It was played on the day the great Tommy Quaid died, and we went from total control to a virtual downing of arms. It was surreal. One minute we looked home and hosed, and the next, Limerick began peppering us with goals.

The story goes that the change coincided with the very minute of Tommy's passing, a strange energy descending upon Semple Stadium. It's a romantic thought, and probably as good an explanation as any for the game turning on its head so dramatically. Tommy was maybe Limerick's greatest goalkeeper and one of the finest of all time. He was also, I gathered, a universally loved gentleman who might well have had access to the deities.

I got one of my favourite goals that day, flicking a ball overhead, past the advancing Limerick goalkeeper. The game was shown on TG4 and I wasn't unhappy when Ger Loughnane nominated it as his goal of the year.

But as soon as that match was over, my mind was already tuning back into Fitzgibbon. I stopped commuting and moved to Waterford full time, into a house on Manor Street, virtually next door to my Uncle Denis's pub. 'Sheff's' was a favourite haunt of students and, over the next four years, Denis would have to keep a few secrets.

Suddenly, life had a degree of pandemonium. There were six of us in a house designed for four. The first four home at night got the four beds. The craic was constant. Another house on the same street had something like eight of the hurlers. 'Oaktown Babes' they called themselves. Don't ask.

It sounds terribly juvenile now, but I suppose it's a kind of rite of passage that third level sets before you. There was a rivalry between the houses that led to childish pranks. One morning we got up to find every last stick of furniture missing from downstairs. Magically, it reappeared in the other house.

My sister Aileen was always very good to us and sent me down a massive pot of chicken curry once. It was gone before we'd had a single spoonful. The house operated more as a hostel, strange faces routinely appearing for breakfast.

You could say we partied as we trained. Everything was full-on. Most of us lived for the hurling and many friendships forged in those college days are still intact to this day. It was a brilliant time of my life, carefree and, yes, occasionally careless.

Academically, I was far happier. Business Studies I could, at least, relate to. It would be two years to get the certificate and, if my mark was high enough, another year to pursue a diploma. All going well, I'd then try and go in search of a degree. And that's how it panned out. Out of 150 people who had started the Cert in Business Studies, just thirty-five of us managed the required fifty-five per cent or over to get back to do a diploma. Of those thirty-five, only six of us survived to do a degree.

We had a cracking team heading to Tipperary for the 1999 Fitzgibbon. The training had been savage throughout winter and I was really feeling the benefit of it. We stopped UCC's bid for the four-in-a-row, winning the final in Templemore with thirteen inter-county players on duty. Serious stuff, with Eamonn Corcoran named Player of the Tournament. I felt euphoric.

Fitzgibbon would change me physically and mentally. We won again in 2000. I had the privilege of being WIT captain for 2002, my final year in college. By then, I was on a different journey and, it's fair to say, living my life by the book. I'd been five years in the college and, of course, played two All-Ireland finals for Kilkenny in the interim.

The house I now shared with Moloney and Geoghegan was about a mile and a half from college and I made a point of walking there and back, twice a day. Six miles, essentially, just to loosen up. I'd had a chastening 2001 and knew I needed to be in better condition. As housemates, we'd really bought into the Fitzgibbon ethos and had started living the life of professional hurlers . . . almost.

The floating of the early days had been replaced by strict adherence to lecture schedules too. I was now pursuing a degree, studying hard. I had twin objectives: leaving college with a degree and winning a third Fitzgibbon would seal the perfect start to 2002. Moloney had finished college, but stayed on as a selector. For months, we talked about little else. It wasn't to be, though.

I got my honours degree, but not the Fitzgibbon. We reached the final in Castlegar, but lost to Brian Geary's University of Limerick. Devastated, I drowned my sorrows in the clubhouse afterwards, and a few of us would miss the bus back to Waterford. I have a memory of a drunken phone call to my old friend, Eamonn Corcoran, from a pub in Galway that evening. Eamonn would have known how bad I was hurting.

He listened like a gentle agony aunt, reminding me that the end of college life was really just the opening of a door. He was right. That August, we'd mark one another in one of the greatest games ever played.

3. Innocent Times

I didn't know Brian Cody and, to begin with, there would be no grand introductions.

My call-up to the Kilkenny senior panel was communicated in a phone call from one of the selectors, Johnny Walsh. Johnny, originally from Ballyhale, was now living in Mooncoin. He framed the conversation in flatly pragmatic terms. It was November of '98 and Cody had just been apppointed manager. I was one of maybe thirty players invited in to training.

I'd be in need of a lift from Waterford.

'I'll collect you,' said Johnny.

The under-21 championship ran late that year, and I'd been told after the Southern final against Mullinavat that Cody had been in attendance. So the call wasn't entirely unexpected. But I did feel like a bit of a schoolboy that first night in Kilkenny CBS, and one thing I will always be appreciative of was what DJ Carey did: he came over, introduced himself and wished me all the best. DJ was a massive star who had temporarily retired that year. Now he was back and, typically, showing that touch of class.

We did some running to have our fitness assessed, then gathered in a classroom for our first meeting with Cody. I would have known Michael Kavanagh and, from Suir Electric, Philly Larkin and Pat O'Neill. But, generally, I was a kid among men.

There were no lightning bolts flying off Cody that first evening. He just spoke of a desire to create a palpable team spirit. It certainly wasn't something destined to happen overnight, as he would lose his first four games in charge of Kilkenny.

Spirit is the kernel of everything he stands for. It's simply what he is all about. To this day, he still talks about that first night and how everything he said back then applies every bit as much today. The years we have failed, in his opinion, were the years when our spirit was found wanting. I share that view.

I made my debut in the Walsh Cup against Wexford on a filthy day in Mullinavat. DJ didn't play so, from the off, I was taking frees. That helped me settle and, as the National League loomed, Brian called DJ and me aside one night at the track in Kilkenny CBS. 'DJ,' he said, 'Henry's going all right on the frees, so we'll leave things for the time being.'

I was shocked. Here was maybe the greatest player of his generation being asked, basically, to watch a novice take on one of his customary responsibilities. But DJ wasn't just gracious. Heading down to our first League game in Cork, I remember him as hugely encouraging.

Cody often jokes that, in the car that day, Ned Quinn suggested to him that a good performance was the main requirement, whatever the result. His response was, 'Feck the good performance, we're going down here to win.'

We didn't, though. Cork beat us by three points.

Clare were setting the physical agenda at that time, Ger Loughnane supposedly getting them to run up hills sheer as the faces of houses. And Cody clearly believed Kilkenny needed toughening in those early days. In time, he would have us jogging around the infield of Gowran Park racecourse and, some nights, climbing our very own Matterhorn over in Bennettsbridge. The latter was, essentially, a farmer's field with a hill and some trees just to the right-hand side of the GAA pitch. We used it for only a single year, 2000; our physical trainer, Mick O'Flynn, got us to run circuits, using the trees as cones essentially. Each lap lasted maybe a minute and they were excruciating. We graduated the following year to Gowran, where we'd run circuits over a hilly section that has since been turned into a golf course.

One thing that staggers me in recall now is that it was quite common for us to train on successive nights. We might be running in Gowran on the Tuesday, then doing these indoor bleep tests in Kilkenny CBS on Wednesday. Flogging ourselves in this small, stuffy hall, maybe ten at a time, then literally exploding out through the fire exit at the end, gasping for fresh air.

Soon as we'd pour out, another group would start. You'd never dream of training that way nowadays, when there's such emphasis on recovery.

It was a different, more innocent time, I suppose. Less scientific. The older lads hated the running and there'd be a queue for the physio's table on those dark nights in Gowran. A few pints would have been commonplace after League games, and it was customary for lads to come back to pre-season training carrying a few stone. Well-padded lads like Pat O'Neill and the goalkeeper, Joe Dermody, would wear two tracksuits during those sessions to sweat off the excesses of winter. Serious men.

If they dreaded the nights of drudgery, it wasn't a problem to a young buck like me. I was juggling college hurling with my new county status and, with WIT winning the Fitzgibbon that year, I settled quickly too into the routine of senior inter-county. Much was made of something I did in a National League game against Wexford that Easter Sunday at Nowlan Park. I scored 1-3 off their corner-back, Colin Furlong, and, late in the game, flicked a ball over his head in front of the old stand. A kind of matador roar lifted to the heavens. I wouldn't have blamed Furlong if he decided to be the bull.

I can still remember that roar and thinking to myself, 'Jesus, I so much want to be part of this . . .'

People often say Cody isn't an especially tactical manager, and it's something that, in later years, I've had a bit of craic slagging him over. But one thing he brought to our game in '99 was the concept of rotating forwards. The idea was that you'd hold your position for maybe three minutes, then the call would go up to move. A couple of the forwards stayed where they were – John Power never left the '40' and Brian McEvoy wouldn't budge off his wing – but the rest of us were interchangeable.

Usually, DJ called the shots. I might be in at full-forward and he'd come jogging over with a simple instruction: 'Right, Henry, out you go!' As the young rookie, who was I to argue with DJ Carey? So I'd trot out obediently to the half-forward line, DJ and Charlie Carter pretty much pulling the strings in a strategy that, to begin with, seemed to bamboozle opposition defences.

I particularly remember our Leinster opener against Laois: their defenders didn't have a clue who they needed to be picking up. We hammered them by twenty-two points that day, DJ the main man scoring 2-3.

For me, it was a pretty gentle introduction to championship hurling and, frankly, not much of a pointer to what it was all about. Before the Leinster final against Offaly, Pat O'Neill called me aside and warned me to expect something entirely different from anything I'd known. It would, he told me, be 'helter-skelter'. We were working together for Suir Electric on the setting up of Lisheen Mine, and Pat, I suppose, felt the need to warn me that the Laois game hadn't maybe been the most educational of assignments.

John Power was back after an eighteen-month absence from the squad, having returned in a challenge against Cork on a beautiful May evening and done really well on Brian Corcoran. The same night, Charlie Carter went to town a little on Diarmuid O'Sullivan. We won the game pulling up, never thinking that the grins on our faces were just four months away from being shoved back up our backsides.

So we were in a good place going into that Leinster final, and Pat's view was that I should let experienced heads like Power and DJ set the tempo. 'Keep out of the way until it settles,' he said. 'Just ease yourself into the game.'

On a sweltering day, I did exactly what Pat told me. DJ scored another 2-3, his second goal a classic on the stroke of half-time to give us an eight-point advantage. By the time I got our fifth goal (my first for Kilkenny and my celebration still makes me cringe), Daithí Regan's dismissal had killed off Offaly's hopes.

I had little enough to do with the emotional dynamic of that game. The lads had been really wired for revenge after what happened in the previous year's All-Ireland. That hurt was theirs, not mine. My priorities didn't extend much beyond just keeping my end up but, at the end, I had 1-6 to my name and was presented with a watch by RTÉ as Man of the Match.

Offaly's backs didn't seem to know what to do against our rotating forwards. Now these guys were no greenhorns, with the likes of Brian Whelahan, Martin Hanamy, Kevin Kinahan and Hubert Rigney to call upon. All were tough, intelligent markers, not known for losing too many one-to-one battles, and I suppose it suited a kid like me not to have to sit too long in any particular back's company.

But people began copping on to the tactic and, by the time the All-Ireland semi-final came around, the surprise factor was gone. There was a six-week break until the game against Clare and, my head full of Brian Lohan, I overdid things. I trained too hard and became too wound up. Clare still had the patent for enormous physicality and Lohan was their emblematic figure in this regard.

The day arrived and I remember charging up the steps of the Cusack Stand tunnel into the light and noise, swinging at a ball and falling flat on my face. People told me afterwards that they knew I wasn't right when they saw it.

Clare didn't spare me. Lohan was ferocious and, when I switched out to the corner for a breather, Brian Quinn gave me a few welcoming digs. The forward rotation just wasn't working, not against such seasoned campaigners. Pretty soon, we just stopped switching and, at half-time, Cody went through us all for a short cut. We were behind because we were effectively being bullied.

The game, like so many others, was eventually settled by a DJ goal. I had gone back to full-forward when a ball came dropping in. As I went to catch it, I took this ferocious slap across the head. Falling to the ground, I looked up and there was DJ pulling the trigger. Top corner.

Rather than follow the flight of the ball, Lohan had come across to nail me, DJ nipping in behind us in the confusion. In the excitement of the goal, no one had really noticed the extent of the blow I'd taken. I was furious. Eventually, I got back on my feet, jogged back in towards Lohan, remarking, 'Brian, if you'd played the ball, you'd have stopped the goal.'

He just stared at me blankly. Probably knew that I was right.

The following day I got a phone call from the team doctor. 'Jesus, Henry,' he said, 'it was only last night, watching the match at home, I saw the slap you got for the goal. Are you all right?'

The day before the final, I went down with my brother Paul to the Shamrocks field and practised frees in the lashing rain. I felt calm.

The weather didn't improve that Sunday and it was undoubtedly a factor in the game degenerating into a pretty dour struggle. I always had the feeling we were going to push on, and maybe, deep down, we all had that same feeling. Willie O'Connor said subsequently that we were probably a bit cocky and that might have been our downfall. We were four points up with seventeen minutes remaining when, slowly, the tide began to turn.

The frees were going well for me but I became increasingly isolated at full-forward. Cork got completely on top in their half-back line and, when they came with their late surge, the crowd started going ballistic. All you could hear was 'CORK CORK CORK . . .'

I was desperate to go out to half-forward, but too shy to make the call. To this day, I feel I might have made a difference physically. Nowadays, Cody always tells us if we feel like doing something different in a game, to go for it. But I was still getting used to him at the time. I hadn't the confidence to make a move. So I just stood there helplessly at full-forward, watching the All-Ireland slip away. And I've never really forgiven myself for letting that happen.

Around this time, I would – routinely – have eaten a fry the morning of a game. When I think about that now it seems almost comical. Worse, I developed an early habit of popping down to the local chipper for a burger and chips on Saturday evenings. Looking back at photographs now, I was pudgy. A dietitian's nightmare.

This would eventually take its toll, and Cody wasn't slow to spot the problem in my second year with Kilkenny.

My form dipped in the early League games of 2000, and I was certainly carrying some unwelcome weight. Putting on my jeans, I'd be aware they were getting tighter all the time. Cody pulled me aside at training in the week we were due to play Tipp and he laid it on the line. 'The lads are saying you're tired,' he said flatly. 'I don't think you're tired. I think you're not fit!'

I was mortified. That Sunday, I remember really bursting a gut to try and impress him. It was to become an unspoken routine across the next decade. If I needed to buck up, Brian would drop a little comment at training. And, almost without knowing, I'd go home that night on a mission to prove him wrong.

In time, I probably needed it less and less. But, in those early days, Cody would have known I wasn't exactly living by the book of Matt Talbot.

There were no long one-to-one conversations between us back then. That wasn't and isn't his style. He might just pass you during a training drill and say something utterly simple like 'Keep it going, Henry,' and it was enough to give you a little extra burst of energy.

People probably imagine he's full of profound wisdoms. But Brian's greatness is a simple matter: he understands hurling better than any man I know. He cuts through bullshit. If another county is doing something he thinks might be of value to Kilkenny (like the hill in Bennettsbridge), he'll adopt it. But he knows the difference between an advancement and a fad.

When we got to that All-Ireland final of '99, he would have been very protective of me from the media hype. I don't actually remember him telling me not to do interviews, but I was aware he didn't particularly want my opinion splashed all over the newspapers. He made it clear he wanted me wrapped up in cotton wool.

John Knox of the *Kilkenny People* rang the house one day and my mother chatted away to him happily. I went ballistic when I saw the article. Looking back, it was a perfectly reasonable, undramatic piece, but I just didn't want to set myself up for a fall.

Sometimes RTÉ still broadcasts snapshots from the end of that final on *Reeling in the Years* and I'm struck by how much of a boy I was at the time. The presentation was on the pitch that year and, as the Cork captain – Mark Landers – makes his speech, I'm visible in the background, crying my eyes out. I took the defeat very badly, worse maybe than was reasonable. I just felt sickened the way Cork had come with a wave of scores to take what I thought would be our title. I can't remember any score individually, just the overall sense of something slipping. In such a tight game, they shouldn't have been able to rein us in without a goal. But rein us in they did, with maybe the smallest man on the field – Seanie McGrath – scoring three points.

So, standing on the pitch, listening to 'The Banks' roared out over the tannoy, I felt I was standing alone, almost, torturing myself with thoughts of what I should have done.

Coming out of the stadium after, some Kilkenny people made a point of applauding us and I couldn't get my head around that. What was there to applaud? We'd lost a game we should have won.

I tried to drown my sorrows that night at our function in the Red Cow and I can remember very little about the evening. But I do remember feeling utterly demoralized at the homecoming. Maybe 25,000 people turned up on a wretched evening in Kilkenny and, again, emotion got the better of me. One of the local newspapers observed that I looked terribly upset. I just felt I had let people down. Maybe I was even in a bit of shock.

That Monday evening is a bit of a blur too, but I do remember Cody speaking from the platform and saying something along the lines of Kilkenny not letting this happen again. The words, I presume, sounded like tokenism. But they were more than that. If we, as players, were angry at this lost opportunity, we were only beginning to discover the inner competitiveness of our manager.

Michael Kavanagh and myself had the small matter of an All-Ireland under-21 final to play the following Sunday against Galway. The team trained in Tullamore that Tuesday night and we were fairly demoralized (and shook) men making the journey over.

Not many people gave that under-21 team a prayer. It was made up mainly of players from junior and intermediate clubs who'd never played minor for Kilkenny. Galway had the Cloonan brothers, Rory Gantley, Mark Kerins and David Tierney. A team of superstars.

At the meal after training that Tuesday night, our manager —
Richie Power — brought in a motivational speaker who showed us a
clip of *The Shawshank Redemption*. It was the segment where Andy is
crawling through the shit. When it was finished, he asked if anyone
had anything to say.

Shawshank is my favourite film and I took this as an invitation.
'Lads,' I said, 'we'll have to be willing to crawl through shit next
Sunday because no way are Michael and I going to go through what
we went through last weekend!'

The Kilkenny crowd got behind us that day in a way I could never
remember them getting behind an under-21 team before, and the
team responded brilliantly. I kept my side of the deal by converting
the frees and Noel Hickey lifted the cup that evening.

Our emotions were running wild. You see, the night before, an
unprovoked assault outside Hayes Hotel in Thurles had left PJ
Delaney fighting for his life. PJ was on the senior panel and had come
on for Charlie Carter in the final. Now we were hearing his chances
of survival were slim.

Podge, his brother, togged out with us that day, but he disappeared
straight after the match. Coming home that evening, we all said a
prayer on the bus for PJ. The following Wednesday, I went up to a
Mass in Johnstown for him and bumped into Brian Cody. Brian said
he'd been told there wasn't much hope. That's how it looked for a few
terrible weeks, but, thankfully, PJ would defy the prognosis and pull
through. The prayers of a county had been answered.

In the Leinster Championship of 2000, we dispatched Dublin and
Offaly by margins of fifteen points and eleven points respectively. I
hurt my AC joint in the Leinster final and had to spend about four
weeks avoiding heavy physical contact. It meant I missed the
under-21 championship and was confined to running on my own in
training while everybody else hurled. This left me mad for action by
the time our All-Ireland semi-final against Galway came around.

Two weeks before that game, we went for a weekend away to
Clarecastle in Clare. There was a real sense of the team being on a

mission. Kilkenny had lost two successive All-Ireland finals and no team in history had lost three in a row. Willie O'Connor, our captain, was an inspirational leader. In Clarecastle, Cody allowed us a few pints after a Saturday night team meeting, and I remember Willie really laying it on the line. Galway had won the League and were unbeaten all year. We couldn't afford a single backward step. And we wouldn't take one.

After a tentative first half, DJ's goal cut us loose. Denis Byrne was unmarkable at half-forward, finishing up with 0-5 from play. We won by eight points, my marker, Liam Hodgins, getting the line for constantly pulling and dragging my jersey.

I had no real fear of Offaly in the final. None of us had. Come to think of it, we had no real fear of anyone. There was just such drive and determination in the group; we had an attitude that nobody would be allowed stand in our way. A year into the job, Brian was more comfortable with the squad and the squad more comfortable with him.

We'd beaten Offaly in three consecutive Leinster deciders and had been as surprised as anyone when they beat Cork in the All-Ireland semi-final. But that result was typical of that Offaly team. They had a gift for the unorthodox, as we well remembered from '98.

All year, though, we seemed to be talking ourselves into a higher emotional intensity. Running up that hill in Bennettsbridge was just the physical expression of a determination to be that bit steelier. At team meetings, everyone was encouraged to make a contribution and there was always a lot of emotion in the room.

If one figure was emblematic of what we were about that year, I'd nominate Eamonn Kennedy. I knew Eamonn from Suir Electric, where he worked as a fitter. He was an old-fashioned centre-half-back, a naturally strong man with a great hand for the high ball. That year, Eamonn was getting up at six in the morning and cycling for an hour and a half before he'd go to work. He got himself into the shape of his life and would finish the year with an All-Star.

One night in Nowlan Park, during the build-up to the final, Brian said he wanted me to say a few words. I was mortified. Back then, I found it nerve-racking to speak in a dressing room and would have been far happier listening to what others had to say. But Cody wasn't offering an invitation, he was issuing a command.

So I talked about the only thing I could, the feeling of devastation I had carried on the train journey home the year before. The sense of embarrassment then of being on an open-topped bus in front of 25,000 Kilkenny supporters who turned out to greet a beaten team in foul weather. 'We can't leave this behind on Sunday week,' I said, my voice beginning to tremble. 'I don't ever want to be staring down at all those people we've let down again.' Much to my embarrassment, I became very emotional.

Other guys who spoke conveyed the exact same message, just in different ways. There was no way we were coming back to Kilkenny without the cup. To do so would have been unthinkable.

There was a bit of controversy in the build-up, as Stephen Grehan was found to have played a soccer match for Spa United the weekend before. He had started every game in that championship, but was then left off the starting fifteen for the final. Brian Cody denied the soccer game had anything to do with his demotion, but there was little doubt playing in that game didn't help Stephen's cause.

By the day of the game, nothing was going to distract us. I vividly remember the Friday week beforehand and a really intense training session. One drill we all absolutely despised was Mick O'Flynn's 150-metre sprints. He might get us to do eight in a row and, by the end, lads would be almost staggering around the place with exhaustion.

But that night, almost to a man, lads were saying, 'We'll do a few more . . .' If there was a stone wall to run through, the wall would have been ground to dust. In some respects, the team was training itself now. Brian has this saying at a certain point in the build-up to a big game. 'There's nothing I can do now,' he tells us.

And, in the week of the 2000 final, there was nothing that he had to.

We didn't spare Offaly. Maybe the fear of having that stigma of being the first team to lose three finals in a row was the trigger. DJ got two early goals and we were eight points clear inside ten minutes.

Actually, that's not strictly true.

DJ's first goal was absolutely brilliant, but I still maintain that his second — technically — was mine. I'd taken a shot that Offaly goalkeeper, Stephen Byrne, partially saved, scooping the ball out just after it had crossed the line. The sliotar went straight to DJ, who tapped it home.

I'd actually seen the umpire reach for his green flag before DJ got to the ball but, no matter, we all wheeled away, celebrating. The following day, I'd get talking to that umpire at the post-All-Ireland lunch for the teams, and he confirmed that the ball had crossed the line.

I've said that to DJ since, but he's having none of it! Anyway, I got my goal in the second half, and hitting the net in an All-Ireland final was a beautiful feeling.

I'll always remember Willie O'Connor at half-time that day, holding a hand to his chest. He'd broken a rib and was in obvious discomfort.

Someone shouted something along the lines of lads having to be willing to die in the second half. 'I won't fucking die,' said Willie. 'But I *will* fucking kill to win this match!' We just weren't for turning.

Charlie Carter and Eddie Brennan also found the net that day, and we ran out comfortable winners. We'd claimed the All-Ireland, winning our four games by an average of almost twelve points. It felt easy. And maybe that was the poison that got into our systems in 2001. The conceit of fellas who felt there was a gap between ourselves and the rest.

In 2001, we steamrollered Leinster again — beating Offaly and Wexford by a combined total of twenty-five points — and arrived at the All-Ireland semi-final against Galway like prize heifers at a fair.

I've made no secret of the self-disgust that, to this day, I feel about my own timidity against their corner-back, Gregory Kennedy, in that game. I needed to cop on. Looking back, I hadn't been hurling great all year and was probably losing focus. And Kennedy did what any smart corner-back would do. He pulled the right strings.

The tone was set from the off when Richie Murray buried Brian McEvoy at the throw-in. Maybe it was a premeditated thing, setting down an immediate marker. It's not something I necessarily agree with and, by right, Murray should have been booked immediately. But it told us something straight away about Galway's attitude to the game. They were determined to bully us that day and, unfortunately, we pretty much stepped aside and let them.

Gregory gave me a running commentary, basically, on how badly I was going. And all I offered in response was the rage of a prima donna. The ref would come across, telling us to cop ourselves on, and all I remember is Gregory laughing. He had me in his pocket.

As a unit, we were horsed out of it that day. We were exposed. Without the requisite hunger, we just weren't prepared for the physical battle. I went looking for protection, berating referee and linesmen, when I should have been man enough to sort things out myself. It was pathetic.

That day, I didn't raise a flag from play. Gregory has joked since that he gave me 'a bit of mental torture'. The truth is, he did nothing untoward other than unmask a child tossing the toys out of the pram.

I thought I was a man but, obviously, I wasn't. I just became more frustrated and irritated with every passing minute, arguing with everyone in sight. I wasn't concentrating on the game and that was a turning point for me. Big deal, someone was pulling my shirt. I do that myself. Yet, the minute the game ended, I slipped into a monumental sulk.

Cody always says hurling's a simple game. He's right. It's all about the ball. If you get side-tracked and your mind goes away from that, you're no good to anyone. That day, I was worried by a guy who wasn't even hurting me. All he was doing was pushing me, winding me up. Nothing more.

There's only one way to answer that. You answer it by getting a score. By looking him in the eye and letting him know you are absolutely indifferent to his bullshit. But that day I looked for umpires, linesmen and the referee for a dig-out.

My own whining and general childishness when presented with a bit of provocation maybe reflected a general preciousness in Kilkenny. Stuff went on in the build-up to that game that wouldn't be countenanced now. There'd been a lot of compliments coming our way after the Leinster Championship, and maybe management bought into the hype.

Generally, the kind of discipline now taken for granted in a Kilkenny dressing room just wasn't there. Players with question marks hanging over their fitness were still getting picked. Fellas who were training out of their skin sat watching this. What Brian had promised night after night was being reneged upon.

Looking back, there was too much craic on the bus to Dublin that day we played Galway. It was laughter all the way, lads cracking jokes as if they were headed to a stag night. The whole operation had become self-satisfied and soft. We got what we deserved.

Personally, it took a while for the penny to drop. I cringe to remember being back down in college later that year and saying in the company of a few Galway lads – Damien Joyce, Cathal Murray and Shane McLaren – that I didn't like the way they'd celebrated beating us in that semi-final.

McLaren shot back at me immediately. 'Would you ever shut up,' he said. 'A bunch of cry-babies is all ye are!'

He was absolutely right. I was being pathetic. Kilkenny were being pathetic, sore losers who'd gone a little precious. That was how I'd played that game. As if I didn't deserve to be pushed. As if I didn't deserve to have someone call me names. As if I didn't deserve to be niggled off the ball.

That feeling even extended back into club action. I remember getting awful stick subsequently in a game against Castlecomer at Nowlan Park. 'You're fuckin' soft, you couldn't do it against Galway . . .' – all that crack. The child in me took the bait. Their goalkeeper was especially verbal and I ran in at one stage and started shouting back. I just didn't want to know. Soon as the final whistle went, I was down the tunnel without shaking a single hand. I was pathetic.

Looking back, I suspect Cody could see all this stuff and he read the implications.

We went back training that November, the usual fitness tests at Kilkenny CBS, then he gathered us in a classroom. He was a different man. He began talking about how individuals needed to buck up their ideas. Then his eyes were on me and I felt six inches tall.

'You,' he said. 'You were too soft, you were pushed around, you were bullied. BULLIED!' I had my head down. My name wasn't the only one being pinpointed but, at that moment, it might as well have been.

I was mortified. I remember thinking, 'Jesus Christ, do you have to do that here in front of all the lads?' I was angry. This was a new Cody, laying down a marker. That night, he made it clear he didn't want to be anybody's friend. There would be no more messing in the group, no more sense of privilege. Never again, even on team holidays, would he be one of the lads.

He was the manager. We were the players. A new arrangement was in place.

I remember going home that evening, spitting fire. Maybe I felt humiliated. I had it in my head that I'd stick those words down his throat, and I suspect he deliberately left me to stew with that thought. There was no coming to me the following night at training and looking to build bridges. If I was angry, that was exactly how he wanted me to be.

4. 'Get the Hell out of Manhattan!'

I watched the 2001 All-Ireland final with a bellyful of grease and regrets from a big Irish bar in the Woodlands district of New York.

Sat on a high stool with Waterford hurlers Ken McGrath and James Murray, spooning down a great fry while Tipp got the better of Galway, I felt seedy and second rate. 'Never want to be here again,' I remember thinking. That afternoon, the three of us played for 'Westmeath' in the county final against 'Limerick', losing by a point. Picked up a few dollars and went drinking.

My memories of that Sunday night all come from a blizzard of blue and gold. Every Irish bar seemed to have been invaded by Tipp's vast emigrant family. Their first All-Ireland in a decade drew an endless siren of whooping joy, every shout reminding me of what Kilkenny had now lost. I hated everything that sound said to me.

The next day, we took ourselves to downtown Manhattan, three Irish culchies on a bit of a tear. I have a blurred memory of a nightclub, a long queue and the suave Mr McGrath nonchalantly slipping a $50 bill to the doorman like our very own Donald Trump.

Tuesday began with the sound of a ringing phone. An Irish lad we'd met had let Ken and me bunk down in his basement flat. Now his voice began scratching at our attention.

'Hang on a second . . .'

The sound of footsteps, a TV being switched on, a short vacuum of sound. Then 'HOLY SHIT . . .'

For the next two hours we sat bolt upright, staring at the live TV news broadcast, searching for New York's famous skyline in a massive, tea-coloured cloud. Maybe it was the sense of watching something straight out of Hollywood, but it took a couple of hours for us to understand our proximity to catastrophe.

'Jesus, we'd better ring home . . .'

Miraculously, we got through. Ken's mother was in tears on the phone. Mine was calmer, but concerned. If anything, they had a better grasp of the scale of the tragedy than we had.

Having made contact with home, we strolled down to Times Square. One of many iconic images from that September morning is of people gathering in the square, staring up at the bank of TV screens broadcasting a live feed from the mass grave that was once the Twin Towers. Ken and I stood in the midst of them. All around us, people wept.

We decided to heed police advice and 'Get the hell out of Manhattan!' But Grand Central station was in chaos. Again it was like a movie scene, thousands pouring on to platforms to get on a train to anywhere. We squeezed on to one just minutes before the station closed.

New York was now, officially, in lock-down.

I had been due to fly home that Thursday, but I ended up having to stay an extra four days. The penny dropped that we were, essentially, in a war zone. I wouldn't pretend it was especially scary or haunting. The scale of what had happened was maybe just too vast to really absorb.

Most of that week was spent drinking beer, watching fresh TV images of the skyscrapers' collapse, hearing new stories of the thousands now officially missing. We tried going to the beach one day, just to break the beery cycle, but the Navy had it shut down. Normal life hung suspended.

We'd spent some time in the pub of a chap James knew from Tallow, nicknamed 'The Thinker'. He'd worked as a firefighter for years in New York and, on the Saturday, he brought us down to the old, red-brick firehouse that used to be his base.

It was deeply moving to watch all the old firefighters present themselves for duty as the toll of lost colleagues kept climbing. The sense of a grief-stricken family was palpable. This particular firehouse had no casualties, but they would have known literally hundreds of the missing.

The firefighters made us feel incredibly welcome at a time when they must have felt like tourist curiosities, passers-by asking them to pose for photographs like you might a giant Mickey Mouse figure in Disney World.

We sat with them to dinner in the firehouse that evening, a great feast of corned beef and spuds. But, just as we began to eat, the shriek of an alarm sounded. In seconds, they were climbing into trucks and swinging out into the streets of Manhattan, destined for who knows where and God knows what.

Staring at their uneaten food, the loss of an All-Ireland felt a pitiably small thing.

I was on a personal mission to toughen up in 2002. Brian Cody's jibe about being 'bullied' the previous August left me bristling through a long winter.

It was my last year at college and, on Saturdays, I started coming home to work as a labourer with my brother-in-law, Larry Cody. This was a hurling decision, pure and simple. I'd seen my brother John's body-shape soften with manhood and I knew some people were thinking I'd probably go the same road.

That couldn't happen. Lifting blocks and mixing cement on frosty mornings asked the questions I needed asked of my resolve to toughen up as a hurler and a man. I was growing up, filling out. I walked everywhere – to college in the morning, home for lunch, back to college, home again. I was eating right, studying hard.

Brian had changed Kilkenny's backroom staff, bringing in Noel Skehan for Ger Henderson. Robbie Lodge was introduced as physio. Brian himself palpably became a little stand-offish. There would be no more cosy cliques in the dressing room. No indulgence of bad habits.

It has pretty much been written into history that the defeat to Galway in 2001 set Cody on a search for a different kind of player. I disagree. To me, a big, self-sufficient hurler had always been his preference. It's what he would have seen in me from the outset in '99, someone big enough and strong enough to win his own ball.

I suspect he prefers hurlers who have the kind of qualities he himself had as a player. He likes fellas who are strong in the air, who don't stand out of contact areas looking for nice, tidy ball. That's what he would have seen in the likes of John Hoyne and Eamonn Kennedy, self-sufficiency. Both were there in '01. The thing that changed after Galway beat us wasn't the style of hurler Cody chose. It was the collective attitude.

Knowing I was captain for WIT's Fitzgibbon campaign in '02, he cut me a little slack, and I missed some of the early League games. But I was back for a meeting with Clare in Ennis that set the standard for our year. They were still in their pomp at the time, a team inclined to test your strength of appetite for battle. Ennis was an intimidating place to go, the crowd practically on top of you, baying for blood.

The team was named at our Friday-night meeting. I was picked at centre-forward, which meant I'd be going head-to-head with the great Seanie McMahon. Peter Barry was centre-back. Derek Lyng started in midfield. There was the sense of a new broom sweeping the dressing room.

Derek's promotion to senior inter-county would be one of the revelations of the summer. We'd gone to college together and were good friends. He'd been on an under-21 panel with me and was a sub on the WIT Fitzgibbon team. Lyng was a good, strong under-age hurler without ever looking exceptional. When I think of the player he became for Kilkenny, I'd be a liar if I said I could have predicted that at college.

But Derek's story probably should be the perfect pick-me-up for any young hurler struggling to make a mark at under-age. He came from a junior club, Emeralds in Urlingford, and his career never seemed signposted for anything spectacular until Brian came to the conclusion that Kilkenny's midfield needed a more robust engine.

Lyng's strength and stamina would become absolutely central to our story over the next decade. This was also the second year of JJ Delaney's life as a senior inter-county hurler. Looking back, you can see a distinct pattern to how Brian was now reshaping the team. Peter

Barry became the role model. Now, Peter would tell you himself that he was never the most poetic of hurlers, but he became the heart of any team he played on.

The guy with the most skill is rarely the one who sets the template in a winning dressing room. It's the fella who works hardest. For us, nobody worked harder than Peter Barry. There's a saying in the Kilkenny dressing room that we're all only holding the jersey for the next fella. Peter epitomized that idea. In my first few years at college, he would give me a lift up and down to training. And just talking to him on those journeys gave me a real education.

He was just so sound, didn't drink and looked after himself really well. The man hadn't an ounce of ego in his make-up, but he was someone you instinctively wanted to follow.

Brian absolutely loved him and, long after he had left the Kilkenny panel, you'd still hear Peter's name come up in conversation. He has long been referenced as a kind of role model in the Kilkenny dressing room. To this day, my conversations with Tommy Walsh about hurling would reference people like Peter, James McGarry and Andy Comerford. They were the leaders that I looked up to and, in 2002, all of them became central to the changing face of Kilkenny.

It's most unusual for us to build League games into anything more than they are, but that game in Ennis was different. Skehan spoke in the dressing room that night, telling us, 'This is where All-Irelands are won.'

We hurled brilliantly on the day and, maybe more importantly, showed a bit of steel. I felt strong, scored 1-4 and didn't take a backward step against McMahon. We were laying down a marker. The question being asked everywhere of Kilkenny now was 'Do they have the stomach?' All year, we would have to provide the answer.

The semi-final of that year's League brought us to the Gaelic Grounds, where Limerick threw the kitchen sink at us. They were a team that didn't hurl to a gentle setting, and Eddie Brennan and Philly Larkin were both sent off in a fairly salty battle. The ref even had to be escorted off the field after our 2-14 to 0-15 victory.

It had been real stand-up-and-be-counted hurling and, again, we showed – even with thirteen men – we were up to it.

We're a curious sort of people in Kilkenny, a bit short on flame-throwing personalities.

You might guess where I'm coming from here, where I'm going to. Let's just say the red-and-white minstrel show that was the Cork team in the noughties never quite rocked our boat. They didn't like us, we didn't like them. Maybe we gave each other good reason.

They depicted us as robotic, conformist types who couldn't locate an original thought of our own. Or, as Dónal Óg would famously put it, 'Stepford Wives'. We saw them as having a little too much of a welcome for themselves. Of being aloof, stand-offish, superior.

In my time hurling with Kilkenny, I'd say that Cork team is the only one with which we never quite managed an adult relationship. You think of the epic All-Ireland finals we had with Tipperary in more recent times, yet there was never any difficulty decommissioning the venom in a dressing-room tunnel and unwinding together like grown men. Some of the most enjoyable nights I've had at All-Star functions have been in the company of those Tipp players that we'd gone to war with the previous September. This never seemed possible with Cork. They radiated an attitude of preferring their own company.

It probably started with the 2002 League final. The GPA had held an EGM two weeks previously, and some kind of agreement was reached between the Cork and Kilkenny representatives that the game would be used as a vehicle of protest.

Cork had been at war with their own county board that year, a war that – by year's end – would plunge them into a players' strike. We had no such issues with those running the game in Kilkenny, and so I suppose we maybe weren't the best candidates for a demonstration.

Andy Comerford, Charlie Carter, DJ Carey and Brian McEvoy had attended that EGM in Portlaoise, but the rest of us didn't know the details of what had been discussed until the Friday night before the League final. Of the Kilkenny men at that EGM, Andy was maybe the only one in a position to beat drums. He was our captain and a strong one. DJ was off the panel, injured. Charlie and McEvoy weren't making the starting fifteen.

So it was Andy who briefed us on the GPA's plan for a protest at the League final. Shirts would hang outside shorts and socks would be worn down around the ankles in the pre-match parade. This outbreak of anarchy-lite would ensure fines for both county boards. A shot across the bows, then, from the workers.

As Andy began outlining the plan to us, Brian Cody stepped into the dressing room.

There was an edge to Cody that year. We'd been bullied by Galway out of the previous summer's championship, and that memory offended just about everything he held dear. He was going to right that wrong and he made clear that no distractions could be countenanced. Just two months earlier, he had culled a few big names from the panel – men like Pat O'Neill and Eamonn Kennedy – making it crystal clear that no one had a divine right to be in his plans.

Now, Cody was like a one-man thunderstorm. He was having none of it.

'First things first, no fucking way are we having any hand, act or part in this protest,' he growled. 'Our only job on Sunday is to win the game. I don't give a shit what anyone from outside this camp is doing!'

Andy tried to hold his ground. 'No,' he said, 'we're going with what was agreed.'

'Not a chance, Andy,' Cody barked, his voice cold as hailstones. And that, pretty much, put an end to it. No more discussion. We looked at our shoes, hoping Andy didn't keep following that bear into the woods.

Deep down, I don't doubt Cody respected Andy for having the courage of his convictions. Andy has a likeable, forceful personality and he was, in every way, a proper leader that year. I'm sure they talked it out privately later. But not at that moment, not in

In Nowlan Park, with an early bit of silverware: the under-13 Schools Country Cup trophy. I'm in the back row, just behind the cup.

In the lounge of our family pub, my younger brother Paul seems to have got the upper hand on me – for once. This was in or shortly after the summer of 1990, to judge from my shirt.

A week after being named Man of the Match for my part in Shamrocks' victory in the 1997 minor county final, I was awarded the same accolade in the 1997 intermediate county final. We had been rank outsiders in both matches.

With my parents on the day I graduated from Waterford Institute of Technology.

In the summer of 1998, having come very close to taking a job in America, I ended up as the free-taker for the Kilkenny under-21s. We were well beaten by Galway in the All-Ireland semi-final, but I scored 3-4, and suddenly I was seen as a candidate for the senior panel (*Ray McManus/Sportsfile*).

My first senior game for Kilkenny, in the Walsh Cup against Wexford, 1999 (*Ray McManus/Sportsfile*).

Celebrating a goal in my first All-Ireland final, versus Offaly in 2000. The goal was credited to DJ Carey, but I still maintain it was mine – and the umpire agrees! (*Damien Eagers/Sportsfile*).

In the 2001 All-Ireland semi-final versus Galway, I let my marker, Gregory Kennedy, get under my skin, and as a team we were horsed out of it. I learned an important lesson that day about the mental side of hurling (*Pat Murphy/Sportsfile*).

Before the 2002 All-Ireland semi-final against Tipp, Eamonn Corcoran and I – good friends from WIT – had to temporarily suspend our friendship: he was to be my marker that day. We won narrowly in one of the truly great games (*Brian Lawless/Sportsfile*).

This image captures the moment when I got past Gerry Quinn of Clare and, with a flick of my wrists from twelve yards out, scored our second goal in the 2002 All-Ireland final, in which I was named Man of the Match (*Damien Eagers/Sportsfile*).

All my Christmases came at once in 2002: in addition to a second All-Ireland medal, I was named Texaco Player of the Year and (*left*) GPA Player of the Year (*Ray McManus/Sportsfile*).

Seán Óg Ó hAilpín and John Gardiner of Cork in pursuit in the 2003 All-Ireland final. I wasn't in top form that day but I kept plugging away, and I took a lot of pleasure from helping the team win (*David Maher/Sportsfile*).

Squaring up to Gerry Quinn of Clare after he caught me in the eye with the butt of his hurl, while Dr Tadhg Crowley tries to attend to me. That was my last action in that 2004 All-Ireland quarter-final replay (*Ray McManus/Sportsfile*).

Contrary to expectations, I made it back the following Sunday for the All-Ireland semi-final against Waterford – and I scored two goals (*Ruth Carter/Sportsfile*).

I was up for the challenge of marking Seán Óg – who would be Hurler of the Year – in the 2004 All-Ireland final, but we were second best: Cork blew us away (*Pat Murphy/Sportsfile*).

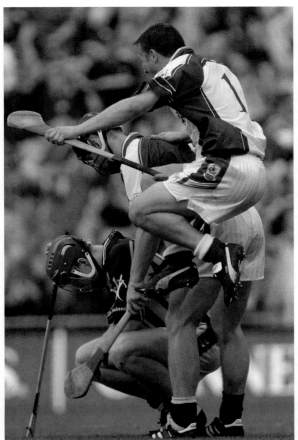

After the final whistle of the 2005 All-Ireland semi-final against Galway, Tony Óg Regan consoled me while Liam Donoghue celebrated. For the second year in a row, we were well beaten (*Brian Lawless/Sportsfile*).

I scored an early goal in the 2006 All-Ireland semi-final against Clare, and by the time I took this late free we had enough of a lead that I was content to knock it over the bar. It was one of my best performances in a Kilkenny jersey (*Damien Eagers/Sportsfile*).

that dressing room, two days before a League final. The subject was closed.

Weakness on our part? If you see it that way, fine. I didn't and I don't. Here's the thing. I was twenty-three, hurling inter-county for my fourth year and, being blunt, completely focused on proving that I wasn't the coward who'd run out the gates of Croke Park the previous August.

As a group, we were bemused by the protest. All the talk of turmoil in Cork simply said to us that they existed in another world. Months later, they went on strike and, reading the newspapers, you'd find yourself thinking, 'What in the name of God is going on down there?'

That was the point of difference. We couldn't understand them. They were fighting about gear, about food after training, about gym-access, about travel arrangements, fundamentally about respect, I suppose. All things we were getting without hassle from our own county board.

As two groups, we were miles apart, and they came to resent this. In time, that resentment led to a depiction of us as virtual robots, just doing what we'd been programmed to do. We weren't. We were doing what we loved.

That League final day in Thurles, Andy went to a few players individually, telling them to make up their own minds. I was one of them. 'Sheff, I'm doing it anyway. Up to yourself if you want to!' he told me. My mind was clear.

The protest died a death, with Andy our lone demonstrator. Only seven Cork lads followed it through, but still, from that moment a gulf began to form: there was a sense that Cork and Kilkenny represented two starkly different philosophies. As they pursued strike action towards the end of that year against a hostile county board, Cork became the definition of the modern, selfless and intelligent GAA revolutionaries. In their own eyes, at least. We were, supposedly, old-world and weak.

That stung, but only like a light brush with nettles. We were winning things, you see. We beat them in that League final and, being honest, didn't exactly see anything in Cork as a template to follow. To our minds, Tipp would have been our nearest challengers. Clare still hadn't gone away. We were driving on.

On a personal level, my life was changing. I'd met Deirdre O'Sullivan the previous December, the two of us spotting one another across a Christmas throng in Langtons bar. Though she'd won an All-Ireland Colleges' camogie medal with St Brigid's Graigue-Ballycallan and had been part of the Kilkenny panel that reached the '97 All-Ireland final, she hadn't a clue about my hurling status. But her sister, Monica, worked locally in Bank of Ireland, knew who I was and, after a typically Irish stand-off, a friend was sent across to make the introductions. Deirdre had been to Australia that year but came home after her father, Michael, was struck ill.

The O'Sullivans were from Callan, close to the Tipp border, and in the run-ups to the All-Ireland finals of 2009, '10, '11 and '14, Michael would make pretty clear to me how unpalatable the thought of losing to the blue and gold would be in their household. Deirdre's brother Adrian hurled minor with Kilkenny and when Michael first heard I had an interest in his daughter, he reputedly advised her to steer clear as I 'needed to be concentrating on the hurling'. Deirdre's other brother, Tom, was into the game too, but destined for a career in what we call special junior!

They were hurling people, then, and our two families warmed to one another pretty quickly. The other change in my life around that time was that I became a tax-paying member of society. On finishing college, I went to work with Bank of Ireland Finance, where I'd already done some work experience. Everything felt natural. I was strong, happy and absolutely determined that there'd be no fingers pointing at me whenever Kilkenny's year was over.

People were giving me more responsibility. Trusting me. I'd been made captain of Shamrocks as many of the older lads slipped away. I suppose I was being challenged to be a man. We played Offaly in Thurles in that year's Leinster semi-final (Croke Park was closed) and Brian made a point of speaking to me, one to one. 'Throw off the shackles here and go let yourself play,' he said. In the dressing room, Andy advised the team to 'Get Henry involved from the off.'

This would be John Power's final year with the panel but, again, I was named at centre-forward ahead of him. He'd been throwing everything into his game that year, really hurling brilliantly. I had a good relationship with John and, the harder he worked, the more he drove me on. To get the shirt ahead of him was a massive vote of confidence.

Up to that year, I'd been mainly a corner-forward for Kilkenny and I found the position restrictive. If the ball isn't coming in, you become a passenger too easily. I'd always hurled 11 with my club. It was a pivotal role and the one I wanted to put a stamp on for the county.

That day against Offaly, I was on fire, scoring 0-7 from play. It was just one of those days when I could feel myself slip into that zone where everything happens almost in slow motion and the ball always seems to find you. I was up against Brian Whelahan, the only modern-day hurler to make the Team of the Millennium. I was so hungry for ball, so strong in my body, they could have set a pack of bloodhounds on me and I probably wouldn't have noticed.

I'd have big time for Whelahan, and he said a few complimentary things about me afterwards in a newspaper article, which meant a lot to me. I was walking on air.

The garlands stopped falling at my feet, though, when we struggled to beat Wexford in the provincial final. Declan Ruth, a former team-mate from WIT, marked me, and Declan always warmed to that chore. He was sticky, knew my game and gave me nothing. In fact, Wexford gave us nothing.

A great score by one of our substitutes, Brian Dowling, helped us fall over the line in the end with only two points to spare. I scored a bagful of frees, but the victory was unspectacular, workmanlike. We didn't really mind. We'd dogged out another victory, shown more steel.

That said, the nature of the win set minds thinking in the dressing room. We'd never looked like opening Wexford up. We lacked explosiveness in the inside forward line, an element of the unexpected. Andy felt we needed DJ Carey back and went to Brian that Monday.

DJ's career was kind of hanging in abeyance at the time. He'd hurt his neck in a car accident towards the end of '01, had been told to take a break from hurling and to avoid all heavy physical contact for a minimum of four months. He also, like so many jet-heeled forwards, had long-standing issues with his hamstrings.

There was a sense that his inter-county career might have been coming to a close. But he was back playing with his club now and Andy was pretty strong in his view that DJ would give us something no other player could. It's a tricky thing, parachuting a player into a team in mid-season, but we weren't talking about any player here. If DJ was even at seventy per cent, he was surely worth the gamble.

He had six weeks to get himself right for a semi-final that set Kilkenny the challenge of trying to record only a second championship victory over Tipp in eighty years. The statistic got a lot of airtime in the build-up, but it didn't signify a great deal. Tipp and Kilkenny Championship meetings were rarities. For me, there would be a far more personal dimension to that semi-final: I would be marking Eamonn Corcoran, one of my best friends at Waterford IT.

I phoned him the Sunday before the game, trying to make light of what was coming. He wasn't talkative. Nicky English had already told him he'd be marking me, whereas, at the time, I wasn't sure. We didn't stay on the line. 'Look, Eamonn,' I said, 'we won't talk next week. Best of luck in the game.' It would be our one and only uncomfortable conversation.

You don't know whether to laugh or cry in those circumstances. Friendship gets suspended. We'd pretty much go to war that day, not in the sense of belting one another, but in just doing our damnedest to win.

It was an epic game too, some felt one of the greatest ever played. We just went at it hammer and tongs. In a sense, Kilkenny had come in under the radar. We were a young team that Wexford had exposed as a little green in some areas. Tipp were defending champions.

I loved the freedom Brian allowed me in that centre-forward role because I could roam into positions that took my marker out of his comfort zone. I was floating, essentially, picking up loose ball.

By half-time, it was pretty obvious the game would go to the wire.

The pace had been unrelenting. I went to the toilet and was standing alongside Peter Barry at a urinal when we could hear DJ begin to make a speech. He was banging a table. 'Lads,' he said, 'I'm after putting in a serious effort these last six weeks to get back here . . .'

I looked at Peter. 'Six fucking weeks?' I said. 'I'm training nine fucking months for this!'

Any other player might have been devoured at that moment. But this wasn't any other player. DJ would go out in that second half and, typically, make the difference. His hand-pass for Jimmy Coogan's decisive goal was a moment of pure genius. Without it, Tipp might well have gotten by us and, who knows, made it two in a row. The story of Kilkenny and Brian Cody could well have petered out that very day.

So winning that game was massive. It didn't just pitch us into an All-Ireland final, it confirmed that the softness of '01 was history. Eamonn and I swapped jerseys at the end and we had a drink up in the players' bar. But, emotionally, we were planets apart that evening.

I rang him the following day, just to see how he was doing. The tone of his voice gave me an immediate answer.

DJ's return was the story of the summer now, and that brought benefits for all of us.

Cody decided to hold an open 'press night', and every journalist seemed drawn to one man. DJ was comfortable with the commotion. He took media attention in his stride and, for the rest of us, there was thus the welcome sense of a low-key build-up.

Despite Waterford wining their first Munster title since '63, they had been snared by Clare in the other semi-final. It was hard to figure out whether, for us, this was good or bad news. Waterford had been spectacular in their provincial final defeat of Tipp, but Clare still had that hard edge of a team that knew how to go to war.

Ger Loughnane was no longer manager, but Cyril Lyons seemed to work off a similar template. We knew, if nothing else, that the final would test us physically.

Cody's plan was to target their strengths, and this meant attacking through the middle. Brian Lohan and Seanie Mac still pinned down the centre of their defence with incredible intensity and we needed to front up here, force them on to the back foot. Martin Comerford was deployed to the edge of the square, where he brilliantly pinned Lohan down all day.

I was invited to do to Seanie what I'd done earlier that year in Ennis. But this wasn't going to happen. Whereas he'd stood right beside me under puck-outs that day, this time he cleverly positioned himself maybe five or six yards behind so that I was always in his eye-line.

I'd decided that I'd run at him, the first ball I got in my hand, and, about three minutes in, it happened. Dipping the shoulder, I barged past, went for my point and – to my disgust – watched the ball drop short. But little things kept going our way that year. DJ, typically, anticipated the flight of the ball better than anyone and nipped in to flick home a goal. Clare never recovered from there. We won comfortably in the end, DJ scoring a point from under the Hogan Stand – two touches, the ball never going to hand – that had the whole stadium swooning.

If you watch the video, I'm running in under the shot, just in case it happens to fall short. And Davy Fitzgerald, with whom I would have my share of run-ins over the years, is giving me a fairly plain-speaking welcome. I've great respect for Davy but, at that moment, I couldn't resist a little bit of return fire. 'That'll keep you quiet.'

After winning the 2000 final, I'd been a bit fed up not to be interviewed that night on *The Sunday Game*. Just an inner child speaking, maybe. To me, at the time, the ultimate place to be seen was sitting in front of the RTÉ cameras, just hours after winning an All-Ireland.

This time more than compensated. I was named Man of the Match and would go on over the next few months to add All-Star, Texaco and GPA Player of the Year awards. The last was a particular bonus, as myself and Kieran McGeeney were the recipients of SEAT cars.

For someone just out of college, all my birthdays now seemed to be coming together. And the ghosts of '01 had all been well and truly exorcised.

5.   Knives Out

We're in a room somewhere in Dublin Airport, Brian Cody on one side of me, Ned Quinn on the other, facing strangers across a table.

It's the spring of 2003 and I'm on trial for doing something stupid. Gave David Kennedy the butt of my hurl into the ribs during a League defeat to Tipp in Nowlan Park. That Monday night I got to see it in slo-mo on TG4 and I felt like a criminal caught on CCTV.

It might have been easier to watch if Kennedy had given me good reason to use timber. He didn't. I was just poor on the day, growing frustrated, maybe listening to too many Tipp voices shouting down our own. If their centre-back said something untoward, I can't recall it. Just remember feeling more and more contrary. Then hitting him a dig.

It's not my style and seeing my frustration exposed on television was plain embarrassing. As luck would have it, TV evidence was now deemed admissible in disciplinary hearings. The Games' Administration Committee kindly extended an invitation for me to come and visit.

The incident didn't really amount to a hill of beans, but Tipp's Brian O'Meara missed an All-Ireland final in '01 for doing much the same. Maybe you have to hurl to understand what's dangerous and what isn't. The men who judged O'Meara clearly didn't.

Now it was the turn of yours truly, Philly Larkin and Ger 'Redser' O'Grady to explain ourselves. 'Redser' had been our chief tormentor that day in Nowlan Park, giving Noel Hickey a torrid time. But, at some point, he'd gotten side-tracked with Philly and the two of them started fighting.

So we find ourselves in this room, just off the main arrivals hall, facing a big, square table with maybe twelve faces behind it. Who did the faces belong to? To this day, I can't honestly say. In my head, they sounded like football men, men maybe representing counties conveniently accessed from Dublin by commuter plane.

Could be I'm just cynical, of course.

Anyway, they kept rewinding the tape, over and back, each new viewing pushing me deeper into my chair. 'Sure, throw the book at me and let's be done with it,' I was thinking. Except for one thing. The video doesn't quite close the deal. You can't actually see the butt of my hurl make contact with Kennedy's midriff.

In a court of law, that might amount to a tiny shaft of light.

Ned and Brian thought so. They heard the questions I was being asked and sensed that they weren't dealing with hurling people here. Little things. The committee men didn't call it the 'butt' of the hurl, they called it the 'top'. Their terminology was like something you'd hear at a post-mortem.

Ned did most of the talking. 'You say it looks like Henry strikes with the hurl there, but can you be definite that he does?'

Brian piped up with mention of my disciplinary record. 'Impeccable' was the word he used. 'If you can guarantee me that's striking, you've better eyes than I have!' he said. The men at the table looked a bit lost. I was invited to go get myself a cup of tea as they asked Philly to step in and explain his fighting.

It was two in the morning by the time we got back to our cars in Kilkenny. The following day, word comes through that we have been declared innocent men, leaving some of the media unamused. They call the GAC decision 'a fudge' and I find myself in two minds. I'm not used to being the focus of negative attention and I know I shouldn't have hit Kennedy. So I am in the wrong and feeling uncomfortable.

But did I deserve a suspension? No, I truly don't think so.

People were saying it's maybe one law for Henry Shefflin, another for everybody else. My face was all over the papers for reasons I wasn't used to. People were judging me, all but dissecting my character. I hated the feeling that gave me.

Next time, I knew, I'd keep the 'top' of my hurl where it belonged!

★

That League ended on a Bank Holiday Monday in Croke Park, a great, eccentric final against Tipp that fizzed with goals and curiosity.

I kicked the winning point, triggering a good quote from DJ. 'Henry was actually trying to kick the ball to me,' he said afterwards. 'But that's Kilkenny football for you!' Maybe 20,000 watched a game that deserved the intimacy of Thurles or Nowlan Park. It felt like Mass in an empty cathedral.

Looking back on the incident with Kennedy and my general demeanour throughout the competition, I wasn't really fit. I was twenty-three, the Liam McCarthy Cup was doing the rounds and, as a young 'Hurler of the Year', I seemed endlessly attached to it like a fancy ribbon. The call would come that it was needed in such and such a place tonight and I'd be, 'Sure, suppose I'd better go . . .'

We'd been to South Africa on a team holiday and Andy Comerford and I had even taken the cup to Australia. My name was out there and it felt more and more as if people were looking for me. The craic was good, the beer invariably free.

In later years, I'd pull back from all this glad-handing. Circumstance – two cruciates, four children – would even see me miss a raft of holidays. But I was nicely insulated in the early months of 2003.

Four times in that League final we trailed Tipp by an eight-point margin. But we were obstinate and, I suppose, innately confident, and we wouldn't let them get away. PJ Ryan had come on for James McGarry and, in the last play of the game, I caught his puck-out. My first real catch all day.

Almost shocked at the feel of leather in my hand, I took off with a small battalion of Tipp men chasing. My intention was to hand-pass into space, but no one came to meet me. This was a problem. The chasers were too close for me to swing and, being honest, my legs were shot. So, from maybe twenty-one yards out, I kicked the ball. Brendan Cummins got a touch, but it scraped over the bar. We'd won another League.

Charlie Carter was our nominated captain for the year but he wasn't starting. DJ, his Gowran clubmate, led us out on the day. But

Charlie collected the cup and made a short speech in the dressing room afterwards. Something along the lines of driving on from there, that it was the championship we'd be judged on. People said afterwards there was a little tension in the room – I can't say I remember. Charlie might have been out of favour but, not for the first time, he'd come in and, effectively, changed the game for us with a goal.

There was a strange dynamic, though, to having a captain who wasn't starting. Charlie would be standing in his tracksuit, saying his few words before a game, and something in Brian Cody's body language told us he wasn't entirely comfortable with Charlie talking. We knew things weren't great between them. We just didn't know the depth of it.

Charlie was well liked in the dressing room and very well-got with supporters. I had big time for him on a personal level too as he'd been very decent to me when I first came on the Kilkenny panel in '99, very open. He would already have known my family from coming into the pub, and he had done some work experience for a local farmer. I'd gone to New York with him for a hurling weekend and stayed in his house the night before we travelled. He was sound as a person and also a serious, serious hurler.

But the tension between him and Brian percolated through the latter stages of the League. The week we were due to play Cork in Páirc Uí Chaoimh, a story did the rounds that Charlie was refusing to travel. He'd been left off the starting fifteen again and, apparently, had had words with Cody the night of the team announcement.

Behind the scenes, a lot of stuff happened that week that the players weren't privy to. We heard subsequently that representatives of the Young Irelands Club had met with Kilkenny's management that Saturday to try and broker a solution. Charlie was on the bus that Sunday. But he'd be an unused sub.

By the start of the Championship, there was no great sense of reconciliation. We played Dublin in a Leinster semi-final at Nowlan Park and won by fifteen points. Again, Charlie didn't get a run.

He'd been putting in a big effort in training and he did make a difference in games whenever he came on. But he had a style of latching on to breaking ball, and I think Brian had decided after 'o1 that he wanted his forwards working harder. Maybe that was where the conflict gathered steam.

Anyway, the night of the Dublin game we were all aware of Charlie picking up his bag in the dressing room immediately afterwards and the sound of a door banging. It was all we really talked about over our few pints that evening. This was a Saturday night but, by Monday, local radio had its teeth into the story. The county seemed split down the middle. Half the county was giving out about Brian, the other half about Charlie.

That Tuesday came an announcement. Charlie Carter had withdrawn from the Kilkenny panel.

I was in the car when I heard it and I immediately rang Charlie. I told him I felt he should just hang in there. Give it another few weeks and we'd all just drive on together. Easy for me to say, maybe, and I knew from the tone of his voice that he was adamant. He'd made his mind up: 'No, that's it!'

As the story gathered legs on local radio and Charlie's statement hit the streets, deep down I suppose I knew there was no way back now. He went on Radio Kilkenny that Wednesday night and said something along the lines of having lost his appetite for hurling.

I was disappointed because I felt, if he'd kept the head down, he'd have been back starting games before the end of the year. To be fair to Charlie, he never tried to drag any of us into the row. The issue was between himself and Brian.

Looking back, I suppose I kept a certain distance from the argument. I was relatively new on the panel, knew that Brian didn't take prisoners and, being honest, I wasn't willing to risk upsetting my career by getting directly involved. If that sounds selfish, I can't dodge the charge. In later years, I'd probably have had the confidence to be more vocal. I certainly felt a little torn watching Charlie go because, when I won my first All-Ireland, it had been Charlie, DJ and me in the full-forward line.

But the moment he went public was the moment I knew his

inter-county career was over. I just couldn't see Brian Cody picking up the phone to try to dissuade him. That's not Brian's way.

He didn't blink. He never does.

There's no doubt some people had their knives out for Cody by that point. If things turned sour for Kilkenny, it wouldn't take long for the flak to start coming his way.

Brian McEvoy had decided to walk too and, in one of the stranger moves, Denis Byrne declared for Tipp, having switched clubs from Graigue-Ballycallan to Mullinahone, just across the county border. I never knew Denis particularly well, but he'd been captain in my first year with Kilkenny and was a top-class hurler.

People were scratching their heads at his decision. The likes of Eamonn Morrissey and 'Shiner' Brennan had previously transferred to Dublin, but they were working in the city. That made sense. In Denis's case, declaring for – of all counties – Tipp seemed a little off the wall.

He would actually play for them in that year's championship, but was spared an appearance against us in the All-Ireland semi-final, which we won by twelve points. We would have won by more but for the heroics of Brendan Cummins. My abiding memory of that game is a goal celebration by Tommy Walsh. It was like something taken from the 1930s, Tommy buck-lepping off the ground like an excited foal. It was Tommy's breakthrough year and, when we met up for a few beers that Monday, we had great craic in Billy Byrnes rewinding to Tommy's moment, everyone in the pub imitating his celebration. Three times, he must have jumped at least five feet off the ground. It was hilarious.

My first glimpse of Tommy had been in a Roinn B under-14 game between Shamrocks and Tullaroan in Callan. My brother Paul was playing and, while Shamrocks had a decent enough young team, everyone's attention in the ground was gradually drawn to the tiny Tullaroan corner-back. Tommy was no more than ten at the time but, already, utterly fearless.

Ball after ball that went into his corner was delivered back out with interest. He was unstoppable. A series of Shamrocks opponents went in to try and subdue him and, one after another, all came back out defeated. Eventually, one of the biggest lads – John Kennedy – went jogging across, but Tommy kept coming out with the ball, side-stepping challenges and clearing with big, exaggerated swings. He just made a fool of every single player that went near him. So it's fair to say that people in Kilkenny became aware of Tommy Walsh when he was still in primary school.

He would go to St Kieran's and win an All-Ireland Colleges medal and, in 2001, he was on a Leinster minor-winning Kilkenny team. But, around the time Tommy was doing his Leaving Cert exam in Kieran's, he was developing a fixation with the Fitzgibbon Cup.

By '02, Cody had begun bringing him in to senior training, but he was essentially just making up the numbers. One year later, he was on the team.

In the lead-up to that All-Ireland semi-final against Tipp, we went to Mount Juliet for a Saturday of team bonding. That evening, we had a barbecue and the management allowed us a few cans to drink. As Tommy got a few down, all inhibition began to lift. I remember him singing this fairly ropy college song, everyone – management and players – looking at one another as if to say, 'Where in the name of God did we get this chap?'

Andy Comerford was slagging him relentlessly about the Fitzgibbon. Tommy had just started in UCC. Every second sentence out of his mouth seemed to be about hurling for the university.

And Andy kept prodding. 'So what's this oul Fitzgubbin thing again?'

Tommy, naively, would start to explain: 'Well, it's . . .'

'And can any oul college enter?'

What he didn't realize was that Comerford had actually won a Fitzgibbon with WIT in the early '90s. Tommy ended up exasperated. As luck would have it, he also ended up without a Fitzgibbon medal.

The great thing about Tommy is that he's the exact same now as on the very first night he came in to train with us. From the outset, he hurled with absolute venom. At one point, I think Brian actually had to call him aside and tell him to relax a little. Maybe because he wasn't the biggest of men, Tommy seemed compelled to mix it with people. He just wouldn't pull back from anything. He needed to be reminded that he was in the squad on merit now. Picked for his hurling, not his temper.

Though we won that semi-final by twelve points, it hadn't entirely been plain sailing. Tipp actually led by two points at half-time and it was DJ who suggested in the dressing room that there were goals to be had if we chased them.

In truth, DJ always seemed to feel that; around this time, he had developed a virtual obsession with goals. It actually became a source of humour in the dressing room how, on occasion, he'd say a few words that would almost flatly contradict a message just delivered by Cody. Brian, you see, was always preaching calm. 'Keep tipping the points over and the goals will come,' he'd counsel. Then DJ would be on his feet and it was as if he hadn't listened to a single word.

'Get the ball in to us and we'll get goals,' he'd say.

Dougal (John Hoyne) and I would be sitting there, chuckling. Brian was never going to pull up DJ for speaking out of turn, was he? And, that day against Tipp in '03, his call to 'Get the ball in, we'll bury them . . .' actually came to pass. Our intent was signposted almost immediately after the resumption when Cummins pulled off one of what would be half a dozen terrific saves, denying Eddie Brennan.

But the floodgates opened once Eddie found the net in the forty-fifth minute and I got our third goal in a second-half rout that had us outscoring Tipp 3-9 to 0-4.

Cork, meanwhile, had got their act together after a period of turmoil and seemed a united group now under Donal O'Grady. They were taken to a replay by Wexford in their semi-final, but won the replay pulling up. We knew we weren't their favourite people and the final probably reflected that tension. They would shoot eleven wides in the first half alone, and we led by six points at half-time.

Despite the scoreline, we weren't flowing. DJ, whose private life had been splashed all over one of the Sunday papers that morning, would be held scoreless in the game. Eddie Brennan barely struck a ball. Apart from frees, I was largely quiet, scoring just two points from play.

When Setanta Ó hAilpín snatched a second-half goal for Cork, Cody sent JJ Delaney back to mark him. With just fifteen minutes remaining, Cork slipped into the lead and we looked in serious trouble. But JJ's switch was the end of Setanta's influence, and Martin Comerford's sixty-fifth-minute goal essentially won the game. Gorta was Man of the Match by a distance that day, giving Diarmuid O'Sullivan a really tough grilling. He finished with 1-4, though Dónal Óg Cusack probably felt he should have kept out the goal.

Tommy has a great saying that it's far better to be noticed playing well in the last twenty minutes of a game than in the first twenty. I think that was the day he formed the opinion. Having started on fire, with three points in the opening twenty, his performance kind of petered out and he ended up being replaced by Conor Phelan.

It was an extremely intense final. I have a vivid memory of O'Sullivan barrelling up the field at one point, Kilkenny's would-be tacklers bouncing off him like roadkill. The crowd loved it. Three striped jerseys hit the ground and I was being lined up as the fourth when the humanitarian in Pat O'Connor interjected, offering O'Sullivan the free. I was only too happy to apply the brakes.

I took real satisfaction from my contribution to the last fifteen minutes of that final. I was involved in a few scores that made the difference, including Gorta's goal. I wasn't in top form, but I just kept horsing myself into the game even when things seemed to be going against me.

When Brian talks about spirit, I'm pretty sure that's what he means. Some days everything might fall right for you, but maybe the ones you take most pleasure from are those where you had to just hang in.

I'd now played in four All-Ireland finals in my first five years of senior inter-county, winning three.

The following January, we flew to Orlando on a team holiday, sated and, on reflection, maybe a little complacent. We didn't know it, but the glory days were about to grind to a halt.

6. The Longest Summer

I wasn't long home from Ardkeen hospital when the man who'd sent me there left a message on my phone.

Gerry Quinn sounded genuine. 'Henry, I'm just ringing to say what happened last Saturday, I never intended. That wouldn't be my form. If you get a chance, could you give me a ring back?'

Before telling the story of what happened next, I should probably rewind a bit, to June 2004 and the Leinster semi-final against Wexford in Croke Park.

Wexford were miles smarter on the day, their wing-forwards interchanging, running diagonal lines over and back. Our half-backs didn't know what to do. Just watching had them dizzy.

Damien Fitzhenry's puck-outs were the key. They could have been radar-guided. He'd stand, watching his wings make these runs, until one of them would suddenly change direction. Next thing, a little prairie of space had opened up and Damien would ping his delivery into the clearing. Alternatively, he'd aim at his midfielders – who took to standing out on the sideline for every puck-out. Wexford played a game that was alien to us, and we ended up a virtual rabble, just fifteen lads shouting at one another, waiting for somebody else to solve the puzzle.

Maybe we'd fallen into the trap of believing what everyone else seemed to be saying about Leinster hurling. It was, supposedly, a one-horse town. Well, now that horse was missing. We'd lost our first match in Leinster in seven years.

True, we almost got out alive. With the game slipping into injury-time, almost inexplicably we still led. Then things started happening in slow motion. Adrian Fenlon went to take a sideline cut from about fifty yards out and we knew that was well within

Adrian's range. 'Jesus, don't,' I remember thinking. Another Wexford point and I felt sure we were facing a replay.

Seconds later, I was sorry he hadn't cut it over the bar. It dropped short to Peter Barry, who, throwing up the ball to clear, had his pocket picked by Mick Jacob. As Jacob's shot hit the net, I could see Brian Cody slump to his knees behind the Canal End goal.

The Wexford crowd went wild. Almost without knowing, we'd been taking Leinster titles for granted and now we weren't even going to make the final.

Cody was absolutely furious. 'I don't want any of you going on the drink tonight,' he told us afterwards in a voice that brooked no argument. He gave it to us between the eyes. We were gone soft, complacent, he said. If we didn't pull our socks up, we were finished. Then, typically, he finished on a positive.

'But be very clear on one thing,' he told us. 'We are going to pick this up, we are going to improve, we haven't gone away. But I don't give a damn who is playing the next day. Because no one has a divine right to this jersey.'

No explanation was needed. Michael Kavanagh would pay for a softish Rory Jacob goal by losing his place for the next game – but every one of us was on tenterhooks.

Looking back, I never felt a hundred per cent that year, even though I always tried to stay fully focused. The day after the Wexford defeat, I texted Fenlon. Just one line: 'Well done yesterday, ye deserved it!' A bad sign of where my head was. At the time, I was thinking of getting a job in the pharmaceutical industry and had been hoping to talk to Adrian about it. Soon as I sent the text, I was mad with myself. Needed to get my game-head back on.

The qualifiers took us down a road we weren't familiar with. After a fairly routine defeat of Dublin, we squared up to Galway in Thurles. Galway had a way of making us uncomfortable. We never knew quite what to expect of them, maybe because they never quite seemed to know what to expect of themselves. All we did know was that, on any given day, they could beat any team.

I always got the impression they liked playing us and, that Sunday evening, you could have cut the tension with a knife. We went to the Springhill Court Hotel for our usual pre-match meal, and I couldn't touch a bite. That's not me. Then, on the bus to Thurles, I sat beside Sean Dowling. Sean's a good pal of mine but he'd just been told he was dropped and was absolutely bulling.

So I'm trying to get my game-head on and the man beside me could probably have done with more understanding company. I was a million miles away. I suppose the newness of it all had us all swallowing hard. All week Brian hammered home the possible implications of losing. It wasn't just the end of our Championship we'd be talking about, but the probable end of half a dozen careers.

Galway bore the brunt of our anxiety. We tore into them. The first puck-out that came my way, I grabbed and won a free. Then Jimmy Coogan put me in for a goal. And, almost without knowing, I found myself running out the field, grabbing the crest of my jersey, bouncing up and down like a madman. The very things we'd shake our heads at when Dan Shanahan, John Mullane or Eoin Kelly did it with Waterford.

That night we just exploded like a firework. Maybe it was fear. We'd won consecutive League and Championship doubles, but the Wexford defeat had exposed an insecurity.

Personally, I was in a zone that evening, scoring 2-11. When I'm in that zone, I'm not really conscious of anything anybody else does. I'm interested only in me and the ball. I don't give a toss who is marking me or what anyone is saying or doing. That's when I'm in the place I need to be.

Much was made afterwards of how animated Cody was on the line that evening. Some journalists seemed to think he might even face some kind of sanction for a couple of altercations with the referee, Diarmuid Kirwan. Truth is, he could have come on spraying machine-gun fire and I don't think any of us would have noticed. When it was put to Brian later that he'd been quite 'wound up', apparently he said, 'I don't do wound up.' I smiled at that.

We were all stepping into the trenches that night against Galway.

Brian has this saying that he's always working off a blank sheet of paper. He constantly lays it on the line that every year could be our last. We'd seen the likes of Pat O'Neill and Charlie Carter cut loose from the panel, so we knew he wasn't bluffing.

That night, every last one of us wore his heart on his sleeve, Brian included. It was Galway's misfortune they just happened to be in the opposite corner.

We were introduced to the concept of seven defenders in the All-Ireland quarter-final by a Clare team managed by Anthony Daly.

Daly's ploy was to pull a half-forward, Alan Markham, back between his two lines of defence. It worked brilliantly. I was playing centre-forward and the extra defender caught us completely off-guard. We were looking around at one another, wondering who was supposed to be marking who. The backs were banging ball up aimlessly and we were constantly outnumbered in attack. It became very frustrating.

On the line, Brian fumed. We kept looking across, asking him where the hell he wanted us to stand. Clare should have beaten us, but we hung in and Tommy Walsh's second-half sending-off oddly helped us, because now we played just two men inside and the extra space suited me. I scored a couple of points off Frank Lohan and got pulled down for a penalty.

On the goal-line, Davy Fitz was giving it loads. 'C'mon, you chicken-shit, are you man enough to go for goal?' I tapped it over the bar, thinking we'd done enough to win. We hadn't. Jamesie O'Connor got a late equalizer.

Cody didn't spare us the following Tuesday. We hadn't just been out-thought by Clare, we'd clearly been out-fought too. They'd roughed us up a bit, and that offended every fibre in his body. That's what he was laying on the line now. 'This time, WE hammer into THEM!' he said.

Daly, it would seem, delivered much the same message to his team. Because, if they were bullies the first day, they were even bigger bullies now. They played like men who didn't like us very much. I was picked at full-forward and, the first ball that came in, Brian Lohan caught me late and high.

We were over by the corner of the new stand and, after the ball was gone, he caught me around the neck and tried flinging me to the ground. I could hear Davy in the goal, mouthing, 'Sow it fucking into him . . .' They were absolutely hyper, banging us hard at every opportunity.

Comes with the territory, presumably.

It's hard to avoid getting dragged into that dynamic. Eddie Brennan got a goal and I wasn't slow in giving Davy a few verbals. There was niggle in the game all day, a lot more heat than light, I suppose. I was getting very little change out of Lohan as we were winning nothing among the half-forwards. I felt starved of the ball inside and asked Cody to bring me out.

Soon as he agreed, I immediately started gesturing towards James McGarry to direct a few puck-outs down on top of me. If James could find me, I felt I could have an impact on the game.

Now, I'm right-handed, which means I catch the ball with my left. Gerry Quinn, who was marking me, is left-handed, catches it with his right. James's puck-out hadn't even arrived when the butt of Quinn's hurl came through my face-guard and I felt two distinct bangs in the eye. Straight away, there was blackness. I was incensed. And scared.

I'd got a bad eye injury before, hurling under-16 for South Kilkenny in a Dublin blitz the weekend of the '95 Leinster final. Helmets didn't have face-guards at the time, and a ball just bounced up, hitting me in the eye. I found myself being placed in the back of an ambulance and taken, on my own, to a Dublin hospital.

It was daunting for a young fella. I didn't know my way around Dublin at the time and, to this day, can't honestly say what hospital I was brought to. But I do remember feeling petrified as this medic began asking questions about an eye that, maybe half an hour after the incident, now had zero vision.

It turned out that a blood vessel had burst and, while drops settled the pain down, it was decided to keep me in overnight. Officials from the county board called in to check on me that Saturday evening but, once they left, I remember feeling incredibly lonely. Mobile phones weren't exactly commonplace at the time and my parents wouldn't have been able to drop everything just to come and visit me.

On the Sunday, my brothers John and Tommy called in with Kevin Kennedy, the Shamrocks groundsman, and Big Tommy Walsh. They were going to the Offaly–Kilkenny game and I asked the matron if, maybe, I could go with them. She was adamant: 'You don't take chances with an eye injury.'

But when she left the ward, I gathered my things and slipped away with the lads. Told nobody. Just walked out of hospital and headed to Croke Park, my eye now offering a bit of blurred vision. Rain was pouring down, but I wore dark glasses to protect the eye from any glare. It was all a big adventure to me, the boys drinking their pints in Quinn's, me looking out at the monsoon through shades, like something out of *Miami Vice*.

When I got home that evening, the condition of the eye worsened and I began to lose all vision again. The matron rang from Dublin, explaining to my mother exactly what I'd done. I spent the next three days in the Ardkeen, being rightly lectured about my stupidity.

Nine years later in Thurles, play continued while I was on the ground. No one seemed to have noticed what'd just been done to me. I threw my hurl away in frustration, panicking at my lack of vision. John Hoyne came across, saw my face and made a lunge for Quinn. A penny was beginning to drop.

Tadhg Crowley, the team doctor, came running in. 'Fuck!' he said the moment he saw my eye. I was shouting now: 'I can't see, I can't see!' Tadhg was telling me to calm down, that everything was going to be fine. But no matter which way I turned my head, I couldn't escape the blackness in my right eye. And I hadn't even got a free!

Now I could hear the anger begin to rise in Tadhg's voice too. A real Kerryman, he wanted Clare people to understand the severity of what'd just been done to me. Decided he'd take me the long way off the field so that we swung down by the Clare dugout. As we went past, Daly and his selectors pointedly refused to make eye-contact. I was shouting, 'This is fucking wrong!'

Lohan was sitting in the dugout now, a pulled hamstring having ended his game. I could see him looking out at me, expressionless. As we swung down the tunnel, my rage gave way to tears and I started crying.

In the dressing room, a steward began asking what seemed pointless questions and I was getting irritated. Tadhg tried to get me to lie on a bed, but I was like a racehorse refusing to go into the stalls. Someone came in the door with an inquiry. Cody wanted to know, would I be able to go back on!

'No chance,' shouted Tadhg.

I was given a bag of ice to keep pressed against the eye and went back out to sit behind the dugout. Ned Quinn was beside me. Ned has a short enough fuse and was letting the Clare management know what he thought of what had been done to me. Insults flew back and forth.

Kilkenny pulled away to win in the end, but the anger didn't taper. Tensions were high, but the priority was to get me out of Thurles now and down to the Ardkeen as fast as humanly possible. I threw on my tracksuit top and jumped into a car driven by Jim Freeman, Chairman of the Supporters Club. The former GAA President, Paddy Buggy – RIP – sat into the back. A garda escort spirited us out through the traffic, and soon we had a clear road to Waterford.

I don't think there was much doubt in any of our minds that my year was over. The conversation was very stilted. Jim sensibly left the radio off as there wasn't much to be gained by listening to coverage of the Thurles fallout. I couldn't see a thing out of the eye and now I had a throbbing headache. The lads knew I was in no real mood for conversation.

I rang Tadhg O'Sullivan, the orthopaedic surgeon, to see if he could get the eye surgeon to see me and, luckily, he succeeded. It being a Saturday evening, I might easily have had to wait until the Monday for an appointment.

To begin with, they tried to open my eye but the swelling made it difficult. So they sent me down for an X-ray, and a torn tear duct was identified. It was at that point the surgeon, Mark Mulhern, told me how close I'd come to losing the eye – maybe a millimetre. As he took me down to theatre to operate under local anaesthetic, he kept accentuating the positive: 'You're a very, very lucky man . . .'

Did I feel it? Can't say I did. For two nights I lay on a bed in the Ardkeen, literally sick with worry about the long-term implications. I'd keep my eye, but in what condition? The vision was still blurred.

I was back home when I got the message from Gerry Quinn. I was still scared about the long-term implications for the eye and my anger hadn't quite subsided. Now I had a decision to make. Would I phone the man responsible? I had a fair idea of what had occurred in Thurles and it hadn't been good. To this day, I believe the strike on me was intentional. Did Gerry Quinn mean to hit me in the eye? No, I don't believe he did. Did he mean to hit me? Absolutely.

Still, I was willing to listen to his explanation. I decided to step out of my parents' house and sit into the car. Best to keep this conversation private, I reckoned.

He answered immediately and, to be fair, sounded remorseful. He asked how I was, a good start. Then he began explaining. 'I genuinely didn't mean to hit. That's just the way I go for a high ball . . .'

I could accept everything he said without absolutely believing it. He was making an effort and I appreciated that. I like to give people a fair chance. Everything he said, I suppose I pretty much expected him to say. Except for a throwaway line at the finish.

'Jaysus,' he said, 'we had mighty craic on the beer all day yesterday.'

I couldn't believe it. Maybe he was nervous and just blurted out the first thing that came into his head, but all I could think was, *Well fuck it, Gerry, you can't have been too concerned about me yesterday so if you were on the beer all day.*

As I hung up, the anger was bubbling away inside again.

Quinn had been pilloried on *The Sunday Game* by Tomás Mulcahy and Larry O'Gorman for the incident and, when he subsequently went public about his 'amicable' telephone conversation with me, the media generally depicted it as a self-serving gesture. Looking back, I think the media – generally – were quite hard on him. I was angry at the time – furious – but I don't actually hold any hard feelings against Gerry Quinn.

I haven't met him since, though I do remember spotting him from a distance at that year's All-Star function. The allowances I'd been willing to make for him had, largely, been undermined by that comment about his day spent on the beer. The funny thing is, I'd always regarded Quinn as a fabulous hurler. Now I found myself wondering if there had been an ounce of sincerity in his apology.

Put it this way, if I saw a lad in my own club pull the kind of stroke Gerry Quinn pulled on me that day in Thurles, I'd let him know in no uncertain way what I thought of him. It was a cheap shot and, potentially, a very dangerous one.

All week, the official line was that I had little chance of playing against Waterford the following Sunday. The first bit of training I did was a few gentle drills on the Friday night. My face was still black and blue but, surprisingly, I felt really good. I'd been putting drops in the eye on a daily basis and my vision was back to normal by the middle of the week.

My nerve? For maybe a year afterwards, people would say to me that I didn't look especially confident under a dropping ball. There's no doubting it: that kind of injury affects your confidence. You start thinking twice about going for a ball. JJ Delaney, like Gerry Quinn, is left-handed and I remember just having that tiny seed of doubt in my mind whenever JJ would be marking me in training.

But Brian put me at corner-forward that day against Waterford and, just a couple of minutes in, I got a goal off Eoin Murphy. Waterford had gambled on a young goalkeeper, Ian O'Regan, making his Championship debut. It was a big ask in an All-Ireland semi-final and you could detect a little edginess in their full-back line.

I took advantage of hesitation to flick home a second goal and, though my legs went towards the end of the game, there was massive relief all round that we were back in an All-Ireland final.

In hindsight, maybe too much. Most of us didn't even go for the meal afterwards. We just headed straight for the bar and were fairly full, getting on the bus home. Already a certain amount of denial was setting in. The 'we're back' vibe was taking over even if the reality didn't really stack up that way because, arguably, Waterford should have beaten us. There was almost a feeling that the job was done. But six games into the Championship, we were pretty much running on empty. The final would be our seventh, almost double the number of Championship games we had become accustomed to.

We trained really hard in the weeks that followed. Brian brought us to the greyhound track at James's Park because, apparently, it was the same width as Croke Park. There were big numbers coming in to watch us train and you could feel their presence on top of us.

Of course, we told each other that we were going well, that we were ready. But we weren't. Our legs were gone.

We were flogging a dead horse.

There was a real edge to Cork in that year's final. You could tell they didn't see much in us to like. Cody asked me if I'd have any issues marking Seán Óg Ó hAilpín, pushing the idea that we were going to target their strengths. I was fine with it. Seán Óg was having a phenomenal season (he would end up Hurler of the Year), but I was now facing my fifth final in six years and I didn't exactly feel like a child on a man's errand.

That said, we were in trouble on two different levels. Firstly, no matter how we tried to distance ourselves from it, talk of the three-in-a-row was everywhere. It hadn't been done by anyone since the great Cork team of the '70s and we seemed to be endlessly reminded that Kilkenny's only previous three-in-a-row had been won in a committee room. Even though it was never spoken about in the dressing room, it was always there, pressing down on us, tugging at our attention. You couldn't escape it.

Our second area of trouble was a little more fundamental: we just weren't hurling well. No matter what slant we tried to put on the season, there was no great flow to anything we'd done. In hindsight, everything about the team was creaking. We were in denial.

After an early Kilkenny score in the final, I deliberately met Seán Óg with a heavy shoulder. Instantly, he barrelled back into me with interest. If I was laying down a marker, he was responding with one of his own: 'You won't fucking knock me backwards!' That message came off every one of them that day.

And Cork blew us away. We didn't get a single score from play in the second half and, long before the end, we might as well have been sitting on the bus, facing home. They'd suffocated us.

I had a goal chance late on when John Hoyne drew the corner-back and threw me a hand-pass. I could feel Dónal Óg advancing and remember thinking, *If I try to catch this, I'll be swallowed up.* So I decided to hit it first time, caught it lovely, but the sliotar bounced up off Cusack's body and he caught it.

In desperation, I threw myself in to make a block and, dummying as if to drive it out of the stadium, he flicked a ten-yard pass to a defender. Great big roar from the crowd. Fuck. Bad enough to lose, but to be a fella's punchline? *Boom. Boom.* Get me out of here.

Now, here's the thing. I've talked about the tension between ourselves and Cork, but I liked a lot of that team as individuals. I've checked and they've no horns growing from their foreheads. I'd have known fellas like Joe Deane and John Browne from my college days. Sound men. I really liked Diarmuid O'Sullivan, even if there were days and games he'd try to terrorize me on the edge of the square. Sully was good company. I got to know him on a few All-Star trips and I'd like to think there was genuine warmth there. Others, like Niall McCarthy and Ronan Curran, I could have a chat with and come away genuinely liking. And how could you not respect Seán Óg?

I actually texted him after that final: 'Congrats Sean Og, better team won. Well done.' I hadn't gotten to speak to him after the game and just wanted to do the right thing. He texted back. My phone didn't turn to sludge.

Unfortunately, my mobile number appeared in some ads in the *Farmers Journal* back then and a few smart boys went to town on me that night. There'd been a lot of criticism of the state of the pitch, with people losing their footing, and, that night especially, strangers texted to tell me I had been 'skating on thin ice'. Hilarious.

The winter ahead would be torture.

7.   The Proposal

Hatred has never been the worst thing a team can encounter in hurling. Ambivalence is.

After the Cork defeat in '04, I think we were terrified of being left behind. People had begun writing us off and there was an attitude that we needed to be on fire from the off in '05 if they weren't going to be proved right. We needed to set down a few early-season markers.

We won the Walsh Cup, blew Clare away in the National League final, then regained our Leinster crown with a thirty-one-point hammering of Offaly and a hard-earned final victory against Wexford. Superficially, all was coming right again in our world. In reality, we were bluffing.

By the time Galway got hold of us in that year's All-Ireland semi-final, the cracks were beginning to show.

We'd struggled past Limerick in a quarter-final notable for our failure to register a goal. Then Noel Hickey was diagnosed with a serious viral infection that was potentially damaging to his heart, ruling him out for the remainder of the season. I'll always remember Brian calling us into a circle at training and breaking the news.

All I could think was that Noel was younger than me. How the hell could this be happening?

The dressing-room banter – 'Jaysus, who'd have known you even had a heart, Hickey!' – concealed a general apprehensiveness. It was decided we should all be screened and, worryingly, Conor Phelan was subsequently found to have a leaky valve in his heart. The cardiologists' advice to Conor was to give up hurling for good.

Looking back, it was a year in which nothing really felt right.

Galway completely blitzed us in the semi-final, scoring five goals and leading by twelve points with around ten minutes remaining. We rallied to pull them back to a goal, but we were just flailing, like a fish on a hook. If it wasn't for Eddie Brennan's 2-4 that day we'd have been obliterated. Our third Championship defeat in eleven months had left us at a major crossroads.

The defeat triggered a lot of negativity and, in some instances, sourness in Kilkenny. Brian's management of the side came under attack. We'd played in five of the last seven All-Ireland finals, winning three. Yet the Galway semi-final defeats of '01 and '05 were being held up as some kind of defining snapshots of our shortcomings.

Brian kept his powder dry but, for a time, we worried that he might walk away.

My own private situation was a mirror of the team's. I'd started work as a pharmaceutical rep and never felt entirely comfortable in the role. Basically, my job was to call in to doctors' surgeries and advise them that they should be prescribing a particular drug. I was working with really decent people, but I felt a fraud and was pretty sure I sounded one.

At times, I might have to wait two hours or more just to get access to a GP. I'd just sit there, doing nothing. The job satisfaction was zero. Other people thrive in the role, but it just didn't suit me. On a few occasions, on my way to an appointment, I actually swung the car round, headed for home and put the head down. The dishonesty of the job sickened me.

Looking back, I had no balance in my life. Everything felt out of kilter. I wasn't eating very much and, as a consequence, my weight fell to under thirteen and a half stone. I was spending most of my time in the car, grabbing a sandwich on the run rather than stopping for a proper lunch. I was too light, too weak and, generally, too preoccupied.

Shamrocks got to the county final for the first time in fifteen years and I took on far too much responsibility in the build-up. Looking back, I cringe at some of the stuff I was doing. It was real 'Charlie Big Potatoes' behaviour, aimed – I suspect – at proving my ability to handle pressure.

The Saturday week before that final against James Stephens, I stood in the dressing room, advising anyone in receipt of media requests for interviews to redirect the call to my number. 'Just get them to ring me!' It actually makes my skin crawl when I think of it now. The lads were perfectly capable of handling themselves with whatever few media requests came their way. But I was trying to play Superman, the big county boy who would deliver his team to the Promised Land.

In the end, I put too much pressure on my own shoulders. I went into the game feeling absolutely certain we would win, my mind already crowding with memories of all the old homecomings from my childhood. But The Village were just calmer on the day, more experienced. They put Philly Larkin marking me, and I had one of those days where I began forcing everything. I was held scoreless, missing about 2-4 from play.

When the final whistle sounded, I bolted for the tunnel without shaking a single hand. The child in me came bursting out. I couldn't find the grace to stay out there and do the manly thing. Everyone saw my little tantrum and it even drew comment in a few newspapers. To this day, I can honestly say that no defeat hurt me more. I just wanted the ground to open up and swallow me whole.

I'll never forget driving down to Langtons afterwards, my three brothers in the car. Paul had been playing, Tommy was a sub, John a selector. The four Shefflin boys together, crawling downtown through the traffic, not a single word being spoken. The silence left a kind of ringing in my ears.

I knew the lads felt sorry for me, sorry for the way my whole year had now unravelled. But the Kilkenny defeats were a million miles from my mind at that moment. The only jersey I could see was the green and white of Shamrocks. I felt I'd let everyone down.

The defeat sat on me all winter. There were times I'd be alone in the car and, without warning, the game would come into my head and my eyes would just fill up with tears. I couldn't get it out of my head. Not just the weakness of my performance, but also the lack of respect I'd shown The Village.

Trouble was, I bottled everything up, didn't speak about it to any-one. I wasn't happy in my work, wasn't happy in my hurling.

Earlier that year, Deirdre and I had spoken about buying a house together and looked at a couple of places in Kilkenny. When I think back, I can only thank God we didn't buy one of them. It was the time of the property boom and everything was a ridiculous price. The houses we looked at were neglected old places that are still sitting derelict today.

In the end, we decided to build in Ballyhale on land owned by my father. And, once the year's hurling ended, I threw myself headlong into that project. We'd just been granted planning permission and, about a week after the county final, I was up on the site, digging foundations. Deirdre could see exactly what I was doing. I was running away, hiding from things.

One evening, she told me so. 'You're only up there because you still haven't come to terms with that county final,' she said. She was right. I needed to grow up.

In many ways, I was in denial. I didn't want to even think about hurling, but I found I was spending so much time in the car, doing a job I hated, that hurling was pretty much all I had in my head. So the house became a kind of escape valve. My brother John is a block-layer and, together, we would do most of the direct labour on site with Cha Fitzpatrick's brother, Donnacha.

I mixed the cement for every single block we laid. It would take a full year to build the house, but I welcomed the physical work and – long term – there's no doubt it helped me get stronger.

And two things happened that November, two things that cleared a lot of fog from my head.

The first was a phone call from Bank of Ireland Finance, inviting me back into my old job. I was euphoric. I'd been thinking of getting back in contact myself, and now it was agreed that I would start back with them in December.

The second was a trip to Dublin for the All-Stars. Truthfully, I had little appetite for it. The year with Kilkenny had ended so miserably, I found it hard to get much pleasure from any personal awards.

The morning after the ceremony, in Citywest, Deirdre and myself went down to breakfast, bumping into Brian Cody and his wife, Elsie. The women, intuitive creatures that they are, soon seemed to realize that Brian and I wouldn't mind getting some stuff off our chests. So they left the two of us in the dining room and, for maybe the next hour, we had what I still regard as one of the most pivotal conversations of my hurling life.

That morning, we talked with an intensity that pretty much shut out everything and everybody else in that dining room. Brian had decided he wasn't walking away from Kilkenny and had very specific plans for the coming year.

I opened my heart to him about my own frustrations: the way my professional life had been so demoralizing, how my loss of weight left me feeling physically weak, and my personal disgust with how I dealt with the county final defeat against his club.

He told me he wanted me to focus on being physically right for the summer of '06. That he wouldn't use me in the National League. The priority for Kilkenny would be the Championship and getting a shot at redemption against Cork.

I drove away from Citywest feeling re-energized. The chat with Brian had been exactly what I needed.

So a lot of little bits and pieces were beginning to fall into place now. But there was still one big one I needed to get right. I'd decided to ask Deirdre to marry me.

To be honest, I suspect she expected a ring over Christmas, but I was toying with a few different dates in my head. At one point, I considered putting the big moment off until Valentine's Day but I knew I probably couldn't wait that long.

So I decided we should head to Lahinch for New Year's Eve. Why? One of the few good things I took from my time on the road as a pharmaceutical rep was my discovery of Lahinch. I loved the place. Had a picture in my head of this beautiful blue sky above a gorgeous, sun-splashed beach as the perfect setting for a proposal.

But it didn't really work out that way.

After checking in to the hotel, I suggested a little walk along the strand. Just two problems: howling wind and rain. Deirdre looked at me as if I had two heads. 'You want to walk in that?' she said.

'C'mon, it's not as bad as it looks,' I lied.

It was worse. The Atlantic looked and sounded like it was going to rise up and swallow Lahinch whole. After a few strides, I turned to Deirdre, got down on one knee and produced the ring. 'Will you marry me?' I asked.

She just started shrieking.

'Is that a yes or a no?' I asked.

'Yes, yes, yes . . .' she replied.

It was only then I realized I'd been nervous as a kitten. I was literally shaking, albeit that could have been partly to do with the cold.

That evening, the storm would knock out most of the electricity in Lahinch. Restaurants didn't open. We had to settle on a local chipper for our celebratory meal of sausages and chips. Not exactly Bogart and Bacall, I suppose.

We were both absolutely drained after the day and barely managed to stay up to see in the New Year. But I have a vivid memory of listening to the roar of the ocean that night and feeling that, finally, my life was beginning to make sense again. I was engaged to the woman I loved, the foundations were down on our new home and I was back in a job I knew I was suited to. It felt like the beginning of the rest of my life.

And I slipped away into the deepest, most contented sleep.

8.   'Hurling is a Simple Game'

Two weeks before we played Galway in the 2006 All-Ireland quarter-final, we went to the Monart Spa resort for a weekend.

Everything felt back on track with the team. The Walsh Cup, League and Leinster Championship had all been secured and now we'd been drawn against the side that dumped us out of the previous year's Championship. It felt perfect. I texted Derek Lyng the evening the draw was made: 'This is the one we want, the one we need!'

There was an edge to us in Monart, born, I suppose, of the realization that we were really just one defeat away from oblivion. Cork going for the three-in-a-row meant that everything about our year would, ultimately, be framed by whether or not we stopped them.

That Friday, we had a team meeting and the dialogue got pretty hot and heavy. I remember Michael Dempsey in particular speaking very well, really challenging the players to take things to the next level. But then he said that some of the lads weren't training as they should. That they were, essentially, cheating.

I challenged him on this immediately. 'Maybe, Mick, you'd be better off going and saying that to these players' faces instead of bringing it up here,' I said.

There was a lot of tension in the room. James Ryall hadn't been making the starting fifteen and suggested that, contrary to what we were endlessly being told, form in training didn't seem to be the deciding factor in team selection. James suggested that some lads were being picked on reputation alone. It was that type of meeting. No place for precious egos.

Then Brian decided to speak. He went for the jugular, talking with disdain about 'some lads in this room with All-Stars, some with "Hurler of the Year" awards'. He said some fellas needed to get their arses into gear and that he personally didn't 'give a shit' what awards any of us had won before. The only thing that mattered was what we planned on winning in the future.

Sitting there, all I could think was that there were only two 'Hurlers of the Year' in the room at that moment. JJ Delaney and me.

I was bulling. To me, Brian had been having a go at me personally. When the meeting ended I stormed back to my room, where Lyng and Michael Kavanagh had to sit listening to me rant. I wanted to go straight to Brian's room and tell him what I thought of him. But, needless to say, I didn't.

Years later, I was reading Donncha O'Callaghan's autobiography and some of his stories about Declan Kidney had me grinning. When Kidney was in charge of Munster, he seemed to do to some players exactly what Cody was doing to us that night in Monart. He'd try to get them angry, then set about harvesting a backlash.

I've no doubt that Brian wanted that anger inside me, maybe inside every one of us. We trained that Sunday morning in Enniscorthy and you could feel an edge to everything we did. At the end of the session, management left us alone and we all pulled into a circle. I remember Noel Hickey speaking. 'Don't ever forget what that losing feeling was like last year,' he said. For him, especially, the previous summer had been a horrendous experience.

A few others spoke in a similar vein before I said something along the lines of not forgetting the winning feeling either, 'Because that's what this is all about!'

But when I got home, Cody's words were still niggling me. Over and over, I found myself saying to Deirdre, 'I'll show him!' Looking back, if I was asked to pick one example of his management that defined Brian Cody's greatness, that weekend in '06 would probably be it.

He had me exactly where he wanted me.

Way back in January, Brian had invited Gerry McEntee down to give us a motivational speech. You could have heard a pin drop in that room as he talked about the situation faced by the great Meath football team he played in after a few sickening defeats by Dublin.

'Everyone's saying ye're gone, ye're finished,' he said. 'Well, what are ye going to do?'

The papers were full of Cork's superior training methods and fitness; the Rebels were 'the best-prepared team in hurling'. But Mick Dempsey, our physical trainer, kept repeating the same message, like a mantra: 'Ignore the propaganda, lads, ye're fitter than them. Trust me, ye're fitter!'

Mick's arrival as our physical trainer had been one of the big backroom changes in '05. I'd be lying if I said he and I saw eye to eye immediately. We didn't. Michael was a member of the Laois football team that won a National League title in '86. Maybe that was the fundamental problem. Football was his game and, to begin with, it seemed to me that his ideas about physical preparation weren't really applicable to hurling.

He'd shown himself to be an accomplished manager, winning three county titles and a Leinster Championship with the Carlow club, O'Hanrahans, and guiding Laois to an under-21 All-Ireland final. At some point, he'd moved to Kilkenny and opened a pub bearing his name above the door on John Street. Then his work with the footballers of Castlecomer and Muckalee brought him to Martin Fogarty's attention.

The view of those who worked with him was, unequivocally, that he knew his stuff. So Fogarty included him in his backroom team when managing Kilkenny to back-to-back All-Ireland under-21 hurling titles in '03 and '04. Those victories led to Martin becoming one of Cody's selectors, and he wasn't slow in providing a glowing reference of Dempsey's understanding of how to train a team.

A massive student of sports science, he came across instantly as being big into weights. Michael is a very serious, focused individual who set each of us a programme designed to improve core strength.

Very quickly, I found myself pulling back from his advice. I was concerned that the weights might make me bulky and I pretty much refused to follow the path he'd set. Maybe, to some degree, I felt a kind of silent loyalty to the departed Mick O'Flynn. Micko, a Corkman, had been part of the Kilkenny furniture. We all liked him and had good craic with him. He was a tough taskmaster and, as we liked to joke, probably fitter than some of the players.

When Brian decided change was needed, bringing in Dempsey and Noel Richardson, some of us felt a bit awkward. We'd still meet Micko in the gym. It didn't feel right somehow that he was outside the group now, given he'd been so heavily involved in our lives. I'd never had a physical trainer until I walked into the Kilkenny senior dressing room. Everything I knew about fitness, I'd learned from Mick O'Flynn.

So, for me, the transition wasn't entirely smooth. Lads like Tommy, Jackie and JJ, who'd been trained by Dempsey with the under-21s, bought into the changeover immediately. They knew how good he was.

Looking back, for that first year anyway, I wasn't giving him the respect I should have been. Brian had, essentially, given him free rein with the physical training and, maybe because so much else in my life was out of kilter in '05, I viewed the change as just another disruption I could have done without.

One night, Brian called me aside and said, 'Mick feels you're not paying him enough attention . . .'

I knew he was right. It doesn't reflect well on me to say it, but I think – deep down – I was looking down my nose at Mick. He'd been training the Muckalee football team and, human nature being what it is, I suppose I just assumed that the job of training Kilkenny hurlers would take him out of his depth.

It took me that first year, essentially, to give him that respect. I had to drop my guard a little and let him into my life. And, gradually, I came to realize that he's actually quite brilliant at what he does. In fact, given the injuries I would suffer down the line, Mick Dempsey became one of the most important people in my career. I became totally engrossed in the whole area of sports science, a subject close to Dempsey's heart. And, happily, I always maintained a good relationship with Mick O'Flynn. Things change and people move on in serious sport. It isn't personal.

One of the things agreed between Cody and me over our All-Star breakfast in '05 had been that my body needed a little kindness. I was having ongoing trouble with inflammation of a groin, and our physio, Robbie Lodge, thought it best that I sidestep a lot of the heavy winter work. Essentially, the only training I was allowed do was some straight-line running and I had minimal involvement during the League.

To begin with, this left me feeling slightly isolated. I would go in to training and just run endless shuttles from one corner flag to another while the session was in full swing. Stop at one end, walk, turn, go again. Pretty monotonous, but exactly what I needed.

All the routine pulling and dragging of winter training had created the groin problem in the first place, and I think Brian recognized that I was at a stage in my career where I needed to be spared the torture. Anyway, with all the work I was doing on the house, my physical fitness wasn't in question. It was simply a case of managing my body with a little more care.

Brian was leaving absolutely nothing to chance in terms of Kilkenny's preparation. We spent one weekend away in Seafield in Wexford and he brought down Nicolas Cruz, one of Ireland's boxing coaches from the 1992 Olympics, to speak to us.

That weekend focused hugely on the importance of sleep and a good diet to us as athletes, Cruz speaking at length about the importance of properly digesting food.

We had a few days free of training the following week and I spent those evenings working, flat out, on the site of our new house. It meant I didn't really have time to head home for a proper dinner and so, one evening, I volunteered to pop down to the local chipper.

As luck would have it, Cha happened to be driving past just as I was pushing in the door.

Later that night, there was a game of poker on up in the Fitzpatricks' house involving Cha, a few of his brothers, John Tennyson and a Clara hurler, Austin Murphy. I wouldn't have had Austin's number, so they sent me a text on his phone, pretending it was from our dietitian, Noreen Roche. It read something along the lines of: 'Henry you were spotted this evening in the chipper in Ballyhale. Cannot believe this after all we talked through at the weekend!'

I immediately texted back a lame apology, explaining how busy I was on-site with the house and promising that I would be back eating properly the following day.

A little later, I received another text – this one sent from Tennyson's phone (another number I didn't have) – purporting to be from Nicolas Cruz. My heart sank. He sounded exasperated, describing it as 'unbelievable' that I could have broken the squad agreement on diet. It was only when I read his final line, 'At least tell me that you digested the chips slowly, Henry', that the penny finally dropped. Bastards.

I was mad for road by the time I got back in for the League semi-final against Tipp and I would score 2-6 (2-3 from play) in the final against Limerick. It brought our fourth League title in five years, but there were enough flaws in the team's performance to give Cody plenty of training-ground ammunition leading into the Leinster Championship.

We didn't exactly pull up any trees with our next couple of performances either. We had fourteen points to spare in an underwhelming Leinster semi-final defeat of Westmeath and, though we beat Wexford by eight in the Leinster final, Declan Ruth held me scoreless from play.

So you can understand the undercurrent of tension surrounding the All-Ireland quarter-final against Galway. Which version of them would turn up was, as usual, anybody's guess.

Naturally, there were a few mentions in the build-up about what they'd done to us the year before but, by and large, we were more inclined to look inward. Brian had been playing Martin Comerford and me as corner-forwards, knowing full well that neither of us was particularly happy there. I felt he was holding me back a little, maybe hoping to get the best out of me as late in the season as possible.

Against Galway I started at full-forward, then moved out to the wing at some point during the game, and that was pretty much the pattern for the rest of the Championship.

We won by five points and, that same Saturday evening, Cork scraped past Limerick by a single point. The 'best-prepared team in hurling' seemed to be showing a few chinks. That was certainly our interpretation and, when they won their semi-final against Waterford by the same narrow margin, we were convinced we'd beat them if we got to the final.

One of the things that really clicked for us that summer was Cha Fitzpatrick's move to midfield from attack. He was an absolute revelation and would end the season named Young Hurler of the Year. Cha's use of the ball gave us another dimension. I knew from watching him with the club just how good Cha could be, but the general hurling public was only beginning to understand the addition he was to Kilkenny.

Clare were our semi-final opponents and, early in the game, I got a goal when Brian Lohan let a ball slip in behind him. I went on to give one of my best performances ever in a Kilkenny jersey, scoring 1-13. Though we won by eight points in the end, the game never felt entirely comfortable. With ten minutes remaining, there was just a point between the sides but, from there, we kicked on impressively. Clare, I suppose, simply weren't the force of old, great men like Lohan and Seanie McMahon pretty much on their last legs.

Whatever about Galway and Clare, our preoccupation with Cork now framed everything. They had recorded thirteen consecutive Championship victories and John Allen had, we heard, brought in Roy Keane to give them a motivational speech.

I remember bristling at the '05 All-Stars function at the way they stuck together on one side of the room. They were champions, the centre of attention. You'd be looking across, thinking, 'Who do they think they are?'

It was around this time they went on a Railway Cup trip to Boston and pretty much decided not to mix. Even their own Munster team-mates really only saw them the day of the game. An atmosphere developed.

Their '05 win had moved them on to thirty All-Irelands, against our twenty-eight. They were chasing three-in-a-row. Their new 'possession' game was being lauded as revolutionary. They were machine-like and polished. You'd swear they'd invented the wheel. When O'Grady left after '04, Allen slipped seamlessly into the manager's role and they hadn't broken stride.

Our manager was very much back to the Cody of January '02. To him, reputations were dust now. He seethed at the depiction of us as some kind of prehistoric force. Years later, in his book, he would refer to a radio comment by Donal O'Grady after the '05 final, suggesting that Kilkenny probably faced a period of struggle. Maybe desperate people file all this stuff away, hoping you can pack it tight like gunpowder. Well, we were desperate people. Everything was on the line now.

We became a team with tunnel vision in '06. Not so much obsessed with getting back to an All-Ireland final as with getting Cork. The rivalry felt personal.

Early that year, James McGarry spoke of building them up in interviews at every possible opportunity. Feeding the fire of their ego. They kept telling the world to form an orderly line and come see how a modern team prepared. We helped arrange the queue.

Fresh-laundered gear hanging up in the dressing room when they'd arrive for training. Drills so sharp they'd take the eyes out of your head. Pre-match warm-ups so finely tuned they guaranteed every player ten thousand touches in ten minutes. Ice-baths. Laptops. Mind games.

For us, that whole season was a long drum roll towards getting a shot at them. Pulling them down to size. Or, as Alex Ferguson might put it, knocking them off their fucking perch.

We came in from the long grass that summer. Cody was being written off, I was being written off. Come to think of it, the whole team was being looked upon as obsolete. It suited us perfectly.

Did we have doubts? Absolutely. That winter, my own head was full of questions. Are we doing something wrong? Are we not training as hard as they are training? Is our style obsolete? In the build-up to the final, we probably talked more about them than we'd ever done about an opposing team before. It felt as if everyone outside the group was expecting Cork to win.

Eight days before the final, we had a meeting and a bit of a stretching session in Hotel Kilkenny. Then we trained in Nowlan Park and JJ Delaney suddenly went down with a damaged cruciate. He was out of the final.

Poor JJ was absolutely devastated, but it was as if we just didn't have time for sympathy. I wouldn't say he was ignored, but you could sense that people were operating now with tunnel vision.

On the Sunday, we had a team meeting and one of the subs, Peter Cleere, decided to speak. Peter would have been very much on the periphery of things, maybe getting the odd League outing, nothing more. But his words were absolutely perfect, and I took them as a sign that the subs were one hundred per cent in tune with the starting fifteen.

Cody had the blackboards out and segregated us into maybe four groups, each one invited to talk tactics. He left the floor open to anyone who wanted to speak and he made it clear he was open to suggestions. Dónal Óg Cusack's short puck-outs were forcing Cork's opponents to think differently. Brian had devised this plan whereby our two corner-forwards would drop back a little, a move that would then be replicated by the wing-forwards and midfielders.

My view was that we'd be better off just marking people individually. If Cusack took a short puck-out to Brian Murphy, so be it. Murphy was a ferociously tight marker, but he wasn't the best striker of a ball. To me, it made sense to tighten up only around those who could deliver a ball eighty yards.

We were very conscious of the damage done by Niall McCarthy in '04 when he'd feign to run one way, then jink back in the opposite direction, losing his marker. This had, clearly, been a pre-arranged tactic: Cusack always anticipated the change of direction and found him with an ocean of ball. My own view had been that so much that went wrong that day had been down to the fact that our legs were simply gone. That said, McCarthy could never be given that kind of freedom again.

Personally, I was trying to tick every conceivable box in terms of preparation. The Thursday before the final, I phoned Jack O'Shea. I'd been on a charity trip to Malawi with him that January and just wanted to pick his brain on how a man who played in so many All-Ireland finals for Kerry kept producing big performances, as if on automatic pilot. This was my fifth final and I wanted to make sure I was in the right place psychologically.

The irony of the '06 All-Ireland final is that we were lauded afterwards for our tactical shrewdness. Allen said he'd never known a more tactical final. But we were so driven in that final, so hungry for the ball, we ended up doing the very thing we vowed not to.

Cork liked to draw you into the tackle, then release quick ball to the man you'd just left. We wouldn't fall into that trap, we said. We'd stay with our men, avoiding the temptation to go rushing in.

We forgot that plan the moment the ball was thrown in. There's a famous image from that day of Seán Óg surrounded by four Kilkenny men. It was likened to the one of Kerry's Eoin Brosnan penned in by half a dozen Tyrone men during the '03 All-Ireland football semi-final. The truth is, we couldn't help ourselves. Anything in red that moved, we just wanted to bury.

I've often joked about it with Brian since. He believes a lot of crap gets written about tactics in hurling and would have bristled at the idea that Cork were somehow managed smarter than us. Yet, just at the very point he was virtually being branded a dinosaur, Cody suddenly found himself lauded for Kilkenny's new tactical refinement. And that on a day we left our tactics in the dressing room.

My view is that, above all else, intensity won that final. It was about as scientific as a bear attack. Our backs were phenomenal, Hickey completely blotting out the threat of Brian Corcoran and reminding us all how sorely his absence had been felt the year before. And Aidan 'Taggy' Fogarty, in his debut Championship, proved the match-winner, scoring 1-3.

As it happened, drawing each line a little deeper under the Cork puck-outs worked perfectly. Their midfielders started going to the wings for puck-outs, only to find themselves marked by our half-forwards. It seemed as if we had a spare man everywhere Cusack's puck-outs dropped.

There was criticism of the pitch and the length of the grass afterwards, but we'd happily have played in a field of corn. Looking back, maybe the high grass suited us. But we were so focused, nothing was going to distract us. Cody talked afterwards of how so many people had written us off. He spoke of Hickey specifically and how he'd been depicted by some judges as too slow.

If there was an unusual amount of emotion in Brian's voice, it perfectly reflected what we were feeling as a group. Everything was on the line that day. Cork had been depicted as everything that we weren't. They wore little motivational tattoos on their arms in the final, which, no doubt, would have been held up as a masterstroke had they won. I suppose there's a pretty fine line between cleverness and bullshit.

Our very existence as county hurlers had been on the line that summer and, really, in our eyes that overrode any need for managerial gimmicks. There wasn't even much roaring and shouting in our dressing room before the final. People knew exactly what they had to do.

Brian Cody's most repeated expression is that 'Hurling is a simple game.' That All-Ireland final offered living proof.

9.   Fr Paul

The difference between first and second is the difference between night and day.

In the end we won everything that year, dominated every awards function. A season that started with doubts about our very futures as county hurlers, one that was marked by the retirements of men like DJ Carey, Peter Barry and John Hoyne, now brought us to a kind of Nirvana.

I collected my sixth All-Star, my fifth in succession. I was named Player of the Year in both the All-Star and GPA schemes. I got the Texaco Award. And then, in late December, the most ridiculous thing happened.

I hadn't intended going to Dublin for the RTÉ Sports Review of the Year function. I was busy with the house and, being honest, had had my fill of functions at that stage. Our wedding date was set for the following March and I seemed to have a thousand and one different things to do.

Only a phone call from RTÉ persuaded me to travel in the end, but I wasn't going with much enthusiasm. It was probably around five in the evening before I even dragged myself off site, covered in construction dust.

The function was in the O'Reilly Hall at UCD, and we had been booked into the nearby Montrose Hotel. I'd seen my face feature in ads for the programme but it hadn't really registered that I was nominated for the overall Sports Personality of the Year award. In any event, the nomination seemed incidental. People of the calibre of Derval O'Rourke, Katie Taylor, Paul O'Connell, Darren Clarke, Bernard Dunne and Kieran Donaghy were on the shortlist too. O'Rourke seemed the obvious favourite, having won gold at the World Indoor Athletics Championships and a silver at the Europeans.

I remember saying to Deirdre as we arrived, 'Look, sure, let's just enjoy the night . . .'

The judging panel was made up of Eamon Dunphy, George Hook, Pat Spillane, Jerry Kiernan, Cyril Farrell and Ted Walsh. Dunphy had come past our table just before the programme started and seemed in high spirits. 'Aaaah, Shefflin, you're a legend,' he told me. I laughed. I knew he had some Kilkenny connection, but I didn't imagine I'd be getting his vote.

After each sport was reviewed, someone from that sport would be called up for an interview. But, when it came to the hurling year, they just showed a few highlights and moved on. It was as if they couldn't wait to get it out of the way. I began to wish I had stayed at home.

Brian and Elsie Cody were at the table with us and I think it's fair to say we had kind of tuned out of things until the voting started.

Then, suddenly, I realized it was a two-way battle between Derval and me. The first four votes cast left us tied at two apiece. Kiernan was visibly seething. I looked over at Cody as if to say, 'Is this really happening?'

Derval had Hector Ó hEochagáin and a camera crew following her every move. It was as if they were there to film her coronation. But a strange sensation went through my body now. A few hours earlier I'd been mixing cement in a Kilkenny field, and this kind of gathering felt a million miles removed from ordinary life. Now I was in contention for the biggest individual award in Irish sport. A GAA player in the middle of all these international stars. I turned to Deirdre. 'Jesus Christ, I couldn't, could I?'

In the end, the deciding vote was Hook's. I doubt he knew a great deal about me but, suddenly, the camera zoomed in on his face and I heard him call out my name. I was incredulous. Next thing, hands were reaching out towards me, offering congratulations.

Ó hEochagáin came over too and I remember him being less than gracious. More or less told me that the judges had got it wrong. I suppose I'd messed up his programme. To this day, I'm still inclined to pinch myself when I look at the award at home. It stands out above all the others.

Years later, I met Hook at a function and he told me that, off air, the panel just couldn't decide on a winner and – literally – made the call live on television. You could see there was real tension there and I doubt Kiernan has ever quite forgiven the decision.

But I was euphoric. Winning it had been beyond my wildest dreams.

There was a stop I had to make on my way home from Dublin the following day that, looking back, offered a jarring reality check.

Monsignor Paul Fitzgerald, as he was known then, was dying. My mother's brother and one of the few real confidants I've had in my life was in the final throes of a three-year battle with colon cancer. He'd hurled minor for Kilkenny before entering the priesthood and tended to take a profoundly stern and sensible view of the game, a view I always welcomed.

Ostensibly, he was a harsh judge. Compliments didn't fall easily from his lips and, where others might dance around the truth for fear of causing offence, Fr Paul tended to be of the view that, long term, candour was the only real kindness.

Formerly the parish priest of Thomastown, he was – I suppose – an old-fashioned man with old-fashioned values. I liked that. I particularly liked the absolute sense of loyalty I got from him. He could be critical of a performance without ever leaving me in the remotest doubt that, in an argument with others, I'd be defended to the hilt.

We grew close over the years. Maybe he was a surrogate for my grandparents, who had all passed away before I was even out of short pants. I always got the impression that Fr Paul was looking out for me. In his vocation, he was a shining light to the family, and our friendship, I don't doubt, had a lot to do with the strong faith I retain today.

This may sound strange, but I don't especially like talking in any great detail about hurling. People have their opinions and I'm more than happy to leave them unchallenged. It's perfectly natural that people who meet me want to talk about this game or that, but I'd never get into anything too heated or too deep. I just feel they're entitled to draw their conclusions, whether or not they happen to coincide with mine.

So, team-mates apart, I tend to pull back from picking through games with people. Fr Paul would have been an exception.

I know he was very proud of the fact that I hurled with Kilkenny, but it just wasn't his style to communicate that pride directly. People who sat beside him during games would say he was a hard man to impress. The day in '04 that I got the bad eye injury in Thurles, he was sitting with my parents. Directly in front of them was Kieran Hoyne, father of John Hoyne. At one point in the game, I – apparently – threw a pass in John's direction that he failed to collect. Fr Paul muttered something about the two of us looking like fellas who were playing on opposing teams.

Kieran Hoyne turned back to my father and asked, 'Henry, is that man supporting Kilkenny or Clare?'

Towards the end, I think people just didn't want to sit with him at matches. He was too hard a judge, too unforgiving. It seemed to escape them that he was also fundamentally fair. Put it this way, when Fr Paul was still alive, there probably wasn't an opinion I valued more than his.

We knew he hadn't that much time left, though, towards the later stages of 2006. The hope had been that he'd be around long enough to celebrate our wedding Mass the following March, but it gradually became apparent that that wasn't going to happen. Fr Tom Murphy, who once played with Kilkenny, would marry us.

A few months earlier, Fr Paul had taken Deirdre and me out for dinner in Mount Juliet, a gesture we both subsequently recognized as a kind of early farewell. It was as if Fr Paul was saying, 'I'm not going to make your wedding, but I'll still be looking out for you both.'

We had no idea of this at the time. To us, he was physically fine. The cancer hadn't gone away, but he certainly didn't seem to be in any imminent trouble. Fr Paul was obviously a lot sicker than he'd let us know, but we had a lovely evening. I remember being parched after a day on the site and downing a pint of Budweiser shandy the moment I arrived – something I'd never ordinarily do in the middle of the season.

Yet, as sick as Fr Paul was, I could see him – literally – glow with pride the morning I called into the hospital in Kilkenny with that RTÉ award. Nice as it was to see that, I could tell – as I could every time I visited – that a little more life had ebbed from him. The medication made him drowsy and there were times I'd just sit with him and watch him doze. The day Cork played Waterford in that year's All-Ireland semi-final, he'd been very disorientated and the two of us just sat watching the game, barely a word spoken between us. It didn't feel awkward. Neither of us had to be anything we weren't in one another's company. Maybe that's the definition of friendship.

That Christmas was a harrowing time, watching his life quite literally ebb away. The Kilkenny team headed away on a team holiday but I decided not to travel. It wasn't that his death seemed imminent, but I just had a sixth sense that, if I went, he might be gone when I came home. I'd have hated that.

He was very set in his ways. They managed to get him a bed in a private nursing home that week but he asked, instead, if he could be brought to the county home. 'Isn't this lovely?' he said when shown his new bed. Luxuries weren't his thing. And, on Christmas morning, he fulfilled what he would have seen as a personal obligation to be on the altar in the home for Mass.

Afterwards, as usual, he came out to our house. He was in a wheelchair and looking extremely frail. Deirdre had bought him a blanket as a Christmas present and he had it across his legs to keep him warm. By now, the smallest things required a massive effort.

When he was leaving that evening, Paul and I had to lift him into the car. My mother put her hand on his shoulder and he flinched. 'Take your hand off my shoulder, Mai, you're hurting me!' he said. And it was probably only then I realized the agony he was going through.

He passed away on the 28th, all of us around the bed.

The following March, in my wedding speech, I made the point that I believed Fr Paul was in the room, looking over us. I still believe that. He is never far from my thoughts now, maybe especially before big games. Usually, I slip into an evening Mass the night before and make sure I'm by the back door at Communion time.

The local priest will invariably wish me and the team the best of luck in his blessing and I always welcome those words. I like to be gone then, just before the congregation leaves.

Fr Paul, I'm sure, wouldn't approve of the quick getaway. But I don't doubt he'd grant me absolution.

10. Shamrocks

Joe Dunphy tells a story about missing the '98 Féile that, I think, goes to the heart of what the Shamrocks mean in Ballyhale.

He would, naturally, have had a vested interest in any young Shamrocks team of the time, given his role as local primary school headmaster. Over a period of nearly forty years, just about every good hurler the club had the benefit of would have come through Joe's nursery first. But he was particularly excited by those under-14s of '98, a team built around a small kid he still considers the best young hurler he ever had in the school, Cha Fitzpatrick.

To Joe's horror, bad planning had him going on a holiday to Turkey the day that team reached the Féile final in Enniscorthy. He was distraught. There was only one place on the planet Joe truly wanted to be that day and it wasn't Kusadasi.

On arrival at the resort, he immediately rang home. Shamrocks, he was told, were the All-Ireland under-14 champions. Joe went back down to the dining room with his news and, in front of maybe fifty people for whom it would have been of little import, suddenly burst out crying.

I often think of that image when pulling on a Shamrocks jersey. Our club is fed by little more than a hundred houses. Hurling glues the community together, giving the village colour and endless hope.

Without the game, it's hard to imagine who and what we would be. It's not as if there's any grand recruitment drive to get kids down to the field before their attention might be thieved by another sport. In Ballyhale, the tug of hurling is almost unspoken. It's just what we do, what families before us have done.

Maybe two-thirds of that '98 Féile team would be on the field in Nowlan Park eight years later when we finally ended a fifteen-year wait to be crowned senior county champions again. To explain what that November day meant to me, I need to rewind a couple of months.

Kilkenny's All-Ireland final defeat of Cork untapped great euphoria across the county. We'd come back from the apparent dead to wreck their three-in-a-row bid and, I suppose, ridicule those trying to depict us as haplessly old-school against the modernity that had become the Cork badge.

It was a victory that electrified the county because our rivalry with Cork had become so personal. As the Scots might sing, we'd now sent them back 'Tae think again . . .'

The following Tuesday, I remember sitting in Langtons and finding myself deep in conversation with John Tennyson. Looking back, I wonder what John made of me that day because I was completely preoccupied with Shamrocks and winning a county final. Maybe even more so, I was obsessed with righting the personal wrongs of '05. I was still needled by my non-performance against The Village in that final and the lack of manliness with which I had met the disappointment. 'If it's the last thing I do,' I said to Tennyson that Tuesday, 'I'm getting a county medal this year!'

I could tell from his expression that he was slightly bemused. The whole county was on a high from the All-Ireland, but I was already moving on. To me, I had a responsibility to honour now and it had nothing to do with National Leagues, McCarthy Cups or All-Stars.

There was widespread speculation that I might be Hurler of the Year again and, driving me into town that morning, my father had mentioned the possibility. It was a lovely thought, but I knew there wasn't a trophy yet minted that would compensate me if Shamrocks didn't win the county. My brother Tommy had retired the year before, but there was still a heavy Shefflin presence in the dressing room. John was a selector, Paul was corner-back and, with Tom Coogan not making the starting fifteen, I was on-field captain.

That said, I'd purposefully pulled back from playing the big-shot. The lad who tried being Superman in '05 now hung up the cape. I was much more relaxed and low-key. I said little in the dressing room before games. We were all in this together and I realized it was on the field that Shamrocks needed my contribution.

Two weeks after the All-Ireland final, we found ourselves nine points down in a county quarter-final against Carrickshock. A big upset looked on the cards, but we rallied well in the end and my contribution of five from play satisfied me that I was showing the real leadership now as distinct from empty speeches.

We beat Dunnamaggin in the semi-final, and so it was down to Shamrocks and O'Loughlin Gaels in the county final. O'Loughlins always had a specific marker for me. Alan O'Brien was really sticky and had a great record of tying me down, so they moved Brian Hogan out of centre-back and set me a familiar challenge.

Barely a minute into the game, O'Brien caught a ball over my head out by the sideline and I met him with a shoulder, shunting him out of play. You could say it was me setting down a marker because, if ever there was a day I needed to stand up, this was it.

The team gelled brilliantly. After a tight enough opening twenty minutes, we gradually pulled away. Two Martin Comerford goals in the opening quarter had kept O'Loughlins in it, but we were always the better team.

We did have a ropy enough third quarter in which they missed a couple of chances and failed to convert a twenty-metre free. But everyone contributed and, when the final whistle went, we were a comfortable eight points clear. I was euphoric.

People routinely ask me what has been my favourite moment in hurling. I'd say going up for the Tom Walsh Cup that day with Tom Coogan. Because Shamrocks winning county finals was such an expectation of my childhood, I felt that going through my own career without achieving the feat would sit as a stain on my record. My earliest dreams had all centred around winning things with Shamrocks, not Kilkenny. Finally, those dreams had been fulfilled.

There was a huge amount of emotion in the immediate aftermath. If I had a euro for every time I've heard a county man saying that winning with club is different, I'd be a wealthy man. It's a cliché, but it's true. By now, our own bar was closed and we all piled into the village's other pub that evening. Only appropriate, too, as 'Andy's' was the name on our jerseys.

I don't have too many clear memories of the night. A lot of drink flowed and there was an abundance of hugging and, I suppose, men getting slobbery with one another, saying things they wouldn't dream of saying in a sober state. The Shefflin brothers were no exception. If I could have bottled that feeling, I would.

For us, winning Kilkenny after a fifteen-year wait felt like a culmination. But it pitched us straight into the Leinster pot: just a week later, we went to Wexford Park to play Rathnure. It created an odd dynamic and our preparation, to put it mildly, wasn't perfect. Basically, we were on the beer all week and, as luck would have it, the All-Star function was on that Friday night in Dublin.

For Cha and me, this was a big occasion. I was Hurler of the Year and he was Young Hurler of the Year. I'd decided I wouldn't drink, slipped away to bed reasonably early and got up the following morning for the customary photo shoot with the previous night's winners. It was about 8.30 when I arrived down at reception and the Sportsfile photographer, Ray McManus, greeted me with a cheery 'We've had your colleague down already!'

I looked at him quizzically. 'Who, Cha?'

'Yeah, he's been and gone!'

It turned out Cha hadn't been to bed. He'd ended up going into town, hitting the tiles in Copper Face Jacks with a Mayo footballer and was at that moment being driven home by Eoin Kelly, the Tipperary hurler. Eoin would tell me about that journey at Tommy Walsh's wedding in 2012. Cha apparently slept the whole way down in the car. Shamrocks, he knew, were training that afternoon.

If I have an abiding memory of the Rathnure game, it's of Cha in the dressing room beforehand, putting an Alka-Seltzer in the pint glass of water he clutched in his hand. He then went out and gave an absolute exhibition. Against all odds, we beat the Wexford champions and that was the start of an incredible odyssey.

On a November Sunday in Portlaoise, we turned in a brilliant second-half performance to blow away Offaly champions Birr, and claim Shamrocks' fifth Leinster club title. This was a momentous win as Birr had been a dominant presence in the province for the previous dozen or so years.

It also had a kind of personal resonance for Shamrocks. When we'd last been Kilkenny champions (in 1991), Birr demolished Shamrocks 2-14 to 0-3 in a humiliating Leinster final. This was sweet revenge.

The victory presented us with a quandary, though. This was new territory for this generation of Shamrocks players and we didn't really know whether to train over the winter or not. It's one of the great difficulties with winning a provincial club title, that you then have three months to wait for an All-Ireland semi-final. Most of our lads just went and played soccer in the interim.

Our semi-final against Toomevara is recalled to this day as one of the more remarkable games in club championship history. I suppose it will forever be remembered for our recovery from twelve points down to beat the Tipperary champions; but, if anything, it probably highlighted the naivety of us as a group.

On our way to Portlaoise, we'd stopped in Durrow for a meal. Afterwards, we had a puckaround, no one really inclined to pay too much heed to the clock. But by the time we got back on the bus, you could sense a certain edginess creep in: we were running a bit late. By Abbeyleix, that edginess was beginning to harden into panic. There was a long tailback and, as we snaked through the town at a glacial pace, someone suggested it might be wise to begin togging out. This wasn't good.

I've always remembered a speech Pádraig Harrington once gave to the Kilkenny team. It was, essentially, about the importance of avoiding clutter in the mind. He talked about having a caddy once who was inclined to rush a lot and do everything at the last minute. The caddy always seemed to be foostering as they headed for the first tee, and Harrington realized that foostering made him tense. They soon parted company.

Well, we were foostering that day in Portlaoise. We eventually got to the ground maybe half an hour before the throw-in, and the dressing room was a picture of fellas rushing about, everyone under pressure.

Did it contribute to our slow start? I'd be doing a slight disservice to Toomevara if I said so. Because they were brilliant on the day, stronger in the tackle and a yard faster than us all over the field. Everything about them in that period reflected the nous and confidence of a side that had won nine Tipp Championships in the previous twelve years.

But we got a vital goal just before half-time and then caught fire in the second half to play maybe the best half-hour of hurling that any Shamrocks team I've been part of has played. In the end, everything turned against Toomevara, and Tommy Dunne, who'd captained Tipp to the All-Ireland in '01, was sent off in his last senior game for the club for a pretty innocuous incident.

The move of Cha, who'd been struggling with flu that week, to full-forward proved a masterstroke and his tally of 1-4 was, essentially, a match-winning return. And I'll forever remember TJ Reid's glorious line cut over the bar with no more than two minutes remaining. If ever there was a pressure shot in hurling, that was surely one. TJ nailed it.

We had our share of luck, too, as Willie Ryan was inches away from a clinching goal for Toome with the game in injury-time.

Now, when people talk about lineage, I suspect I know what they mean. Because, if this was new territory for us as a group, we now found an insane confidence. It was as if we considered this to be Shamrocks' natural environment: an All-Ireland final on St Patrick's Day.

If anything, there was a giddiness in the group. Two weeks before the final, we were allowed a twenty-minute run-out in Croke Park and, for a lot of the lads, it was a real novelty to be down in the belly of the stadium. Everyone was laughing and kidding about. Loughrea would be our final opponents, but it was as if we could see no danger.

The Reids proved our scorers-in-chief again, contributing a

combined 3-7 of our 3-12 in a game we won easily. I was marked by Gregory Kennedy, the Galway player who'd given me such a torrid time in the 'o1 All-Ireland semi-final. He was sound this time, never opened his mouth, and yet I didn't get a score from play against him. That aside, this was a much happier experience. My focus was just on getting on the ball, bringing others into a play, using my head. A game we never really looked like losing was won by seven points, Loughrea getting a consolation goal in added time.

That evening was like a snapshot from my childhood. It was Shamrocks' fourth All-Ireland crown, which meant we were now joint top in the roll of honour alongside Birr. We stopped in Carlow on the way home, bringing the cup through the lobby of the Dolmen Hotel to huge cheers. And the whole parish was out when we got home.

Our county final victory meant that I would be Kilkenny captain in 'o7. The day after that All-Ireland club final, we were having a few drinks in Andy's when Brian Cody texted his congratulations. I slipped out the back of the pub and phoned him. And, for maybe three-quarters of an hour, we chatted about the year ahead.

'Your work is done with Ballyhale now, Henry,' Cody told me. 'This is where it starts with Kilkenny.' And, standing there at the back of Andy's, the responsibility of my new status slowly began sinking in.

11. Vanessa

On the night before the 2007 All-Ireland final, I visited Fr Paul's grave in Thomastown cemetery.

It had become a comforting place since his death and I got into the habit of calling on the eve of big games. My faith is strong and just walking through those black gates, where the old Dublin road dips down into the town, rinses my mind of clutter.

The priests are buried over to one side of the graveyard, well in off the road. When Deirdre and I arrived, my mother was already there. As we stood together, heads bowed, we became aware – almost simultaneously – of James McGarry. He was at the grave of his wife, Vanessa, just inside the gate, a little to the left.

Maybe we shouldn't have, but we felt awkward. Would we go across, or just leave him with the privacy of his thoughts? Where James now stood, a coffin was sunk into the ground that shouldn't have been there. Just six weeks earlier, he'd carried his wife to her final resting place. In a sense, the whole of Kilkenny carried Vanessa to that spot. We were still raw from the experience.

I couldn't imagine the world at that moment through James's eyes.

Vanessa's accident happened on a Thursday. I was in the bank on the Waterford quays with a customer. My mobile kept ringing but, out of courtesy to the customer, I was ignoring it. It rang four times in quick succession, the ringtone sounding more urgent each time. I glanced down at the name on the screen. Brian Cody.

Trouble.

Excusing myself, I dialled his number. The rest is a blur. 'Vanessa McGarry was killed this morning in a road accident.' I put the phone down, the customer still sitting in front of me, waiting for business to recommence. A normal man living a normal day. I cut the process short as politely as I could, packed my bag and left. Apart from a short, disbelieving call to Deirdre, I spoke to no one.

Where do you go with news like that? What do you do? I drove home in a trance, took our dog, Guinness, for a walk and ended up sitting on a ledge in the garden, staring into space. Vanessa was gone. Killed on the N9, just three kilometres from Thomastown where she worked in a pharmacy.

Another great Kilkenny GAA woman, Mary Lonergan from Paulstown, also died in the accident.

After a time, I began phoning people, team-mates that I'd be closest to. We recycled the same expressions over and over, helpless, futile words. You're thinking of James and what he was now going through. And you're thinking of poor Darragh, their son, who was such a familiar presence to us at training, and who had survived the accident. You're wondering if there's any tiny comfort you might offer, knowing – deep down – there isn't.

Vanessa had been on countless team holidays with us. She was loved by all the girls and was utterly devoted to her family. I could see so many simple similarities between her and James and Deirdre and me. Newly married, building a house, planning a future.

Those similarities had now been brutally removed.

That evening, I went into St Luke's hospital with Brian, Mick Dempsey and Martin Fogarty, barely a word spoken in the car as we drove up. Darragh was in a bed, a bandage across his forehead. James was being James, thanking us for coming in, radiating a lovely, quiet grace.

We hugged and, pretty quickly, the words dried up. What to say?

Clumsily, I tried lightening things and said something to Darragh about getting him and his daddy up the steps of the Hogan Stand in September. Later, that thought would strike a certain chord with me. But, at the time, it signified nothing more than my own helplessness. It might even have sounded crass.

We all felt out of our depth in that hospital room, talking only to avoid the uncomfortable spaces of silence. Wishing that it was all just a terrible dream.

Instead of the usual training session at Nowlan Park on the Friday night before an All-Ireland quarter-final, we were now gathering to discuss a funeral. To begin with, we didn't even know if the game against Galway was off or on. Brian was adamant it should be postponed and asked me, as captain, what was the view of the players.

I hadn't a clue. Hurling was the last thing on our minds and I can honestly say Galway hadn't featured in a single conversation since we'd heard the awful news. 'We'll do whatever we have to do,' I said weakly. My head was gone.

Looking back, it seems daft we were even having the conversation. How could we have possibly played? The shock was paralysing.

That Friday, Brian's words were perfect. He told us that the only thing that mattered now was being there for James and Darragh, paying our respects at the funeral and giving them our support. 'Hurling doesn't come into it,' he said.

Later that evening, the postponement of the match was confirmed. Instead of heading to Croke Park that Sunday, we'd be gathered in a country cemetery.

We formed a guard of honour at the removal and, again, at the funeral Mass and burial. As captain, I found myself pushed to the front, right beside the chief mourners. Standing there, I couldn't imagine what they were going through. My coping mechanism was to switch to autopilot, going through motions, willing away time.

Once Vanessa was laid to rest, we had to get on with the pretence of normality.

It felt inappropriate to even talk about hurling at first. Brian called us into a circle the first night back training and he spoke beautifully. Just something simple about how all we could do now was be the best that we could be. Vanessa was remembered, Mary Lonergan too.

He could, I suppose, have come out with stuff about trying to honour their memory by winning the All-Ireland. But, then, would that mean you dishonoured them if you lost? If anything, we now realized more than ever that, for all the fretting and obsessing we did about hurling, it was just the colour in our lives, not the fabric. Life was about family.

And yet, maybe we needed that colour more than ever before. What else had we to carry us now? To offer escape?

Nothing really made sense that first night back. James, obviously, was missing. The atmosphere was desperate. We went through the motions. Brian conveyed a message from James, insisting that he wanted us to drive on now. But you can't just flick that switch when your mind is a million miles away.

In the end, maybe we took refuge in cliché. I found myself talking about 'doing it' for Vanessa. It's strange, you find yourself saying these things, but you're not getting in your car and driving over to James's house in Bennetsbridge and seeing if there's anything you can actually do.

I felt helpless. I wasn't in the habit of calling to James in the past, so it would have been hard to do it now without making him feel uncomfortable.

Martin Comerford was one of James's closest friends, and he became the squad's main link to him. The rest of us left them to get on with it. I decided if there was anything I could do, it would have to be on the hurling field.

The Friday night before the rearranged game with Galway, James came to training. He didn't tog out. Just stood by the side of the field, watching us going through our drills. But his presence felt huge. No one went over to him because we knew the last thing he wanted was people crowding him and being awkward again.

I can't overstate how important simply seeing him was to all of us. He hadn't been making the starting fifteen that year, but he'd been a major, major figure in the dressing room. The typical quiet man who didn't speak often, but always spoke well. Just having him stand on the line that night closed off a critical gap in the dressing room. It made us feel one again.

★

I could say that the 'cause' of Vanessa's memory carried us to victory that quarter-final Sunday against Galway and, subsequently, all the way to the All-Ireland. But that would be a lie. We just carried on with our lives, all the time tiptoeing around the heartbreak without ever understanding it.

I got credit for my speech after that final, but to be honest I never had a plan. Maybe from the moment of Vanessa's death, the speech had a subliminal presence in the back of my mind. If so, I kept running from it.

Deirdre and I had gone over to James that night in Thomastown cemetery, and Deirdre talked about Vanessa in a lovely, open way that I felt put James at ease. Then we left him to his space, exchanging almost breezy 'see ya in the morning' goodbyes.

It was when we got home that Deirdre brought up the subject of the speech I'd have to make if we won the final. She had a sheet of paper and she thought it might be a good thing to prepare a few bullet points. 'You'll have to remember . . .' she began and I just snapped. 'Jesus, don't you think I've enough to be worrying about,' I shouted. 'I mightn't have a speech to make!'

We were strong favourites to beat Limerick but, all my hurling life, I've dreaded that status. Now I feared we were tempting fate. Wouldn't I feel a right fool with these bullet points in my sock, standing down on the Croke Park pitch while Damien Reale went up the steps of the Hogan Stand to take the cup?

So Deirdre took the brunt of my anxiety and I left her there, with her pen and paper. Of course, she had been right. The following day, I made a point of stuffing that sheet of paper she'd been writing on in my tracksuit pocket. Just in case.

And then, as it turned out, my injury meant I had a bit more time than anticipated to think about what I might say. As I sat in the stand, watching us ease away to a convincing victory, I began thinking about the people that needed to be remembered in my captain's speech. Suddenly, I wanted Deirdre's slip of paper. But it was in my tracksuit bottoms. In the dressing room.

When the whistle went, I rushed down on to the sideline to

embrace Brian and a few of the players. A steward had hold of my arm, but I broke away from him and nipped down the tunnel. Into the dressing room, picked up Deirdre's bullet-points, took a few deep breaths. I could hear the muffled roars outside, but I wanted to compose myself, make sure I got things right. Then, after maybe a couple of minutes, out I went to collect the Liam McCarthy Cup.

As I was gathering myself, one thought dominated. That clumsy suggestion I had made in St Luke's hospital the day Vanessa died. I wanted James and Darragh to come up those steps with me.

Outside, I tracked James down and asked: 'Will you come up and get the cup with me?'

He was adamant: 'No, no way!'

'C'mon, James, I want you up there . . .'

'No, Henry!' He wasn't for budging.

'Will Darragh come up with me?' I asked.

'No,' James answered on his son's behalf. But I knew, looking at Darragh, that he wasn't strictly averse to the idea.

'C'mon, Darragh . . .'

When James saw the two of us go towards the steps, I think the protective father in him took over. He followed us up but, typically, only at a bit of a distance. If you look at the photographs during my speech, he's actually standing to the side, doing his damnedest to fade into the background. There isn't a man I know with less interest in being the centre of attention and, in those seconds, I can just about read his mind: *This should be Henry's moment, not mine.*

So there was no grand plan. Just a sense of growing spiritual momentum to the year that culminated with me grabbing one handle of the Liam McCarthy that September day and young Darragh McGarry grabbing the other.

It was an important moment for me. Did it soften their pain? No. I knew I had nothing in my power to do that. I couldn't do anything for Vanessa. I couldn't bring her back. I couldn't really do anything for James or Darragh either. Couldn't even say anything to make things better.

But, at last, I felt finally I'd contributed something more than a

Mass card and a few mumbled, inadequate words. Please God, Darragh will cherish that moment for the rest of his life and James will, in time, see in it the absolute respect and care Kilkenny people felt for him through that terrible year.

We'd won the two-in-a-row, but lost something of our innocence. Something that could never be recovered.

12.   Storing the Hurt

Hard to know what to make of an All-Ireland-winning year that leaves you feeling equivocal. There was a barely perceptible cloud over everything from the morning of Vanessa's death.

Earlier that year we'd lost to Waterford in the League final, then retained the Leinster Championship without finding out much about ourselves. If anything, I was a little uncomfortable, a little embarrassed going up into the Hogan Stand to make a speech after we'd beaten Wexford in the provincial final by fifteen points. Not too many people hung around for the presentation and, maybe, you can see a little sheepishness in my smile as I lift the Bob O'Keeffe Cup above my head. It was our ninth Leinster title in ten years and, no matter how we dressed the arithmetic up, it was another anticlimax for the public. Two goals in the opening eleven minutes just seemed to knock the stuffing out of Wexford.

In my view, they didn't really help themselves when their manager, John Meyler, took off Declan Ruth after just fourteen minutes. Ruth had a decent record of marking me, so they introduced him to the unfamiliar setting of full-back when they saw me starting on the edge of the square. Declan was a fish out of water there and the experiment didn't work. He was a centre-back, one of the best in the country.

If I had been Meyler, I'd have made a few switches but left a man of Ruth's experience on the field. He didn't. We pretty much scored at will in the game, Willie O'Dwyer catching the eye with 2-3 and Martin Comerford and I both chipping in with a lot of scores from play.

The media focus afterwards wasn't on Kilkenny, though. A headline in the *Irish Independent* bellowed, 'Stop this futile madness now'. We were almost made to feel guilty for having won again. It seemed the only consolation to the general public was Dublin beating Kilkenny in the minor final.

Next up came Galway, now managed by Ger Loughnane, in the All-Ireland quarter-final. During the build-up, Loughnane engaged in what could be best described as a little mischief. Himself and Cody go back a long way, all the way back to teacher-training college in Drumcondra during the 1970s. At one time in their lives, they were team-mates and – I would imagine – friends. But there wasn't much mutual affection expressed after Ger gave an interview in which he essentially depicted Kilkenny as a dirty team. That was our interpretation anyway as he talked about us systematically flicking the hurl across opponents' wrists with a game plan he described as giving opposing players 'a ferocious barracking'. We were living on the edge, apparently, which – naturally – compelled referees to be extra vigilant and strong-minded. It wasn't terribly hard to break down what Ger was doing. Cody, I know, was furious but chose not to really reference the comments in any team-talks.

Galway put it up to us in Croke Park and, for an hour, the game was an absolute humdinger. Then we got away from them in the last ten minutes, to win by a decidedly flattering ten points. I was held scoreless from play, but Cody would subsequently describe my performance as one of the greatest he had seen in a Kilkenny jersey.

I'd certainly put in what I considered a decent shift in terms of unselfish work and willingness to take pain. But Brian only made the observation after my cruciate went in that year's All-Ireland final, so I think it might have been interpreted by some as an expression of sympathy more than anything else.

This wouldn't strictly have been the case. When I look back on my career, it's games like that one against Galway, where I just hung in there, that give me the greatest satisfaction. A lot of energy had been sapped out of me by events of the previous week, but I kept going.

If there is one thing above all that unites Brian Cody and me, it is the belief that a career is defined by how you deal with adversity. The days when everything just flows are great but, ultimately, they seem easy too. On the hard days, you learn what really lies within.

Bizarrely, Wexford were our semi-final opponents, having shocked a Tipperary team deemed good enough by their management to leave Brendan Cummins, Eoin Kelly and Shane McGrath sitting in the stand. Again, fortune seemed to be favouring Kilkenny. Being honest, Tipp would have been far more worrying opposition from our perspective.

So we won that semi-final by ten points and, in the showers after, I remember Richie Power joking about my personal tally of 0-14: 'You weren't going to be held scoreless from play today, Henry!' He was right, I suppose. I'd gone into the game feeling it was time to step up to the mark.

We'd beaten Wexford in the manner universally expected, and that's when Ger Loughnane came back into the story. The day before the final against Limerick, Ger gave an RTÉ radio interview in which he reiterated the points he had already made about our supposedly unscrupulous style of hurling. This was below the belt. If we could just about swallow the charge as a little gamesmanship before a contest in which Ger himself would be directly involved, this was of another parish.

There was a brief mention made of it on the bus to Dublin, but Brian clearly didn't want us sidetracked from the job of beating Limerick. We had plenty of other issues to concentrate the mind in any case. PJ Ryan had broken his arm in the semi-final and was a doubt right up to the weekend of the final. At one point, the possibility of James McGarry starting was being mentioned. Given what James had been through, this wouldn't have been ideal. I don't think any of us doubted for a second that he'd be able to cope with it, but would it be fair to ask?

The problem was that PJ had had a plate inserted in his arm and four weeks, clearly, was less than the appropriate recovery time. As it happened, PJ got the nod, but I don't suppose playing with a plate in your arm is a common medical recommendation. To this day, I think he suffers pain as a legacy of that injury.

We would also lose Noel Hickey just over twenty minutes into the game with a recurrence of hamstring trouble but, in reality, the game was already won by then.

We had decided to attack Limerick where they were strong and set down some early markers. Their big players against Waterford had been men like Stephen Lucey, Brian Geary, Andrew O'Shaughnessy and, particularly, young Séamus Hickey. The view was that we needed to get at them early and test their mettle.

It's funny, I was reading a quote from Hickey before they played us in the 2014 Championship in which he threw us a back-handed compliment. Something along the lines of 'Everything I know about physicality I learned from a Kilkenny jersey.'

The message in a Kilkenny dressing room is always the same. Put your marker under pressure, ask questions of them and see how they respond. And the final of '07 was no different.

Any worries I might have had about us not being fully focused were blown away when we opened with an unanswered 2-3 in little more than ten minutes. Limerick didn't know what had hit them. Much was made of a heavy shoulder I gave Hickey early in the game. The insinuation seemed to be that it had been premeditated. It wasn't. But the attitude throughout the team was to meet Limerick physically, to make it clear we wouldn't be taking any steps backward.

Did Ger Loughnane's attack on us have any impact? I can't honestly say, but Limerick were awarded eighteen frees in that final to Kilkenny's seven. Perhaps people can draw their own conclusions.

After our early scoring burst, the game settled into a relatively even contest without ever looking like it might slip away from us. I was enjoying it tremendously when, approaching half-time, my knee collided with Peter Lawlor's and something popped. I was moved to full-forward for the last few seconds of the half, but Robbie Lodge sensed immediately that I was in big trouble.

In the dressing room, he brought me out to a warm-up area and told me to jog in a straight line. 'Now turn,' he said. I did and immediately fell over. 'Look, that's you gone, Henry!'

I went into the medical room in floods of tears, then back out to the boys. It was suggested that maybe I might say a few words, but I couldn't bring myself to talk. Then someone said something along the lines of doing it 'for Henry'. And I thought, of all the causes we had to fight for that year, mine was easily the least important.

My team-mates went back out and won the All-Ireland with something to spare.

I experienced one of the most precious nights of my life the following Tuesday when I, literally, brought the cup home. Kilkenny had never lost a final with a Ballyhale captain and I was now the sixth man from the village to lift the McCarthy Cup. It is a memory I will always treasure: the bus pulling up outside my brother John's house on the main road through Ballyhale, where my mother and father stood behind the gate with my brothers and sisters.

I brought the cup down off the bus for a few precious seconds and, for all the public glare of an All-Ireland homecoming, that felt incredibly precious and private.

As a kid, I would have seen other Ballyhale men bring the Liam McCarthy Cup down that same road. But here, as the leader of a winning team, I was now bringing it to my own family.

Something I will never forget.

13. The Perfect Storm

They want us 'nose to nose', they say. Preferably glaring.

John Mullane and I would prefer to be anywhere but here right now, but there are obligations to meet. It's a photo shoot for PUMA on Waterford's quays, maybe two weeks before the '08 All-Ireland final. We make small talk and laugh at stupid things, the two of us togged out in our match gear.

Horns beep, passers-by shouting out their bold predictions. The banter is good. 'We're coming to get you, Sheff!' That sort of thing.

Ordinarily, Mullane and I get on great, but this gig's different. The PR guy becomes our safety valve. You see, if John and I talk directly to one another, the conversation is sure to drift into uncomfortable territory. So we address everything to this young chap in a suit, crowding him with attention.

'Did you come down from Dublin this morning?'

'Is that new boot selling well?'

I don't particularly want to know about Waterford's training and I'm sure John doesn't want to know about Kilkenny's. So there is a clipped awkwardness to how we address one another. This is too close to game-time now, neither of us especially comfortable in the other's company.

So we stand there for the cameras, having this ridiculous stare-off. Cringe-inducing stuff. The weeks leading into an All-Ireland final, you're not exactly thinking warm, cuddly thoughts about your opponent. There's an aggression building that needs to be channelled into the right energy. The thought strikes that, if I was a back, this sudden proximity to Waterford's main attacking threat mightn't be especially wise. Because I'm sure John would quite happily toss me over the quay here and I wouldn't have a problem reciprocating.

That's hard to explain when all that people see is flags and bunting.

To players, this is the best and worst time imaginable. You are in the place your entire year has been geared towards delivering you to. But you are also now fearful of doing anything that might be detrimental to the team.

So you spend a lot of the time dodging contact with other human beings. Training becomes the only natural outlet, because training is the one environment in which you are with people going through exactly the same thing.

Until that photo shoot, I'd just about managed to keep the hype of the final at arm's length. Working for Bank of Ireland in Waterford, I could see the giddiness everywhere. I had a lunchtime ritual of slipping down to Dooley's Hotel around 2 p.m. in the hope that the rush would be over, and I'd always sit in the corner, my back to the rest of the dining room, a newspaper up to my face. I'd be in and out in maybe half an hour, refuelling as inconspicuously as I could. Behaving like a spy.

I just didn't want to engage with people. Waterford's supporters are brilliant, but they were incredibly hyped up by the county's first appearance in an All-Ireland final in forty-five years. I had no interest in communicating with anyone on that level. To me, this final was about anything but hype. It had to be about cool heads and hurling.

Every day at work, I could see the hysteria building. The Waterford people didn't know any different. They couldn't. I was hearing stuff back about their 'open day' and how the players couldn't get off the field for two hours afterwards because of the demand for autographs. Crazy stuff. You'd meet people in the street and they'd literally have tears in their eyes talking about what it meant to them to see Waterford in the All-Ireland final.

Local radio constantly played their 'anthem', Journey's 'Don't Stop Believin''. Davy Fitz, their new manager, was getting a lot of attention, having taken over from Justin McCarthy in mid-Championship. Waterford were *the* story.

Then I'd slip off home to Kilkenny in the evening and it was like entering a monastery. Not many flags to see and few enough people even coming in to see us train. We were injury-free, low-key, yet going for the three-in-a-row. Waterford seemed to be soaking up every ounce of available media attention. It felt perfect.

So, staring into John Mullane's eyes on the Waterford quays, the only voice I can hear in my head is saying something along the lines of 'Beam me up, Scottie!'

The moment the photo shoot ends, I make my excuses and dance across the street to the Tower Hotel, where I've left my work clothes. The bank will have to wait, though.

I take myself straight to the gym.

Sadhbh was born that March and life, suddenly, found a different balance.

Fatherhood is an odd condition. That first time you close the door behind you, having brought a newborn home, is, I suspect, one of the more terrifying experiences a man can go through. I certainly felt out of my depth. All the big, high-pressure games I'd come through over the years dwindled in significance when set against the realization that I was now responsible for a little girl.

It certainly meant that Deirdre and I had more to talk about than my knee. Which, for her, I'd imagine, was a good thing.

At first I was complacent about the injury and the rehab, maybe even a bit cavalier. The pain was pretty full-on at our function in the Citywest Hotel after the final, but beer and adrenalin compensated. If anything, I was looking on the injury as a bonus. I'd get a break now. The body could re-charge.

I remember Gorta and Noel Hickey putting me up on their shoulders and there being no real sense of me carrying a serious injury. Might as well have been a mildly sprained ankle. The first time I used crutches was the following Friday and, by then, the knee was big as a pumpkin.

I drove down to Tadhg in the Whitfield Clinic and, surprise, surprise, it was too swollen to do anything. So I spent maybe four weeks doing basic exercises, just to get myself ready for surgery. Hobbling around as the wounded soldier.

Shamrocks had won the county final again and there were pictures from the day of myself and Cha on the line, two invalids now surplus to requirements. Cha had broken his foot and needed crutches too. The Reids shot the lights out that day against St Martins and TJ was quick to slag me afterwards: 'We don't need you any more, Henry!'

It was early October by the time I went under the knife, and I slipped into a winter rehab programme without any great sense of urgency. Trouble was, I had no real deadline. There was no chance of playing for the club, no matter how far they travelled. And I wouldn't exactly be busting a gut to get a run in the National League.

The injury meant I couldn't drive, so I was off work until after Christmas. It all fitted conveniently into place. My game-face was gone. I was going to the gym five days a week, but I wasn't killing myself. My mind was in neutral. Deirdre had given birth to Sadhbh the following March and she was still in hospital when I got a first real sense of how far I still had to go.

I was in the habit of dropping over to her parents' house in Callan and taking her St Bernard, George, for a walk. Just a few hundred yards from the O'Sullivans, I slipped on the road, badly wrenching the knee. It felt like I'd done something serious, the pain so bad I had to ring Deirdre's brother Tom to come and collect me.

It was a false alarm, but the lack of flexibility really worried me now. I didn't understand the dynamics of the cruciate. In a sense, I was rehabbing blindly, following instructions without asking questions. I wasn't sure whether to hold back or push harder. I did a lot of flexibility work in the pool in Hotel Kilkenny and, once I went back to work, in the Tower Hotel in Waterford. Every lunchtime, jogging over and back in the water. Running to stand still.

I had company at first, Tennyson and Richie O'Neill having snapped cruciates that same summer. We became the three amigos. A trip was organized for us in November to Sunderland through Niall Quinn. We'd meet the Premier League club's chief physio and talk through the processes of rehab. We'd take in a game.

It proved a great weekend, if not a great match – a 1-1 draw with Newcastle. We stayed in the team hotel that Friday night, an old country house that had none of the five-star opulence I expected. We watched the players arrive and, having imagined that I'd envy them, I found myself thinking how boring so much of the professional footballer's life must be.

The physio came down and spoke to the three of us individually. He was excellent. But we all had one eye on the lift-door, waiting for the manager. We'd been told Roy Keane would be down to meet us, but he never materialized. I was gutted. I'd be a fan of his. Wouldn't necessarily agree with everything he's said and done in his life, but I do respect the conviction he carries. If he believes in something, it's non-negotiable.

I suppose we didn't gain a whole lot from the Sunderland experience. We just had our few pints and embraced the sense of adventure. If anything, Tennyson summed up our mindset when checking in. 'Will you look after these for me?' he said, handing his crutches over to the receptionist. 'I'll get them back off you tomorrow.'

The three of us were together a lot in the early months of '08 and, inevitably, comparing progress. This wasn't good. Of the three, I seemed to be making the slowest progress. Tennyson had been last to have the operation but he was running with more freedom than me. Richie, who was Kilkenny's third goalkeeper, was moving even better. While Tennyson and I were just running laps at county training, Richie was back hurling.

Brian Cody actually put him out corner-forward one night and he pulled up with a hamstring strain. This wasn't surprising, as the operation involves taking a graft from your hamstring to bind the cruciate. Richie hurled with his club soon after and I'll never forget the phone call from Tennyson.

'Richie's cruciate snapped again tonight!' My blood ran cold.

So the incident with Deirdre's dog set off all kinds of sirens in my head. Robbie tried to reassure me, saying it might be a good thing if it took away some tightness. I wasn't convinced.

I didn't play any part in the National League, which Tipperary won, and I arrived on the doorstep of the Championship feeling anything but bullish about my fitness. We'd always targeted the Leinster opener against Offaly in Portlaoise on 15 June and I suppose

I was cutting it fine by getting my first start with Shamrocks just two weeks earlier in a Championship game against Young Irelands.

I didn't feel right. I can remember one of my first nights back in Nowlan Park, catching a ball over JJ Delaney, turning on landing and feeling that the leg might give way under me. I was coming back from a physical injury, but the challenge was largely mental. Deirdre became my private psychologist.

I'd scored three points from play in that comeback against Gowran in Thomastown, but went into the Offaly game feeling more nervous than I think I've been before in any game in my life. This was strange territory for me.

And, for half an hour, Offaly absolutely threw the kitchen sink at us. I got the first score from play, but it would prove my only one. It was real helter-skelter hurling and, approaching half-time, we had managed only to edge a few points clear. Then PJ Ryan found me with a puck-out on the stand-side and I took off on a run. It ended with an offload to Martin Comerford, and Gorta scoring a goal. Maybe the one time that whole day I actually forgot the knee, and I'd managed to set up a vital score. The goal put us seven points clear and seemed to have a crushing impact on Offaly. Their challenge absolutely collapsed.

We pulled away to win by a deceptive eighteen points in the end, Brian switching me out to centre-forward, where I was studiously diligent in avoiding physical contact. Just floated about the place, enjoying the fact that Offaly's fire was spent and I didn't have to make any tackles.

The big bandage on my knee still seemed to dominate my thinking, though. Coming off the field that evening, I was delighted to have seventy minutes under my belt. But they hadn't been what I would regard as a genuine seventy minutes. I was still inclined to mind myself. Not a good state of affairs during the Championship.

We hammered Wexford by nineteen points to retain our provincial crown. There was a gap between the two of us as teams and, every time we met, that gap was coldly accentuated on the scoreboard. I actually remember little enough of that final. Cody had me back in the left-corner, easing me through things. The bandage was still there. I was playing tiptoe hurling. Bluffing.

Two weeks before we played Cork in the All-Ireland semi-final, we went to the Seafield golf resort outside Gorey for a weekend. In those days, it was always a bit of a guessing game when you got on the bus outside the Springhill Hotel, wondering where we were headed. Brian wouldn't tell us the destination – he liked to keep things interesting.

He also liked to spring the odd surprise guest to speak to us, as with Nicolas Cruz before the '06 semi-final. This time, though, we would do the talking among ourselves.

We stayed in chalets and I was billeted with Derek Lyng and Cha, who was our captain. No one said as much, but I could tell that people were beginning to doubt me.

On the Sunday, we trained at Buffers Alley and I decided it was time for a change. I left the bandage in my gear-bag and went out on the field without stopping off first for physio. Just felt I was using too many mental crutches. For six months, I'd practically lived on Robbie Lodge's table. This was my first serious injury and I just couldn't seem to shake a lingering sense of tightness in the knee. It was wrecking my head and, deep down, I think I had almost come to depend upon the physio's table for psychological support as much as physical. It was time to move on.

Robbie came out to me before the session got under way.

'Henry, do you need a rub?'

'No, Robbie, not today.'

We lined up for a training match and I found myself in Tommy Walsh's gentle care. Litmus test. 'I'm forgetting about this knee now,' I remember saying to myself. There could be no more mollycoddling.

Before long, I had 1-3 scored off Tommy and the two of us were wrestling on the ground, the ball at the far end of the field. There were a few locals in to watch and I'd say they could hardly believe their eyes. But I was delighted. Tommy was thick because I was gaining the upper hand and I knew, if I had Tommy Walsh pissed off, I couldn't be that far off the pace.

A few lads pulled us apart and, listening to their pleas for us to calm down, I was almost struggling to suppress a grin.

The Wednesday night before the game, Michael Kavanagh spoke at a team meeting. He talked of some older players 'not going great' and there being pressure on them to produce a performance now. I've known Kav almost as long as I've been hurling and I recognized he was directing the comment at me.

His words knocked me back a little. I suppose I wasn't used to people casting doubt on my contribution to the team. But he was right. A lot of people in the game had already formed a view that I wasn't the same player since injuring my knee. Some suspected I might never be again.

Everything Michael was hinting at was, I knew, fundamentally true.

I couldn't afford to be half-baked playing Cork. There was a sense of the Championship really only starting now, and you could still feel that palpable edge between the teams. This was clearly it for them. We knew they'd be on a mission. I was told I'd be marking Seán Óg, which, even at my best, was always a severe test.

That said, it wasn't Cork I felt I needed to challenge. It was myself. From the Leinster final on, I went out to Tramore every lunchtime and just walked up and down the strand, breathing in the fresh air. I could feel the pressure building, but I had learned how to push myself again. I was ready to throw off the shackles.

There was just one small complication to overcome first.

My brother Paul was getting married in Kenmare the Friday before the semi-final and I was to be his best man. He'd booked the date on the basis of the previous year's calendar, not realizing there'd been a change. I broke the news to Cody immediately after the Leinster final. He seemed unperturbed – 'Look, we'll arrange something' – but it wasn't perfect.

Paul and I are extremely close and I was conscious of not wanting to let him down. One thing I've become pretty good at in recent times is compartmentalizing things, dividing my focus between different needs. So I brought the hurls and a ball with me as Deirdre and I made the long drive to Kenmare with my parents that Thursday. My sister Helena had already phoned back to say that the hotel was noisy at night and I might be better off checking into a smaller place across the road. She made the booking.

On arrival in Kenmare, Deirdre and I went straight to the gym. That was my mindset. Everyone knew the focus I was desperate to keep.

At the same time, I had a speech to make and didn't want to let Paul down on that front.

The wedding went off well, and a plan had been quietly hatched to get me home as painlessly as possible the following morning. Michael Dempsey arranged for the Carlow businessman Stephen Murphy to collect me in his helicopter. This was a godsend as Kenmare is a monster drive from south Kilkenny and the last thing I needed was the knee stiffening up in the car.

Heavy fog that Saturday morning meant my brother Tommy had to drive us to Killarney for the pick-up. That would be our only hardship. Maybe half an hour after Stephen collected us, Deirdre and I were touching down in a field across the road from our house in Ballyhale. As I was walking across the avenue, I rang Tommy.

'Thanks for that, worked out great.'

'Why, where are you?'

'Home.'

'Jaysus, we're not even back in Kenmare!'

Now, if I ever win the lottery . . .

The first twenty-five minutes against Cork were about as serious as Championship hurling can be. The match had an incredible intensity and was played at breakneck speed. The ball was fizzing around and you could tell from the sounds of the crowd that they felt they were witnessing something special. It was hard to catch your breath.

There is no feeling in the world to match being in the heart of a Championship game like that, sensing the electricity it is creating all around you. That is what I know I will miss most of all in retirement. The sense of being part of something special.

Cork threw everything at us, we threw everything back. Then, approaching half-time, Eoin Larkin got a goal and you could see Cork's body-language change instantly. It was as if they were thinking, 'Jesus, we'll never get rid of these bastards.' We were like a confident boxer, inviting his opponent forward, challenging him: 'C'mon, we'll take anything you've got!'

A couple of Kilkenny points followed and, incredibly, we went down the tunnel eight points clear. For Cork, that was the end.

Just after half-time, I broke on to a ball that Cha and Seán Óg were rushing towards. Just busted past them and landed a big score. There was a photograph of me taken immediately after, hand in the air. In some ways, it's an image of redemption. Because that was the moment I knew I was hurling as I could again. I finished the day with nine points, three of them from play.

I was back in the land of the living.

What in God's name possessed Waterford? Even now, I am inclined to ask that question of a team that, having looked as if it had reached new levels of maturity in its semi-final defeat of Tipperary, literally tried changing personality on the biggest day of the year.

It was inexplicable. Having lost their previous five semi-finals, the win over Tipp seemed to speak of a wiser, calmer Waterford, capable of winning nerve-racking battles. Then they came back to Croke Park on the first Sunday in September and completely lost the plot.

Some of their best, most honourable players got sucked into an apparent attempt to soften us up. This wasn't clever. Eddie Brennan and Tommy Walsh both took hits before the ball was even thrown in and, all around the pitch, the Waterford players were literally snorting with aggression. The hype had seeped into their group mindset and, mentally, they were just gone to another place.

Quite early in the game, I went out to the Hogan Stand side to take a '65'. Davy Fitz stood on the line, barking at me like a madman. We made eye contact and I just shook my head, as if to say, 'Davy, would you ever shut up?' He was still ranting as I stood over the ball. I nailed it.

Running back into position, I made a point of looking back over at Davy. He was visibly sickened. I didn't have to say anything. If Waterford honestly thought a bit of physical and verbal abuse was the way to beat Kilkenny, they were about to be disabused of the notion.

I don't think they'd have beaten us with sixteen, even seventeen players that day. We were in the zone. We'd gone back to Seafield for a weekend and you could almost feel our performance brewing. A lot of different people spoke, including lads that mightn't normally. Donnacha Cody, Brian's son, had only just joined the panel, but even he stood up.

We talked of the previous year's League final, in which Waterford had beaten us to claim their first title since 1963. I have a memory of sitting on the bus afterwards, waiting to get to hell out of Thurles (which is always a bit of an ordeal), and our attention slowly being drawn to the Waterford bus, which was parked maybe fifty yards away from ours. They had the cup on board and it might have been our imaginations running wild, but they seemed unnaturally keen to draw our attention to the fact. A couple of their players kept shaking it in our direction, like they were prizefighters with a precious belt. We sat watching them and, to a man, began to boil.

Now I'm quite open to the possibility that the Waterford players in question didn't even notice their proximity to the Kilkenny bus. It could be they were just in a private state of euphoria, oblivious to the outside world. But we took their rowdiness as a determination to needle a beaten team.

I can't remember exactly who was sitting beside me, but I do remember turning to him and saying, 'Look at the fuckers, the way they're rubbing our noses in it!'

The day after we beat Galway in that year's All-Ireland quarter-final, Waterford drew a wonderful contest against Cork. One week later, they won the replay in an equally spectacular contest. It was a massive victory for them and they were all pretty animated on the pitch afterwards.

Immediately before that game, we had secured our place in the All-Ireland final with a comfortable defeat of Wexford. Now, sitting in the stand afterwards, we got the impression that one or two of the Waterford players were staring up at us, desperate to catch our attention. It was as if they were saying, 'Coming to get you next!'

Of course, seven days later they were out, Limerick blasting five goals past them.

If you perceive, rightly or wrongly, that someone has disrespected you, the best thing to do is store that hurt for another day. Looking back, I'd have to say the Waterford lads did nothing particularly untoward on either of the occasions I've mentioned. But, in sport, you're always looking for that extra edge and the instinct is to make use of whatever may be to hand.

So, in the run-up to the '08 All-Ireland final, there was a kind of stalemate to our training that, on reflection, showed just how ready for battle we were. Like, I felt I was absolutely flying, but I'd be marked by JJ and he was flying too. So many people were on fire, to a man they were cancelling one another out. And Waterford thought that they might bully us!

We blitzed them. If there's been a perfect performance from Kilkenny in my time, that was it. They could have worn hurls off us all day and I honestly don't think we'd have felt it. Brian Hogan tossed me an early ball and I pinged it over almost from the sideline. We were all in perfect synch. When they were done with abusing us, Waterford had nothing else to give.

We were seventeen points ahead by half-time, but we weren't letting up. In the dressing room, the subs were literally hopping off us, everyone hungry for physical contact. It wasn't about the three-in-a-row, I'm pretty sure of that. I don't know what it was. But we were hungry as dogs. Even the quiet lads in the squad were shouting: 'Keep fucking going, no fucking let-up!' Going back out, we were like fellas going to war.

If Waterford thought the bad news might stop coming, they were mistaken. They didn't manage a point from play until the forty-sixth minute, by which time I suppose the black-and-amber tassels were already attached to the Liam McCarthy Cup.

Tommy and JJ mopped up Clinton Hennessy's puck-outs as if they could read his mind. Hennessy started drilling them to midfield instead, and I remember anticipating one, cutting across, swivelling in mid-air and bringing the ball down on the hurl. There was an audible reaction from the crowd, as if what I'd done shouldn't have been possible.

To be honest, I was thinking much the same: 'How the hell did I do that?' But that's what happens when all the planets are aligned, I suppose. You feel anything is possible. I took off on a solo run and I could hear Lyng charging up beside me. I gave the pass, he scored.

We just went away from Waterford. Out the gate and into another galaxy. In the entire game, I think we only shot two wides. Of our 3-30 total, 3-24 would be scored from play. Brian brought on James McGarry for his last county appearance and the rest was all high-fives and bear hugs. We got our three-in-a-row with twenty-three points to spare. Nine of us would finish the year with All-Stars.

We'd whipped up the perfect storm.

14.   Creating a Monster

Sometimes I find it difficult to recognize myself on television and in newspapers.

Maybe that's the lie in the story of 'King Henry', a virtual cartoon cut-out. In the real world, my world, I am a husband, father, son and brother who has bills to pay and everyday human worries to overcome. I am King only in a world of media make-believe.

The man looking back at me every morning from the shaving mirror has a lot going on in his head. Sometimes, the higher I seem to fly in hurling terms, the starker the demands I place on myself. Play a great game, then beat yourself up over the need to be as good the next day. It's a trap my personality sets on impulse.

I feel compelled to back up what I do. Endlessly.

Maybe there's a streak of conceit in that. I mean, I love the life I live but my personality is so intimately linked to what I do, it seems natural to wonder who I will be when I'm no longer Henry Shefflin, Kilkenny hurler. Will I need an element of re-invention?

People see something that I don't always see. They see certainty and utter calm. It's a privilege being a household name in Irish sport, but the flipside of that privilege is that people presume things, people expect things.

That sort of presumption came to feel a bit of a millstone in my life around 2009 and 2010, until I found a way of dealing with it.

People's expectations can press down on you like a boulder on the chest. The more they tell you how good you are, the more hunted you feel. I can understand if that sounds like a contradiction, but let me tell you about '09, the chase for the four-in-a-row and how All-Ireland final week almost broke me.

*

All year I feared we were creating a monster.

It started with the National League, when we painted a bullseye on our foreheads. I've always had mixed feelings about dishing someone a hiding when you know, the next day you meet, that team will feel as if they're almost going to war.

And, in the GAA, there is always a next day.

We saw that from the outset in '09. Our second League game brought us to Walsh Park and a nice, swift reunion with the Waterford team we'd humiliated the previous September. We knew there'd be a backlash, and we weren't disappointed.

They applauded us on to the pitch, then tossed away all courtesies. Everything about Waterford's body language from the throw-in bellowed, 'We've no respect for ye.'

They were wired and, sitting in the stand that day, I could feel venom in the local desire to right what they perceived as the wrongs of September. Tommy Walsh and Eoin Kelly were both sent off after a little outbreak of hostilities and, to great, proud roars, Waterford held on to win by four.

Being honest, it didn't bother us unduly. Those League points clearly meant a great deal more to them than to us and, by the time I made my return to competitive action in a comprehensive thirteen-point victory over Clare in Ennis, we'd also hammered Galway in Salthill and given Tipp a bit of a drilling in Nowlan Park. I had been due to make my comeback in the Tipp game, but I came down with flu that week and ended up watching it from home. Gorta scored three goals, one of them a nonchalant flick over Brendan Cummins's head. It was real exhibition stuff and I can't say I particularly enjoyed it.

We were hurling at a level now that just seemed to be overwhelming our opponents. That Tipp game was won by seventeen points and we had twelve to spare in the victory over Galway. Next up after Clare was that visit of Cork to Nowlan Park, on the Cork players' first day back from their well-documented strike.

Fast-forward to the autumn of that year, when Dónal Óg Cusack published his book.

I was at a media function in Dublin one day and the journalists were fussing for my reaction to Dónal Óg's 'Stepford Wives' line, which was all over the newspapers. I hadn't read the book at that time and, at that point, I wasn't sure what 'Stepford Wives' signified. I asked the journalists to turn the tape recorders off because I had no intention of commenting on something I didn't understand.

About a month later, I was at home with Deirdre when one of the *Stepford Wives* movies came on the TV. I remember texting Tommy Walsh as it was starting: 'I see we're on TV Tommy!'

A short text back: 'So I see!'

Watching, the penny began to drop. I was bulling. I saw what Dónal Óg was implying. We'd no minds of our own. We just followed the leader. We were lapdogs. To me, he was out of order. Dónal Óg knew next to nothing about us as people. He was writing from a position of ignorance. I would have massive personal respect for Dónal Óg as a hurler and as a man. I've done a few GPA gigs with him and found him hugely likeable. But the 'Stepford Wives' thing made me angry.

Look, if Kilkenny players seemed unusually compatible with our county board, maybe it's because our county board was unusually progressive. In that context, I couldn't speak highly enough of Ned Quinn. Cork's story – their long battle for better treatment and facilities – was light years removed from ours. We'd see John Gardiner appearing on *Prime Time* and none of it made sense.

Let me say this. I absolutely accept Cork's argument that they were fighting for a principle of better conditions for all teams, not just their own. In time, maybe less successful counties benefited from that stand. Maybe a lot of people now have the right mileage rate, the right food after training and the right gear because Cork raised their heads above the parapet.

Could we have done more in Kilkenny? Maybe we could. But I'd be the first to admit that, when it comes to hurling, I was always one hundred per cent selfish. It's tunnel vision. I focused on getting myself right and pulled away from anything that might disturb that focus. Like, I didn't train young lads down the field in Ballyhale because I'd neither the time nor the reserves of energy. I looked after number one. My view was always that, after retirement, I'd start giving back. But as long as I was playing, I had three priorities: family, work, hurling. If that makes me a selfish person, fair enough. But I have a mind. I make my own choices. In the Kilkenny dressing room, nobody is led anywhere by the hand.

I suspect what differences that existed between Cork and us became magnified in their minds as we kept on winning and they slipped into decline. Dónal Óg's recollection of the National League game in '09, in which we beat them by twenty-seven points, certainly went to a place I didn't recognize.

We were a three-in-a-row team, they were coming back from yet another civil war. Planets apart. As we set about them that day in Nowlan Park, Dónal Óg read things into our body language that didn't exist.

I'll admit we were as psyched that day as we would have been for a Championship match. This was no run-of-the-mill League game. There had been massive media focus on it because it was Cork's first day back from a strike. We knew it was different.

Then again, nothing specific was said in the dressing room before or after. Nothing was necessary.

When it was over, the attitude of the players was very simple. 'That's us, that's Kilkenny, that's how we do our talking!'

Were we going for the jugular? Absolutely. But do you honestly think we'd have been any less motivated to put up a big score if it was Tipperary in front of us? Or, say, the Clare team of the 1990s? I've never once stood in a dressing room and been told to ease up on a struggling opponent. You have a team on the back foot, you nail them. That's bred into us.

At the same time, as the score ran up that day, I did feel a stab of unease. The pessimist in me reasons that a big win will always, one day, come back to haunt you.

When that game ended, I walked over to shake hands with Dónal Óg. He would write of that moment, 'He looked me in the eye and most of what he was saying to himself was, "There you go now, Cusack, twenty-seven points. Take that home with ya!"'

I read that, thinking Dónal Óg maybe sees me as a far deeper person than I am. The truth is that I shook his hand because I respect him. I will admit there was a lot of whooping and hollering, the crowd going absolutely ballistic. That's what they do when we hurl out of our skins against a team regarded as a threat.

I consider Dónal Óg an iconic GAA figure. He brought goalkeeping to a new level, and the courage he has shown off the field will forever be recognized by anyone with a healthy GAA brain. But he misread us in Kilkenny.

Going into that year's League final against Tipperary, all the hype was about us. We'd won four games in a row by a cumulative total of sixty-eight points. At a function in Dublin, Anthony Daly joked that it might be 2020 before Kilkenny lost a match again. Journalists were openly questioning if, maybe, the season should just be declared over and all the trophies deposited in Nowlan Park. After that Cork win, our price to win a fourth All-Ireland in succession was down to 1/2. The whole thing was slipping out of control.

And then Tipp gave us the root up the backside that, I suppose, all of hurling wanted them to.

The League final was spectacular in some respects, a bit of a farce in others. We would hear afterwards that Tipp had cuttings of that seventeen-point defeat pinned up on their dressing-room wall, and we had little difficulty believing it. They came after us like bears after raw meat.

The game was played under experimental rules. Two ticks in the referee's notebook was the equivalent of a yellow card, and a yellow card brought dismissal (albeit the departing player could be replaced). Thurles was no place for laboratory mice that day in a game played at Championship intensity, if not sometimes beyond. Four players would get the line, myself among them.

It was hot and heavy stuff, Tipp lacing into us right from the off with some huge hits. They had two goals in the opening fifteen minutes, during which time we lost our centre-back, Brian Hogan, with a broken collarbone. No question, we were taken aback by their ferocity. There was serious belting going on and we were, largely, on the receiving end.

James Woodlock got their opening goal after what we perceived to be a foul on James Ryall by Micheál Webster. The referee, John Sexton, let it go. He let a lot go that same day.

Were some of the hits over the top? No question about it. That said, we should have been better prepared for that than we were. A few weeks earlier, we'd humiliated Tipp. If they had anything in them as men, they were going to come after us physically. We were down by five points at half-time, the Tipp lads – reputedly – dancing on those newspaper cuttings in their dressing room.

Now, personally, I've always preferred a referee to let things flow. My view is that he should always play the advantage and then blow the play back if it doesn't accrue. Admittedly, circumstance dictates your view of things. Sometimes it might feel as if the head is hanging off you and, seeing the ref's arms waving 'Play on', you're thinking, 'I'll have to be shot here today before I get a free.'

That day in Thurles, I got an early knee to the groin and never really shook it off. Next thing, Pádraic Maher was catching balls over my head and, with every catch, the pressure began to build for me to come up with some kind of response. I got my first tick for pulling a jersey. Then, forty-two minutes in, I was ordered ashore for what would be the first of only two occasions in my adult career.

A high ball was dropping short and, as Shane McGrath got in front of me, I flicked the hurl in the general vicinity of the ball and his hand, catching him on the top of the helmet. It was late, but I didn't intentionally hit him. That said, it was a straight yellow in its own right and Sexton produced the card. I was off.

With me gone, Richie Hogan had to step up to the plate and, on absolutely every level, he did. With a free from the right-hand touch-line and on the '65', he put Kilkenny a point to the good with time almost up. Seconds later, though, Noel McGrath equalized with a Tipp free, and so we had a period of extra time in which the temperature didn't drop a single degree.

We won in the end by 2-26 to 4-17, the post-match debate focusing almost as much on the sendings-off (Gorta was put off within thirty seconds of entering the field) as on the tumultuous physicality of the contest. Still, I felt good collecting the cup. We'd stood up to Tipp, you see. Everybody had stood up. Fellas like TJ Reid and Richie Hogan had taken responsibility when some of us more experienced heads were no longer on the pitch.

For Cody, especially, I think the day was perfect. Tipp's performance put an end to the nonsense suggesting we would coast to another All-Ireland win. The threat of complacency had, suddenly, retreated. Our first night back at training, we felt pretty sure what the manager's opening words to us would be.

'I told ye so!'

As it happened, we misread him. Actually, we weren't long back training after that League final when we all found ourselves drawn to the conclusion that Brian Cody was leaving us.

He just called us into a huddle one night in Nowlan Park and broke the news that he was doing a book. The way he explained it was that he'd been told someone else was contemplating writing the story of the Cody era. Rather than let a third party have free rein, he'd decided to do something about it himself.

We were staggered because we couldn't imagine him co-operating with a book while he was still Kilkenny manager. It sounded suspiciously as if he was preparing a farewell. That night he set about reassuring us that the book would in no way interfere with his focus on our pursuit of another All-Ireland. He just wanted us to hear it, he told us, 'first hand' from him. 'This is the last you'll hear about it from me,' he said. 'My full concentration is on driving this on now . . .'

Still, after training, it was the only topic of conversation. Most of us agreed that it had to be a definite sign that, after eleven years at the helm, he now intended packing it in. The shock in the dressing room was palpable.

We hadn't seen this coming.

★

I scored 1-14 in the All-Ireland semi-final against Waterford, 1-6 of that from play. Here was one of those games that leave you thinking, 'That's why I do this . . .'

The easiest way to describe the zone you slip into is: you get a feeling of lightness in your feet. I'd gone into that game with the balance absolutely right. Why? Well, that's the slightly perverse thing. I'd played poorly in the Leinster final against Dublin who, effectively, operated with seven backs that day. They'd seen us win a pulsating semi-final against Galway in Tullamore, when a burst of ten consecutive points completely turned the game. Anthony Daly put Michael Carton on me and he never left my space, just pulling and dragging me all day. Nothing he did should really have been a problem, but I hadn't anything in my legs. I'd trained too hard in the build-up. Early-morning walks and stuff like that. I'd gone over the top.

We never really looked like losing the game, but it was Gorta who made the difference, scoring 2-4. And that's where the perverse side of things kicks in. Playing badly against Dublin had given me the launch pad for my performance against Waterford. A little bit of anger with myself. The sense of having something now to prove.

Cody decided to move me in to full-forward from the wing. People said afterwards that this was a deliberate tactic to target the young Waterford full-back, Aidan Kearney, who'd done well on Joe Canning in their surprise quarter-final win against Galway. It actually wasn't. It was simply an acknowledgement that I hadn't gone well the last day and that a change of scenery might suit me.

The first ball that came in, I just sensed it was going to be a good day. Dipped down with one hand, caught it, straight up, bang, over the bar. On these days, it feels as if the hurl is part of your body, as if what you're doing is the most natural thing. It's like the ball is following you around. You keep going to the right place, doing the right things. You're floating.

The semi-finals of '06 and '09 were two games that gave me that sense of power, of being capable of doing virtually anything I chose. It's an intoxicating feeling. You'd like the game to go on for another hour because there's not a shred of fatigue in your body. The only thing tugging you back is a voice in your head telling you to save something for the final.

And that's the first inkling of your new problem.

Sadhbh was now seventeen months old, and Deirdre was expecting again. I'd describe myself as a modern father in that I'd happily change nappies, do my little bit. But the week of a big game I suppose I'm not exactly hands-on. Psychologically, I go to a different place.

If training is at seven, I like to be in Nowlan Park at six. So I'm gone from the house at half five, which means about fifteen minutes after getting in from work. Fifteen minutes of fatherhood. By the time I'm pulling back in the gate, everyone's in bed and asleep.

If I'm tetchy, as I occasionally am in game-week, that bit of space is welcome. To be woken by a teething baby in All-Ireland-final week is to feel a rising panic. What if I don't get back to sleep and end up feeling drained? The more you think that way, the more likely it will come to pass.

Leading up to the final against Tipperary, I could feel a nervousness build and little things began to bother me. When little things bother you, your energy leaks away like grain from a punctured sack. I'm not sure if it was the four-in-a-row in this instance or the fact that it was Tipp in the other corner. Maybe it was a combination of both.

Tipp didn't have any particular relevance in my world, maybe a little banter at college with Eamonn Corcoran and Enda Everard, but nothing more than mischief and one-eyed slagging. Yet, all around now, I could sense a desperation to beat them. Deirdre comes from Callan, right on the border with Mullinahone, and her father would always be saying, 'Whatever happens, THEY can't beat us . . .'

At training, any of the players living close to the Tipp border would be delivering a variation on the same theme. Fellas like Derek Lyng, Taggy Fogarty, PJ Ryan. They'd speak in the dressing room, almost with tears in their eyes: 'Lads, we can't lose this one . . .' The whole tradition of the rivalry seemed to be telling people that this final was bigger than others.

I've never been into reading about the John Doyles or Lory Meaghers, but you'd know that Tipp and Kilkenny had history.

Maybe it was somewhere back in the mists of time, but it existed. I had vivid memories of the '91 final, John Power reefing his hand on the Cusack Stand wire and Tipp just about getting over the line in a poor game. I started secondary school in Kieran's the following day and would have stayed in town to see the homecoming. Paul Phelan, our club captain, was up on the bus and we happened to catch each other's eye. I was eating chips, Paul was hungry. He gestured for me to throw him up a few chips. My service to the county had begun.

Eighteen years later, Tipp were back in the Kilkenny cross-hairs. On the Thursday before the final, we went to Deirdre's parents for dinner. I was a little agitated and distracted. The night before, we'd been training in a threatened apocalypse at Nowlan Park. Thunder and lightning. Torrential rain. Sheepish gazes in Cody's direction. Except from me.

Even from the dressing-room tunnel, you could see large parts of the field were under water. But I wanted to be out there, practising frees. Eventually PJ Ryan agreed to come with me. Next thing, I'm standing there in the lashing rain, tossing questions in PJ's direction. 'As a matter of interest, PJ, what way does Brendan Cummins hold the hurl if he's facing a penalty?'

PJ offered a quick imitation of the Tipp goalkeeper, reassuring me of something I pretty much already knew. 'No harm, just in case,' I said, explaining myself. The weather eased a little and Tommy Walsh appeared, dressed in this ridiculous over-sized hoodie. Then the others followed. We trained for fifteen minutes and then aborted. The whole thing just seemed pointless.

Little things.

So Deirdre and her family didn't have the most responsive of dinner-guests the following evening. Coming home, she said something to me in the car and I, quite literally, didn't hear a single word. My head was wrecked from thinking about what was coming. I was in another world, becoming a bit of an Antichrist.

Deirdre reads me like a book at these moments. She says she can tell if I'm in a good place. Sometimes, I try to fool her – I put on an act, pretending to be all things to all people – and she sees straight through it. This time, there was no act to unravel.

I don't normally suffer bad nerves, but this was different. Three days to go and I was sinking into some kind of personal panic. It felt like the panic was making my batteries run down, literally stealing the strength from my legs. When we got home, I went upstairs, lay on the bed and felt like weeping.

Deirdre came up to find out what was wrong. I tried explaining.

'My legs, they're like jelly. The strength is gone from them completely.' I'm looking at my wife now, tears beginning to form. 'What am I going to do? I can't fucking play if I'm like this!'

Deirdre calmed me down, insisting it was all just a natural build-up of pre-match pressure as we pushed for four-in-a-row. I was just trying to play the game three days early and everything felt like it was coming unglued. Eventually, I took on board what she was saying.

But only in the comfort of a new day.

It is half-time in the All-Ireland final against Tipperary. My voice probably needs to be heard, but I haven't the gall to speak.

I'm a passenger here. People are being kind and that kindness probably translates into worry. I'm not really doing it for my team. I've put over a few frees and invited Brendan Cummins to make a half-decent save from an early shot, but this game will pass me by entirely if I don't find a way of getting myself involved. We lead by two points. The four-in-a-row is glistening right in front of us.

Brian Cody circles the dressing room, gently coaxing more out of different individuals. He stops at me. 'C'mon, Henry, we need you this half, we need you to up it . . .' It's a gentle way of telling me to buck up my ideas. God knows, I've been trying. I've been working as hard as I've ever worked in a game, shipping punishment, throwing my body into dangerous places. I got one block in on Conor O'Mahony that resulted in an Eoin Larkin point. I'm hoping people noticed.

Jackie Tyrrell's voice breaks across the room. 'Look at the way

Henry's blockin' and hookin', we all need to do that,' he says. Jackie's words mean an awful lot to me. I look at my boots. Whatever is in me needs to come out now.

But the game resumes and it's still not happening. That Thursday-night panic attack wasn't all just down to an overheating mind. My legs feel as if they're made of rope. I've no strength in them, almost no feeling. So I do what I've taught myself to do. I keep sticking my body in the way of things, keep trying to be of nuisance value. Something tells me it won't be enough.

PJ Ryan is pulling off saves straight out of Lourdes to keep us in it. It's as if he knows what the Tipp forwards are going to do before they do it. You can see them shaking their heads, wondering what it'll take to beat him. I'm directly in line behind Séamus Callanan as he hits one and it looks like it's going for the top corner, only for PJ to get to it spectacularly. He has nights like this in training where absolutely nothing gets past him. But this is an All-Ireland final. A goalkeeper is going to be Man of the Match and Kilkenny are about to have an All-Star in the number 1 jersey for the first time since Michael Walsh in '93.

It's funny and, I suppose, a little strange that that's happening to PJ so soon after getting the jersey from James McGarry. To my mind, James was the best goalkeeper in the country for at least five or six years, yet never won an All-Star. McGarry, I suspect, suffered because he never went for the spectacular. Where other goalkeepers dived, James always stood. He was always on his toes and his reading of a game was extraordinary.

With twenty minutes remaining, Tipp lose Benny Dunne to a moment of madness on Tommy Walsh but, if anything, it emboldens them. Ten minutes after Benny's departure, they lead by two points. I'm still hitting the frees, but all the momentum is theirs now.

We've ten minutes to rescue the dream.

Richie Power is fouled and, when the penalty is awarded, my first reaction is terror. 'Christ, no, do I really have to do this?' The game is on a knife-edge and what I do in the next minute is almost certain to decide whether we live or die here. If I were hurling well, I'd probably devour this opportunity. But all I have in my head right now is doubt.

It's the old 'King Henry' thing. The people in the stands see someone entirely different from the man speaking in my head now. I'm trying to gather myself. Separate myself from the consequences.

I don't even see Cummins come running out from the goal to try and psych me out. The referee is in my ear. 'Take a second, take a second . . .' I'm actually facing the other goal as he's speaking. You see, I'm not a natural penalty-taker – at least not in the way, say, DJ Carey was a natural, or TJ Reid or Anthony Nash. I wouldn't have anything like their strike of a ball. My record with penalties isn't particularly good.

People don't realize, but – twenty-one yards out . . . three big men on the line . . . a huge crowd waiting – the goals can look as small as a doll's house at that moment. The one thing I have learned is to make a decision about where to send the ball, and stick to it. A gift of experience, I suppose, that has survived the nearly two decades since Niall Nevin's save during that under-14s game in Thomastown.

I want to go to Cummins's left. The way PJ showed me how he holds his hurl confirmed my opinion that he'd probably prefer something straight at him or to his right. So this is it. This is where the science ends and everything is pared down to hitting a sliotar as hard as is humanly possible. Just keep the head down, give it everything . . .

The net jumps and the roar is beautiful, but I don't even celebrate. I turn and go sprinting back into position. All I feel is absolute relief, as if I've dodged a bullet here. My legs still feel barely able to support my body's weight. Just look at the video of what follows.

Within sixty seconds Gorta is scoring another goal. Watch as Eoin Larkin cuts inside to give the ball to him. The nearest man to the goal-scorer is Brendan Maher, who I'm supposed to be marking. We'd both gone sprinting after the play but, at the point of arrival, Maher had twenty yards gained on me. That was my day pared down to a single moment.

Back in the room at Citywest that night, my body was covered in welts and bruises. I felt as if I'd taken a hundred belts for the cause, the kind of belts you never get when you're on your game. Looking in the mirror, my torso was covered in a red jigsaw. Against Waterford in the semi-final, nobody had laid a glove on me. That day, I was floating like a butterfly.

My first reaction after all these games was always to analyse my own performance. If we'd won and I'd played well, the feeling was perfect. If we'd won and I'd been poor, it was a different, equivocal satisfaction. So I was a small bit disappointed in myself, heading down the stairs that night to celebrate the four-in-a-row, a feeling I would never tolerate from myself again. I was also completely wrecked.

A massive crowd had gathered outside the function room and, at one point, I innocently tried to make my way out there to buy a drink. It would have been easier get into Fort Knox than get through the celebrating throng to the bar counter. The sight of a player coming through the doors almost triggered a riot. Pretty soon, I aborted and slumped back down at the table.

'Jesus, lads, it's impossible out there . . .' I said, suddenly feeling a little bit old. The younger players were clearly only warming up for the night ahead. I looked at Deirdre, heavily pregnant, and could see the tiredness come over her in waves. The two of us were totally shattered.

So we got up from the table, slipped out a back door and went up to the room. It was maybe one in the morning and I was only too happy to fall into bed. Downstairs, the party would keep going all the way through till daylight.

I know that because I didn't sleep a wink.

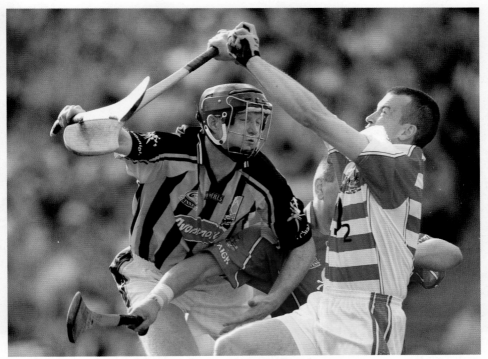

Jostling with Dónal Óg Cusack in the 2006 All-Ireland final. That summer, Cork were going for three in a row, we were being written off, and the rivalry felt personal (*Ray McManus/Sportsfile*).

Shaking hands with Ronan Curran after the match. We won that final on pure intensity (*Ray McManus/Sportsfile*).

After a disappointing 2005 club season, when I tried to do too much as captain, I was determined in 2006 to win the county championship with Shamrocks – something I hadn't yet achieved. I still think of this as one of my best ever victories (*Pat Murphy/Sportsfile*).

My greatest match: Deirdre and I were married in March 2007 (*John McIlwaine*).

I got to the ball just ahead of the Limerick goalkeeper, Brian Murray, to score our second goal in the 2007 All-Ireland final – one of the best of my career. I sat out the second half with an injury, but my day was not done yet . . .

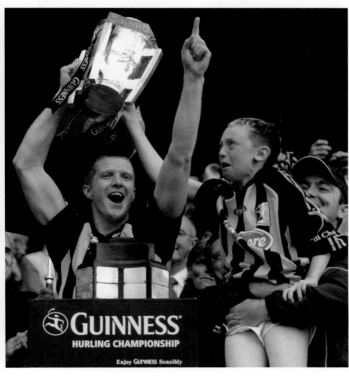

As Kilkenny captain I was proud to lift the cup along with Darragh McGarry, James's son, at the end of the summer when he lost his mother, Vanessa (*Pat Murphy/Sportsfile*).

With Deirdre and my parents at the christening of our first child, Sadhbh, in March 2008.

Sprinting away from Waterford's Eoin Kelly and Stephen Molumphy in the 2008 All-Ireland final. We put in a near-perfect performance that day (*Brendan Moran/Sportsfile*).

After a tough day in the 2009 Leinster final against Dublin, I was in the zone in the All-Ireland semi-final against Waterford: everything clicked (*Daire Brennan/Sportsfile*).

In the All-Ireland final against Tipperary, by contrast, nothing was working for me: my legs felt leaden. I didn't much fancy taking this late penalty, and I felt no joy to score – just relief (*Brian Lawless/Sportsfile*).

A sweet celebration with James McGarry after Shamrocks won the 2010 All-Ireland club final against a star-studded Portumna team that was going for three in a row (*Brian Lawless/Sportsfile*).

Landing awkwardly in the first half of the 2010 All-Ireland semi-final against Cork, I tore the cruciate ligament in my knee. For about thirty seconds, the pain was unlike anything I'd ever experienced (*Oliver McVeigh/Sportsfile*).

Although the official line was that I had no chance of playing in the final, Ger Hartmann did amazing work to help me get fit to play in a training match – and I did enough to get picked for the final (*Diarmuid Greene/Sportsfile*).

After thirteen minutes of the final against Tipp – during which I probably touched the ball more often than I had in the whole of the previous year's final – my knee gave out on me. Tipp went on to win and I wondered if I'd done the right thing by playing (*Matt Browne/Sportsfile*).

Being introduced by the Taoiseach to President Obama in May 2011, just a few days after I'd met the Queen: an amazing week (*Maxwell Photography*).

Celebrating an early point in the 2011 All-Ireland final – against Tipp, for the third year in a row. We put in a great team performance to win our fifth title in six years (*Brian Lawless/Sportsfile*).

15.   Catching Eddie

Three weeks after the All-Ireland final, we gathered at The Hub in Kilkenny for the formal launch of Brian Cody's autobiography.

There was a real sense of the Big Top coming to town as over a thousand people swamped the place, desperate to get their hands on a book we still feared might be a signal of his imminent departure. A giant screen behind the stage was showing the victory over Tipp in its entirety again, and the thing that struck all of us was how it drew the attention of the hall as if the match was a live broadcast.

The players had a slightly different focus. As soon as we got copies of the book, lads began leafing through the pages almost manically, desperate to discern just how many dressing-room secrets Brian might have chosen to divulge.

I flicked through it myself, but decided not to dig any deeper. To this day, I haven't read *Cody: The Autobiography* because I didn't especially want to explore too deeply anything Brian had to say that might (a) upset me, or (b) give me a swelled head. That's just the way my mind works. As long as I was still hurling for Kilkenny, I felt it best to push the book away.

Others had no such insecurities, and pretty soon the word was coming back that Brian hadn't leaked any state secrets. This was reassuring. He likes to leave it until November before making any announcement regarding his future intentions, but the book certainly created no obstacle to him staying on.

My own fretting over a poor performance in the final had pretty much evaporated by that point. I had started copping myself on as early as the morning after, when our customary trip into Crumlin Children's Hospital brought us into contact with some kids facing desperate personal circumstances. Deirdre had gone home early to collect Sadhbh, and I found myself feeling slightly pathetic, meeting these children, some of them terminally ill, when I'd been beating myself up over not playing great in a game of hurling.

I had also come round to the idea that, in scoring the penalty, I'd played a pivotal part in Kilkenny securing the four-in-a-row. We'd all been left a little bemused immediately after the final whistle when the GAA's plan to have the presentation of the McCarthy Cup take place on the field had to be summarily aborted because of a pitch invasion.

As the crowd came spilling in off Hill 16, an announcement for stewards and gardaí to resort to 'Plan B' went out over the tannoy. A planned fireworks display had to be abandoned and the whole thing descended into a slightly dangerous farce.

The President of the GAA, Christy Cooney, suggested afterwards that they might have to make the place 'Ceaușescu-esque'. This was the moment, I suspect, when that big, see-through barrier that today pens in Hill 16 became reality. It's a pity they had to do it but, from a players' viewpoint, it has made those seconds immediately after an All-Ireland final a little bit saner and, undoubtedly, safer. I remember running to embrace PJ Ryan when, like the banks of a river breaking in a flood, this mass of people suddenly came pouring over us. Just getting to the sanctuary of the Hogan Stand was an ordeal.

The Thursday after the final, I did something I wouldn't normally do. I sat down to watch the game again in its entirety. The madness of the week had begun to ebb and there'd been such a broad consensus that it was one of the greatest finals ever played, I wanted to watch it in the quiet and privacy of home.

It was incredible to see the pace and quality of the hurling, the massive physical intensity with which the final was played, because – when you're in the midst of a game like that – you've no way of making a judgement on its quality.

Meanwhile, my focus was turning back to the club.

After winning the All-Ireland in 2006, Shamrocks had struggled to keep standards up. Some lads, perhaps, had become a bit big for their boots.

It wasn't an overnight thing, just something gradual that crept up on people. You wouldn't even notice it at the time but, with hindsight, there had been some giveaway signs. With Cha and myself on crutches, Shamrocks were still good enough to retain the county title in '07, beating St Martins by ten points in the final.

Even though Birr got the better of us in a subsequent Leinster semi-final, we were now unequivocally top dogs in Kilkenny. And, given Kilkenny were top dogs in the country, that status carried weight.

We made it three-in-a-row in '08, winning a tight final against The Village, then gaining revenge against Birr to claim another Leinster title. The following February, this set up an All-Ireland semi-final against the reigning champions, Portumna.

They had a star-studded team, with a precocious teenager their biggest star of all. Joe Canning had exploded on to the national consciousness the previous summer with a remarkable first Championship for Galway, scoring 2-12 of his team's 2-15 in an All-Ireland qualifier defeat to Cork that July. He was already, clearly, a seriously accomplished talent.

I'd never met Joe, but now, suddenly, the Shamrocks–Portumna semi-final seemed to be distilled in media minds down to some kind of straight shoot-out between the two of us. The newspapers went big with stuff about 'The King and his Pretender', and that nonsense began to play a bit on my mind.

When he scored an early goal in the game, a voice in my head was saying, 'Jesus, you need to do something here . . .' To be fair, I felt I was doing reasonably. Seven minutes into the game, I caught a high ball and ran for maybe fifty yards before offloading to Eoin Reid for a Shamrocks goal.

Trouble was, Portumna were just obliterating our full-back line. They had two goals scored inside the opening six minutes and would nail another brace within eight minutes of the restart. As a team, they were on fire. I remember at one stage making a run up along the sideline and being shunted into touch by a combination of three Portumna players. Joe was one of them, a great roar erupting in the stand.

You could tell it was a big moment for their supporters whereas, for me, it proved absolutely sickening. All those roars amounted to a singing declaration that Joe had got the better of me, that the so-called King was gone. I suppose it comes with the territory of being so high-profile: everything you do gets over-analysed.

Portumna were by far the better team on the day and our backs just couldn't contain what their forwards were doing. Canning and Damien Hayes especially seemed to have this almost telepathic relationship on the field. Joe finished with 2-5.

It was a bad day for Shamrocks and one, in hindsight, we should have seen coming. We were very disorganized, nowhere near as well prepared as we needed to be. Looking back, I just don't think we were mentally on the same planet as Portumna.

I remember a heavy fall of snow in January and our normal training venue in Piltown was closed. We ended up going to our own field and just throwing snowballs, everyone messing and joking. Ours was a real rural club attitude. A 'we have the hurlers' type of delusion.

That night said a lot about our mental preparation for Portumna. We just weren't tuned in and, surprise, surprise, they blew us out of it.

I was disgusted with some of the things I saw in the immediate aftermath. It seemed to me that, with a lot of the lads, there was no great sense of disappointment. Some fellas seemed to be of the view that they'd done enough for Shamrocks already. It made my blood boil, watching them take defeat in their stride that evening, planning the night ahead as if there was still something to celebrate.

Now I'm not a big man for having a local as I don't take a pint on any kind of regular basis, but all the old-timers were down in Andy's that evening. Men like my father, Big Tommy Walsh, Kevin Kennedy and Bobby Aylward. They might even have had waspish tongues on them but, to me, they were entitled to give their opinions.

No more than a handful of the team showed up. There was Aidan Cummins, Bob Aylward, my brother Paul and me. This was symptomatic of the way we'd been that day and it sickened me. Somewhere along the journey we'd become disjointed and, individually, a bit selfish. Unfortunately, most of the team headed straight into Kilkenny, oblivious to the fact that the pub sponsoring the team might have done with the bit of business.

Now some of the lads might read this and say, 'Well, you don't give Andy's too much business yourself!' It's true, I don't. But, on an evening like that, I believe you should always go back to your own people. Those small things matter. Get them right and the big things will look after themselves. Maybe it comes down to something as simple as having respect for people.

It just struck me that we had perhaps forgotten what and who we were representing when wearing the Shamrocks jersey. Our early victories and losses had always ended with us being together. That unity represented a basic sense of place that, maybe, was now missing.

Going into that semi-final, I suspect we'd actually lost respect for ourselves. Our standards had dropped and, through the team and subs, a slight lack of interest had taken hold. Maybe we'd just become too accustomed to winning. For Cha and me, that loss to Portumna was our first club championship defeat since the '05 county final. That kind of consistency is very hard to sustain at club level. Inevitably, your hunger recedes a little and standards tend to drop.

The defeat jolted a few people out of their comfort zones and there was a sense that management perhaps needed freshening up. Maurice Aylward wasn't averse to the idea of rejigging his selectors, but he had underestimated the appetite for change. At a team meeting to discuss the coming season, the view of the group was that we needed more variety and intensity to our training drills. Maurice was agreeable, saying he'd been thinking along the same lines.

But, suddenly, Maurice's own position as manager was being put to a vote and, after three successive county titles, the players' vote went against him.

James McGarry and Michael Fennelly Sr were installed as co-managers and there was a real sense of mission now. Straight away, you could see a lot of Brian Cody's management style in McGarry. He was maybe quieter, a little more pensive, but he brought the same intensity of focus, the same sense of seriousness about what it was we were trying to achieve.

We kept alive the possibility of another shot at Portumna by winning a fourth consecutive county title, beating The Village by three points in a tight final. James's arrival had been just what we needed in terms of a different voice, selling fresh ideas. He's brilliant in a dressing room. As a goalkeeper he'd be very much into the importance of a good first touch, and his drills are all obedient to that duty.

The Kilkenny Championship ran late that year, and winning it catapulted us into a tightly condensed Leinster Championship. Henry Junior was born the week after the county final and, just seven days after retaining that crown, we survived a massive Leinster Championship scare in Wexford Park, coming from nine points down against Oulart the Ballagh to win in extra time.

Liam Dunne, the Oulart manager, came into our dressing room after the game and joked that things had been difficult enough for Wexford hurling, coping with one Henry Shefflin without having to deal with another!

It was already November now and reasonably comfortable victories followed over Ballyboden St Enda's and Tullamore to give us our third provincial title in four years. This put us joint top of the Leinster roll of honour alongside Birr on seven titles.

Henry Junior's birth meant I skipped the Kilkenny team holiday to Thailand and, being honest, it suited me. We had drawn Newtownshandrum in the All-Ireland semi-final and, if we won, I didn't doubt Portumna would be waiting for us in the final. Beat both of those, and we knew we could rightly declare ourselves the best club team in the country.

Video analysis wasn't something we did too much of with either Ballyhale or Kilkenny but, prior to that Newtown game, McGarry focused in great detail on our opponents' short-passing game. That ran against the grain of everything we knew as hurlers. The old way was just to get yourself as right as possible and not worry about the opposition. But James's use of the video was brilliant in that Newtown would have no surprises for us when we met. Right through the team, you could feel a solid flow of confidence. I scored 0-13 and got Man of the Match, but it had been the performance of our goal-keeper, James Connolly, that really made the difference.

For the final, no great analysis was required. Portumna were going for three-in-a-row, and James confined the video work to a replay of the first half of the '09 semi-final. Nothing more was needed. Our body language had been shocking that day. Even in the way we walked on to the field, we had the air of a beaten team. Looking at the video, you could see we'd lost the game before we even left the dressing room.

In one sense, it wasn't surprising. Portumna had one of the best club teams going, but I don't think they understood what was coming their way this time. Everything about our preparation was so smooth, so professional, we were maybe becoming stronger than the sum of our individual parts.

The squad went to Youghal for a bonding weekend and, even though I was sick, I still drove myself down to be a part of it. Everyone was incredibly clued in and you could feel the big performance brewing.

On the day, Portumna just couldn't match our hunger. In fact, if it wasn't for Joe Canning's 0-12, we'd have won pulling up. As it happened, we had five points to spare in the end, the exact tally I scored from play. After being beaten so emphatically by them the year before, this was one of the sweetest victories in Ballyhale's history.

Man of the Match that day was our corner-back, Alan Cuddihy. Young, cocky and fearless, Alan represented the exciting young breed now coming on the Ballyhale scene. On the bus leaving Croke Park, he got to his feet, turned to me with the award in his hand and grinned, 'I bet you don't have one of these, Henry!'

He was right. I didn't.

That homecoming is one I will always remember because it brought home to me how much my life was changing. When we'd last come home as All-Ireland champions, in '07, I was a single man. Now I was coming home to a wife and two children and, as the bus swung around towards Carroll's Hotel in Knocktopher, to see them

standing in the street outside Heaslip's shop made me quite emotional. As I waved down at them, little glimpses of my own childhood
began to flash through my mind. There was a sense of my life having
turned full circle.

The 2010 National League took a long time to climb out from under
a winter blanket.

Club duty excused me from the early hardship and I was at home,
sitting by a warm fire, the night Kilkenny's opening game with Tipperary in Thurles was called off because of a dramatically heavy fall
of snow. It was surreal, watching the pitch slowly disappear during
the TV build-up, a penny slowly beginning to drop that hurling
would be impossible in Semple Stadium that night.

They re-fixed the game for the following Tuesday but, again, the
weather forced a postponement. Ireland was in the grip of a big
freeze.

I wasn't that bothered about the League, and I suspect Brian Cody
wasn't either. Nobody was willing to admit it, but the five-in-a-row
was splashing around in everyone's mind. Our year would be defined
by whether or not we delivered and won a unique place for ourselves
in history.

On a personal level, the All-Ireland run with Shamrocks had been
a massive distraction. The day Kilkenny played Offaly in the League,
I was so tuned into club stuff it was nearly evening before I even
bothered looking for a report of the game.

Henry Junior's arrival had reinforced for me the beauty of having
real balance in your life. For years, hurling just consumed me. I was
probably thinking about it far too much. A bad game would leave me
stewing for days, thinking about the things I could or should have
done. It was a destructive cycle that often left me drained.

Now I was leaving hurling at the front door, doing family things
and loving the fact that two of the most important people in my life
couldn't care less if I never lifted a hurl again. Sadhbh and Henry just
wanted their daddy to play with them. It probably helped that so
many of my Kilkenny team-mates also seemed to be settling down at

the same time. Martin Comerford, Michael Kavanagh, Eddie Brennan, Derek Lyng and Noel Hickey were all recent newlyweds now. Everyone's personal circumstances seemed to be changing. Or, as we put it in the dressing room, fellas were 'dropping like flies'.

The League passed fairly undramatically for Kilkenny, defeats to Tipp, Cork and Galway meaning we failed to make the final for only the third time in nine years. Any disappointment didn't linger. Championship was our solitary focus.

We blew Dublin away in the Leinster semi-final on a day I became the highest scorer in Championship history. At the start of the day, I was three points behind Eddie Keher in the all-time records, and I'd be lying if I said it wasn't on my mind as I lined up my fourth free of the day. In fact, I have a picture at home of me lining up that free, and I was really chuffed to get it.

But then I remember having a little conversation with myself to put that stuff out of my mind. The time to be thinking of awards or records was when I finished up. That's not for a second to play down the satisfaction I took from that milestone. I know how special Keher was in a Kilkenny jersey. He was a scoring machine at a time when forwards probably got it tougher than we do today.

Eddie's also a thorough gentleman and a massive hurling man who regularly comes in to watch Kilkenny train.

He called up to me in 2012 to have a jersey signed and, for me, it was a real privilege just having him in the house. That's the kind of thing I will always remember when my career is over, the surreal sense of sitting there, having a cup of tea and thinking that the two of us were the highest scorers in the entire history of Championship hurling.

He actually told me that he'd love to be in contact more often but, while I was still playing, he wanted to give me space. To me, that was a measure of the man.

The Leinster final pretty much summed up what you could call the Galway enigma. After the ferocity of their challenge in Tullamore the previous year, we thought they'd come out against us now with all guns blazing. They didn't. There was something strangely lethargic about them and, while we never quite pulled away from them, there was never a real sense that they believed they were going to win. Offaly had taken them to a replay in the semi-final, and it was as if that experience ripped away a lot of the belief Galway had built up through winning the National League.

I scored a goal in the first half, and the game really just fizzled out. The story of the day became their struggle to get Joe Canning involved. They tried him everywhere – wing-forward, centre-forward, corner-forward, full-forward. No matter where he went, Joe struggled to get the ball in his hand. Our backs just held their positions. There were no special arrangements made for any player. Cody just trusted everyone to hold his end up.

That faith was repaid in spades but, personally, I felt like a car not quite running on all cylinders. There was more in me, I felt absolutely certain of that. Just needed a little tinkering.

16.   The Battle of Wounded Knee

An August night in Nowlan Park and I feel like a trapeze artist preparing for the applause of the Big Top.

I step from Robbie Lodge's room into the dressing-room corridor, my insides churning. The crowd outside is the kind you'd expect at a county final. 'Nothing wrong with you now, Henry, the injury is in the past,' says Brian Cody. Lads are patting me as they go past. Eyes shine with recognition.

I'm like a religious relic about to be checked for authenticity. Canice Hickey steps into the tunnel with me and as we emerge, blinking, into the autumn glare, loud applause erupts. 'Jaysus, Canice, they're glad to see you tonight,' a voice chuckles.

I slip into a line and begin pucking balls across the field. There's a hum in the place like people are waiting for a theatre curtain to open. Eight thousand pairs of eyes burn into me. I could combust here if I don't start breathing slower. I could die.

We do the drills, now the match. Cody throws me a bib. 'Centre-forward,' he says. I will have the pleasure of Brian Hogan as my jailer. A few weeks ago, Hogie and I sat into a stranger's car outside Croke Park and got driven to Wexford, down to the cryotherapy chamber in Whites Hotel, Hogie with his busted hand, me with my ruined knee.

A ball comes dropping towards us now, I put up my hand and it sticks. The crowd convulses. 'Jesus,' I think to myself, 'not too bad!' The plan is to play twenty minutes, but I've ceased being anyone's special project now. I'm either right tonight or I'm not.

I get to half-time and Cody approaches. 'Are you playing on?' he asks. It's not really a question. I play to the end and stride off to grand applause. Haven't exactly pulled up any trees but, apart from one queasy moment of instability under the new stand, haven't felt like an invalid either.

We shower, change, have a little talk and nobody mentions the knee. It's history now. Then I slip out to the car, which I've parked tight against the wall of the old stand to facilitate an inconspicuous arrival and departure. I reach across to my phone with two calls to make. Deirdre and Gerard Hartmann.

Then I spot the windscreen. Someone's left a 'good luck' note. As my wife's voice comes on the line, I'm lifting the wiper to retrieve it. Everything is good, I'm telling Deirdre. I'm back in the frame for Tipp. Then I look down at the sheet of paper in my hands. A parking ticket.

Fuck, is this an omen?

The sequence of events? Four weeks before the All-Ireland semi-final against Cork, I was like a boxer desperate to add a few pounds to his punch. Went to Mick Dempsey. 'There's more in me if you can just give me a little more power,' I said. Mick devised a programme of squat-jumps to get some speed and sharpness into my legs. So I'd head into the Nowlan Park gym before training and do them before we started.

Maybe it's all in the mind, but I felt fantastic. On the Friday before the semi-final, we had the customary team meeting in Nowlan Park. Brian named the starting fifteen and said his few words. Sometimes I speak at these meetings, sometimes I don't. That night I spoke.

'Two fucking words, lads,' I shouted. 'Stepford Wives. We'll fucking show them!' Everyone just turned and walked out the door.

That Sunday, we did show them. I seemed to run on spring-loaded feet in that semi-final, setting up Eddie Brennan for a goal, knifing through the defence and passing perfectly with my weaker hand. We were ripping Cork to pieces. Next thing, I launched myself at a diagonal ball and, when I looked at this moment later, a thought struck that I'd never seen myself jump so high.

But, on landing, my left knee met a sledgehammer and I felt something pop. I knew instantly. The pain for the first forty seconds or so of a torn cruciate is shocking, then it just settles into numbness. Robbie and Tadhg came out to me with spray and reassurance.

'Relax, Henry, you're grand.'

'I'm not grand, it's gone, it's fucking gone!'

I cried, once I got to the tunnel. Big, gulping tears of resignation. This was my year over, maybe my hurling career. I should have gone straight up to the subs in the stand, but I couldn't bring myself to do that. Tadhg got me to gather myself, come back out and be a man. Next thing, Marty Morrissey was standing with us.

Marty, I'm sure, needed to feed an update to the lads doing the television commentary upstairs. He began to ask a question. 'Feck off Marty, leave him alone!' roared Tadhg. Marty didn't linger.

John Crosbie was the kind stadium steward who offered to drive Hogie and me to Wexford. We hadn't even showered, were still in our Kilkenny gear and united by a foul humour. 'Sure, turn on the radio,' we suggested, to break the silence. Crosbie couldn't. The radio in his Mercedes was broken.

So, with maybe twenty minutes to go in the All-Ireland semi-final against Cork, we were driving through the north inner city, this perfectly nice man from Edenderry trying to make conversation with two Lucifers.

That night, after the cryotherapy session in Wexford, John would drop us both home, me to Ballyhale, Hogie to Thomastown. As soon as I got inside, I went straight for the phone, dialling Tadhg O'Sullivan. So I was standing by the fireplace, chatting to my surgeon, when, with almost comic timing, he said, 'Hang on, here it is!'

He was watching *The Sunday Game*. So was Deirdre. I could see myself on screen, launching into the air, then crumbling. Could hear Tadhg's voice.

'Aw, Jesus. No, that doesn't look good, Henry!'

So Hogie and me were back with the cryotherapy the next morning. Three more sessions at a temperature that would freeze oil. Then back to Kilkenny, where the lads were meeting for the ritual few Monday pints in Billy Byrnes. I just had a Lucozade and some food. James Ryall was inquisitive.

'I'm gone, James. I know it!'

The enormity of my disappointment was pulling me down now. I felt a million miles removed from everyone. The papers were full of Kilkenny's demolition job on a team that had once had such a huge presence in our world. Only Tipp stood between us and a place with the gods now. But I wasn't going to be involved.

I drove home, lay on my bed and cried. Poor Deirdre, still in her work clothes, might as well have been trying to lift the *Titanic* off the floor of the ocean.

We waited for the swelling to go down before Tadhg O'Sullivan had a look that Tuesday, at the Whitfield Clinic. He seemed non-committal. There was suspiciously little swelling now, so he suggested an MRI.

And as I lay there in that tube, listening to the familiar clicking, banging sounds, I actually dared to hope. Tadhg then called me into a side-room where the radiographer stared at a small assembly of screens. He was peering over her shoulder. Then his verdict hit me like a meteorite. 'Ah, Henry, it's gone. It's completely gone.'

The phone calls I made then were short and devoid of small talk. Deirdre first, then Brian. On the road between Ballyhale and Mullinavat, I had to pull in. My head was gone. I rang Tadhg Crowley. I was making calls like a drowning man making lunges for the shore.

Eventually I drove into Kilkenny, meeting Deirdre for lunch. Chicken fillet roll, bag of crisps, Mars bar and a Coke, sitting in the car. No need for a nutritionist now.

Then Tadhg Crowley called me back, maybe out of pity. Asked me to go and see him. That evening he gave me a set of crutches and suggested trying to rehab the knee. I lay on his bed, protesting. 'For Christ's sake, what's the point, Tadhg?'

And that's when he mentioned Ronan O'Gara. And a man with magic hands.

I walked into Gerard Hartmann's clinic on crutches that Wednesday and came away without them.

Ger's first trick was a trick of the mind. He began working on my good knee, asking me about old surgery and a legacy of stiffness. I was lying on the bed, thinking, 'Jesus, my fucking left leg is the problem!' It was all psychology. Maybe even distraction.

By the time he got to my left, he was into the story of O'Gara. I'd read Ronan's book and knew where this was going. Sometimes you can just build up the muscles around a damaged cruciate and, essentially, make do without the ligament. Ger mentioned Kieran McGeeney as another example. Every test he did on my knee now produced an equivocal conclusion.

'There's a bit of give there, but I don't feel it coming the whole way . . . It's really interesting that there's no swelling . . . Jesus, Henry, I don't know . . .'

As he worked on me, he was taking copious notes. He had me doing functional tests. Walking. Squats. He rubbed the knee endlessly, almost as if the problem could be erased through friction. And, with every sentence from Hartmann's lips, I could feel a little more light spill into my world.

He told me to forget about the crutches. He couldn't promise anything but was willing to take me on as a project. But only on one condition: 'You go for this one hundred per cent or you don't bother.' There were four and a half weeks to the All-Ireland final. To have a chance of playing, I knew I'd need to be able to train in three and a half.

'Come back in tomorrow morning,' he told me, 'and bring your training gear.'

Rackard Cody, our kit man, had driven me down, and he was now bringing home a different man. When he'd collected me that morning at Carroll's in Knocktopher, I thought we were heading to Limerick, essentially to plan rehab before surgery. Now a whole new possibility opened up.

I rang Brian on the way home. 'Sure, give it a lash!' was his attitude. If there was a one per cent chance of facing Tipp, where was the harm in chasing it? But I suspect he thought it a pipe dream.

Anyway, that's how it began. Back down that Thursday for maybe four hours of physical and mental rehab. Hartmann would bury his thumbs into the muscles around the knee, opening them up, waking them, causing my body to lift off the table with pain. He has a little gym off his treatment room, and he'd get me doing body stretches and squats. Really simple, basic exercises, just bearing my own body weight. Ordinarily, I'd be doing them with maybe a hundred kilos on my back. But everything was a building block for the mind now.

His colleague, Ger Keane, stepped in occasionally, studying what I was doing and telling me, 'Jesus, Henry, you're flying it!'

The positivity was phenomenal. They gave me a programme of daily exercises to follow and told me to be back down the following Monday. That Saturday, I took myself into the gym in Nowlan Park, where I knew I could get some work done in privacy. Cody heard I was there and decided to see for himself.

I remember doing these one-legged squats on the bad knee, the perspiration rolling off me. I'd stand on a box, pushing my body weight up and down with a medicine ball in my hands. Cody arrived with Mick Dempsey and Martin Fogarty, and I could see his surprise. 'Jesus Christ, I can't believe what I'm seeing.'

That evening, I went home to Deirdre in great form. There was no swelling in the knee. No hint of a negative reaction. I knew Cody was starting to think what I was thinking: 'This might not be so far-fetched after all . . .'

The following week, John Tennyson was dispatched with me to Limerick. John's cruciate had gone too and now he became part of the same project. It was exhilarating and exhausting. The treatment was incredibly intense, two consecutive days of non-stop work, then back home with a programme to follow.

We might finish at seven on a Thursday evening and be straight back in on Friday morning for more of the same. Hartmann has a house on the University of Limerick campus, and Tennyson and I would stay there overnight. We were like giddy students, lying there in the evenings with tea and fig rolls, icing our wounded knees.

Tennyson was more sceptical than me. 'Henry, we haven't a fucking chance,' he'd say. We'd be in the car on the way back to Kilkenny and the little exchange would start. When I spoke it was as if the voice that came out was Ger Hartmann's. 'No, John, this will work, stick with it.'

Hartmann and Keane could read our differing mindsets. They

thought John a little negative, worried that he was dragging me down.

They were wrong. I was actually enjoying the banter with Tennyson, and the truth is that nothing could drag me down at that point. I had bought into this, big time. Every glimpse of progress made me work a little harder. And, even if Tennyson had his doubts, he was still going with me, stride for stride.

The arrangement was strictly covert: publicly, there was absolutely no question of me being in the running to play against Tipp. Even my family was kept in the dark. When the first rumours began to slip out, one of the selectors, Martin Fogarty, knocked it emphatically on the head. 'Not a chance,' he told the media. 'Sure, the cruciate is gone!'

By the third week, Hartmann had me jogging on the UL indoor track, and that's when the story gathered some traction. I remember, one morning, a few lads playing basketball beneath us and, suddenly, word leaked on to the internet. My sister Cecilia spotted it and mentioned it to my mother, and that evening I found myself pleading the Fifth Amendment.

'Look, I wouldn't pay much heed to it . . . we'll just see how it goes . . .'

For three weeks I was off work, training as a full-time athlete. The moment Deirdre was out the door in the morning, I'd be on the floor, doing my exercises. I was pulling on boots and running now. Every new day brought another lift in confidence. Even the hurl was back out and in use.

Two weeks before the final, Cody took the team to Wexford for a weekend while Tennyson and I headed to Limerick for one of our final sessions. I was glad that I'd soon be making the journey for the last time. There is no good stretch of road going from Callan to Clonmel to Cahir to Tipp town and, finally, into Limerick. The travel was beginning to wear.

As media curiosity heightened, Tennyson and I had taken to wearing hats to conceal our identity. Our last Limerick session was on the Tuesday, twelve days before the final. Hartmann split us up.

By now, he was working as much on my mind as on my knee. I was due back training in Nowlan Park the following night, and everything he said was designed to flush away any self-doubt. 'You're good to go, Henry. I can see you grabbing balls tomorrow night, scoring points for fun!' I jumped on every word like a lottery ticket.

I knew I had done everything I could. I was ready.

I'd gone back to work in Waterford two weeks before the final, and the exertion of everything combined left me looking like a ghost. The Thursday after my big night back in Nowlan Park, I had followed my usual lunchtime ritual: dipped into Dooley's on the quays around 2 p.m., found a seat with my back to the room, pulled open a newspaper. And there, on the back page, was a photograph of the miracle of Henry. The size of the crowd was mentioned. The atmosphere of elation. Reading it had made me nauseous.

The following day would be my last visit to Hartmann's clinic, and I think he saw enough in my face to convince him not to do very much. My body and mind were virtually at breaking point. I was yawning on the bed as he worked.

At training the following day, it was agreed that I would start the final. The relief at the end of that session was enormous. Deep down, maybe it should have been a giveaway. Another session without breaking down – that's how I was thinking. My nerves were raw. I went up for a ball with Brian Hogan the following Wednesday night and he broke a finger. Jesus Christ. I decided to sit out Friday's session.

Maybe I had a sixth sense. Sitting in the conservatory the day before the final, I said to Deirdre, 'Look, whatever happens now, I've done everything I can.' It wasn't the most hopeful observation.

Funny thing is, I would get my hands on the ball more in the first thirteen minutes against Tipp than I had maybe in the whole of the '09 final. I was feeling good. Then I went to pivot on a breaking ball and my left knee went from under me. It wasn't especially painful and I didn't become emotional.

I just hobbled off what had begun to feel like a movie-set. Shane McGrath delivered a consoling tap on the backside as I made my exit. And, watching me leave, the Tipp crowd seemed to join in a generous applause. Looking back, that moment means an awful lot to me. The rivalry between our counties gets incredibly intense and I know full well that people on both sides can be very blinkered in how they read it. But, of all the compliments I have taken in my hurling career, I look back on that moment of collective applause as one of the most precious.

Of course, maybe they just reckoned they were seeing the last of me.

I was led to a seat in the stand and given ice, everyone around me commiserating. After about ten minutes, a man in a yellow bib approached, a steward looking for me to autograph something. 'Would you ever fuck off,' someone roared. I told him I'd do it later.

In the dressing room at half-time, Mick Dempsey and Martin Fogarty called on me to say a few words, but I didn't have the heart. 'C'mon, Henry, c'mon.' I made a stab at something, but could feel myself getting emotional. Someone interjected, 'C'mon, we'll do it for Henry!' Where had I heard that before?

And they tried, but they couldn't. As the five-in-a-row began slipping away, I found myself drawn towards the pitch. We were chasing the game, leaving gaps. I could see Tommy and JJ getting dragged too far forward and I hobbled down to sit beside Cody and Ned Quinn. I was warning against leaving too much space inside. At one point, I even went up to the sideline and roared at JJ to 'get back'.

It was horrible, the five-in-a-row slipping away and all I had left to contribute was a few shouted instructions the lads probably couldn't even hear. Then the whistle went and I remember feeling just like I had in the seconds before Paul Phelan's late goal for Ballyhale in the '89 county final.

I was standing in the last place on earth I wanted to be.

The regrets of 2010 eased with the passing of time. People I respect in the game, like Peter Barry and Eamonn Corcoran, made me realize that it would have been worse to have never tried. To have been left wondering.

But the experience exhausted me. I'll never forget arriving back at the hotel and all these supporters cheering us in the door, patting us on the back. 'Why are they clapping us?' I was thinking. I struggled up the big, grand stairs out of the front lobby and there, standing at the top, were Ger Hartmann and Ger Keane. The two of them had waited a couple of hours to see me. I really respected them for that. The easy thing for them would have been to just head for the hills now. Leave me to my disappointment. For all the positivity of the weeks before, they knew this had always been a possibility. But they also knew how much I'd put in, both physically and emotionally, to play in the final. They looked devastated that it hadn't worked out.

When Deirdre and I got up to the room, I didn't want to face the evening function. I just wanted to go home and curl up in a ball, become invisible. The five-in-a-row was gone and now I was facing more surgery, more rehab. A thought struck that I might never play for Kilkenny again.

There's always a pre-dinner drinks reception, restricted to the players, their wives and girlfriends. We were the last ones down and I remember going in on the crutches, thinking, 'I shouldn't be here, I can't even walk!' A massive crowd had booked into the hotel, I suppose in expectation of history. They applauded us every step of the way into the function. I felt agitated. The cup was in the Burlington, decorated with blue and gold tassles.

The cruciate apart, I'd also ripped cartilage in my knee. The pain began to throb and my leg was swelling badly. After a while, supporters came pouring into the function and I knew I needed to get out of there. The hotel's deputy manager showed us a way out a back door and through the kitchen. As we left, I glanced back and could see what looked like a thousand faces peering after me in pity. The weight of the world was back on my shoulders.

Cody had told Deirdre to make sure to keep my spirits up and she certainly had a job on her hands. Mentally and physically, I was broken.

★

At 4 a.m., as I lay, wide awake, on a hotel bed in Citywest, my knee screaming out for the comfort of painkillers, there was a knock at the door. Deirdre was beside me and in a deep sleep. Last thing I needed was a chat with a beery stranger who couldn't find his room. (I heard subsequently that it was Dr Tadhg Crowley knocking, armed with something to dull the pain. He'd spotted the missed calls. Sums up my weekend, really.)

I waited for the first, faint glow of morning and dialled Rackard Cody's number. It was a safe enough call as Rackard doesn't drink. I didn't particularly want to head downstairs without familiar company.

Then I rang my sister Aileen for a lift. The Kilkenny routine here is for lads to reconvene for a few pints in the front bar before checking out. Hair-of-the-dog stuff. But by the time the texts started flying, Deirdre and I were already home in Ballyhale. I headed to bed for a few hours' sleep.

Later, Deirdre drove me into Kilkenny to meet the team off the train and show my face at the homecoming. I owed that to the supporters. But I'd had a bellyful of this All-Ireland, and the pain soon hunted me out of the function in Langtons.

We gambled and we lost. What should have been about a bid for immortality and the five-in-a-row became my very own Lourdes experiment. Do I regret that gamble? On that morning after the final, I'd never regretted anything more in my life. In time, I would come to realize it was a chance I simply had to take. But in the immediate aftermath, I was consumed with something that felt like guilt.

17.   Hello, Mister President

Tadhg O'Sullivan is standing over me, a tiny bottle in his hand. 'Here's what was causing the pain in your knee,' he says.

There's a lump of cartilage in the bottle. My cruciate had been hanging by a thread after the All-Ireland semi-final and it snapped with such force in the final that it took out cartilage with it. So this grey lump of matter was just rolling around inside my knee, jabbing nerve ends. Agony.

It took a month for the swelling to go down and surgery to become feasible. That month felt like a small eternity. I couldn't work because I couldn't drive, and into the vacuum came a flood of bad thoughts. It wasn't so much me thinking that my career was finished as a growing suspicion that everyone else believed it might be.

The lost five-in-a-row was immaterial now. Sure, there were days when it crept up unexpectedly and the sheer scale of what, as a team, we had almost achieved would hit home. That was our chance of immortality, of separating ourselves from everyone else in GAA history. To do something that no team had ever done before. But this was 'could have been, should have been' territory. A place I needed to avoid.

The pain was tearing at me badly now and, on the Tuesday morning, I had to be driven to the Whitfield for Tadhg to drain some blood from the knee. From there, it was back into town, to Billy Byrnes, The World's End and, finally, back to Langton's again on a pub crawl that left me pretty exhausted and ready only for my bed around nine that evening.

My batteries were completely flat now, the mental side of everything having taken its toll. I would need weeks to get any real energy back into my body.

We were all devastated at the loss, but maybe I was inclined to personalize it more than others. Would Kilkenny have been better off if a line had been drawn under my season after the semi-final? How had the circus surrounding John Tennyson and me affected the others? Was I more culpable than anyone else for our loss?

Tennyson, for his part, had lasted the whole final. I look back at the video and can see he is clearly compromised whenever he has to turn. In normal circumstances, he wouldn't have played. But Brian Hogan's broken finger meant these weren't normal circumstances. So he just about held his own at centre-back, without ever really driving the team forward as he can.

I suppose I envied him that consolation at least, the feeling of having survived.

It didn't help that I knew what was ahead of me in terms of rehab after surgery. Dark days would be unavoidable. There were other implications to consider too.

In August, my boss in the bank, Pat Creed, had spoken to me about becoming national sales manager, with ten people working under me. It would have been a big step forward in my career – but that, obviously, had to be put on hold. I was due to start in September; now we were putting it back to January. Pat, as ever, was unbelievably supportive. My absence for two months was going to put work colleagues under severe pressure, yet he organized an automatic car so I'd still be able to drive.

To prepare for surgery, I reverted to a familiar exercise designed to strengthen muscles around the cruciate. It involved manipulating a ball behind the injured knee. Every now and then, this would produce a bolt of unmerciful pain. But I had to do it. The idea is that you keep the muscles tense and firing so that they contract. Hence, when you come out of surgery, they are quicker to respond.

I'd started hounding Tadhg to do the operation so that rehab could begin as soon as possible. Slowly, all the negativity of losing to Tipp began to shrink in the face of an absolute compulsion to go again. I couldn't leave things as they were.

Tadhg relented in October, by which time I already had tunnel vision for my recovery. Before I went under, I issued a few

instructions. In my previous cruciate rehab, I had become familiar with an ice machine that you strap to the affected area to bring
down swelling. The county board has two 'Game Ready' machines
and, in recent years, I've claimed virtual ownership of one. I'd
asked the physio if it would make sense to use it immediately after
surgery and he reckoned that it would. So I told the nurses to attach
the 'Game Ready' to my knee as soon as the operation was complete.
This meant it would be doing its job before I even came out of the
anaesthetic.

I was in a lot of pain when I did wake up and, being honest, I probably wasn't the best person to live with in the days that immediately
followed. I became hugely impatient to be doing stuff that, deep
down, I knew might not even be possible for months ahead. I was
also approaching my thirty-second birthday. Unless I did everything
by the book (and even if I did), there was clearly a distinct possibility
that my career in top-flight hurling was over.

Some newspaper articles at the time certainly implied as much.
The tone of everything was one of sympathy. It seemed as if I
was being spoken of only in the past tense now. It's funny – for all
the reams of good stuff written about you in a long career, I've
always found it's the snippets of bad stuff that you most readily
absorb.

A picture from the Cork game, of me on the ground in tears,
seemed the only one being used of Henry Shefflin now. I felt the
world had written me off. And, psychologically, that was probably
no bad thing.

The loss of cartilage is problematic because it's there, essentially, to
protect the knee. I have an area now where it's bone on bone, and that
needs constant management and care. Still, the 'Game Ready' did its
job and I quickly settled into a morning routine of getting the kids
out the door with Deirdre, then heading straight to the gym in Hotel
Kilkenny, where I'd spend the rest of the morning. After lunch, I'd
do an hour in the pool, then home. I was, effectively, in full-time
rehab.

I had to be on crutches for twelve weeks, but I started 'spinning' sessions on a bike at first, using no resistance. Just getting the legs active again. To begin with, the knee felt really strange, almost wobbling while I spun. So how did I respond? I did what any lunatic would do and decided to add resistance. Disaster. The next day my knee was the width of a piano leg.

This happened about four weeks after the operation and it coincided with a call to the house from Ger Hartmann and Ger Keane. They just wanted to see how I was doing, but their timing couldn't have been worse. As Hartmann ran his hand over the knee, I could see concern in his expression.

'Jesus, that feels very hot!' he said.

I told them what I'd done and I could see from the way they were looking at one another that they thought I needed protecting from myself. But I wasn't their problem now. I made them some tea. They left.

'Look, take it easy . . .'

Another brainwave I'd had by then was to stop taking the painkillers. There is something in my make-up that leads me to the feeling that, maybe, I can read what's happening with my body a lot better when there's no concealment. Anyway, I sometimes have problems with my stomach when I take them, so what harm would a little pain do, so long as it proved educational?

I'd been told to take the tablets for two weeks, but I stopped after three days. By day six, I was in pretty serious discomfort and rang Robbie Lodge. Robbie knew me well enough to sense this wasn't exactly a question for *Mastermind*.

'Did you stop taking the tablets?' he asked.

'Yes.'

'Start taking them again.'

Then, just as I began to make progress, the snow came. For a week, we were trapped in Ballyhale under a great white blanket. Couldn't even get the few hundred yards down the hill to my parents' house. I'll never forget it. The two kids were sick, Deirdre was pregnant and I was now, officially, useless on a pair of crutches. All I could hear was a ticking clock again. I had cabin fever and I started panicking.

Mentally, I needed the gym now more than ever, but the roads were undrivable. We'd just got a delivery of coal, so I took myself out to the garage and improvised a weights session. Started doing squats with a forty-kilo bag of coal on my back and a tin of paint in each hand. At some point, Deirdre noticed I was missing from the house and came looking. When she found me, I could tell she was a little emotional. I suppose I looked pathetic, covered in soot from head to toe.

The harsh winter continued out through March, but I'd gone back to work in January and, although really busy with the job, I made sure to get in some kind of session every day. Once, in February, I had to do an overnight in Westport and, after doing a gym session on arrival in the hotel, started asking around for a suitable place to do a morning run.

The receptionist was looking at me as if my hair was on fire, but I was up the following morning at seven and, in darkness, drove around town until I found the GAA pitch. The gate, naturally, was locked so I climbed over and began running laps, watching the lights come on in the houses around the field as people got up for work. At this stage, I was having to strap the knee because of what they call a 'pikey', a little catch at the top of it causing discomfort as I ran.

When I think of my desperation to get back, that's probably one of the lonelier images that come back to me: sitting in the February blackness, shivering in my car as I applied the strapping. The moment the run was finished, though, all that loneliness slipped away. Getting work like that done before the day has even started always has that effect on me. That morning, I went back to the hotel, happy that I'd earned my two bowls of porridge.

If it all sounds a little obsessive, it's probably because it was. My moods were directly related to my training. Always have been, really. I have this thing that, if team-mates are training five times a week, I'll see to it that I do six. It's a psychological trick I play on myself, always looking for an edge. You see, when I'm coming back after injury, I know the others are expecting a bit of a wreck to come through the gate. The big thing for me is to disappoint them.

That would have been very much my mindset when I went back with Kilkenny towards the end of February. My first night back, I just did the running and was up the front all through. Cody was nervous I was going too hard and had to tell me to stop. Jackie Tyrrell said to Cody afterwards that he couldn't believe how good a condition I was in and it meant a lot to me to hear that. The lads had been expecting some kind of sickly child through the gate that evening.

Over the weeks that followed, I started doing a bit of hurling in training with Shamrocks. One night, I went for a ball and Patrick Reid came in under me. Neither of us saw the other coming and, as I caught the ball, we collided heavily. My heart skipped a beat as I fell. Just that horrible sensation of thinking everything could come undone here. But, thankfully, I picked myself up without any great difficulty and it was a big psychological boost to get that first fall out of the way.

I'd started going in to the home League games, if only to let everyone know that rumours of my demise had been slightly exaggerated. Little did I think those rumours were, suddenly, about to switch from me to the whole team.

'CROKER CHOKERS' ran one newspaper headline the week after our League final mauling against Dublin.

The appetite to have Kilkenny washed and laid out on a slab before summer even came was palpable. But to call a team that had won four of the last five All-Irelands 'chokers'? It was bewildering in one sense, gratifying in another. We were wounded animals and you just got the feeling that people were ready to turn their backs.

A little personal selfishness kicked in too. As one of 'the injured' who'd sat out the League, I was entirely exempt from blame. Better still, people were talking about the number of missed frees Kilkenny had against Dublin. I felt needed again.

I'm not trying to downplay the problems we had, because they were pretty self-evident. To win their first League in seventy-two years, Dublin devoured us physically. They looked a yard faster, were stronger in the tackle and, most worrying of all, hurled with far superior discipline.

The images that came from the final flew in the face of everything we like to think we stand for. Over the years, Kilkenny might, almost habitually, have been accused of excessive physicality, but we have never been considered hotheads. Eoin Larkin was a little unlucky to get a straight red card that day, but the most worrying lapse came on the stroke of half-time, when John Dalton tangled with Dublin's Conor McCormack.

The pictures didn't do John any favours and, while the incident wasn't seen by referee Michael Wadding, video evidence was subsequently used to impose an eight-week suspension. In some respects, that was the beginning and the end of Dalton as a county hurler. Paul Murphy's emergence meant he didn't get his place back on the team and John would retire, prematurely in my mind, at the end of the Championship.

Maybe there was a perception of Rome burning while Nero fiddled as Cody batted away talk of a crisis, but I can honestly say he was absolutely calm in the dressing room afterwards. I'd been sitting in the stand alongside Tommy Walsh and Michael Fennelly, and all of us were agreed on one thing: this defeat was dropping us into the long grass. If people wanted to write us off, all the better.

I'd brought my gear with me that day and, while the boys were having their pre-match sandwiches in the Airport Hotel, I did a session in the gym. After the game, I'd gone on to the field with Tommy, the two of us looking up at the cup presentation. I won't pretend there weren't doubts fizzing around our heads as John McCaffrey made his speech.

But it was obvious that Dublin had been far more up for the final than us. I felt it would be hard for them to replicate that performance, whereas we knew we could raise our game a good few notches.

A few days after the final, Jackie Tyrrell gave a newspaper interview in which he was quoted as saying that Kilkenny 'seemed to be going backwards'. Brian, I know, wasn't best pleased. His whole demeanour in the dressing room after the game had been restrained and positive, a 'we'll sort this out' kind of certainty. Now Jackie was in the press talking of 'slipping standards' and the 'worst perform-ance' given by Kilkenny in his time with the team.

A text went out to all the players afterwards, reiterating a policy of media interviews needing to be cleared with management first. There was a lot of negativity around and I suppose the feeling was that Jack-ie's outburst was adding to it. But he'd just been speaking his mind, and I certainly had no issue with anything he said.

Actually, with the gift of hindsight, I think it was a good thing that Jackie said what he did. He's someone I have massive time for and who is very straight in what he says. I don't doubt management would have preferred a more diplomatic line, but there is so much respect for Jackie Tyrrell in the Kilkenny dressing room, I think his outburst was a positive.

We took two weeks off after the League final and I remember a cer-tain apprehension going in, the first night back. Just a feeling that we were walking into a backlash. Maybe that's where Cody's intelligence comes to the fore. He's never predictable. Our two-hour session was tough, but nothing daft. Then he was absolutely positive afterwards in the team meeting. No recrimination, no scapegoats, no panic.

'This is where we are now,' he said, 'and we're going to get better. It won't happen overnight but, believe me, we will improve and, what's more, we'll keep improving . . .'

The outside world might have seen us as a team in crisis, but the man at the helm clearly didn't. That night, I believe, was the turning point of our season.

I'm watching Jedward chat up my wife and she isn't putting up much of what I'd call an argument.

John and Edward are not what I expected. Nobody is. I look around this room with its plush sofas and tall refreshment trolleys, and it is virtually paved with famous faces. It feels like I might be hallucinating here. Brendan Gleeson has been over, talking about the GAA. Daniel Day-Lewis sits chatting in a corner.

I've been shooting the breeze with Danny from The Coronas, who – it turns out – knows his hurling. I say hello again to Pádraig Harrington. Brian O'Driscoll moves easily from group to group, hands clamped on the Heineken Cup that Leinster have just regained in Cardiff. I like O'Driscoll. He comes over and says hello with what feels like genuine friendliness.

We're in a VIP room at the back of the Bank of Ireland building on College Green, waiting to meet the US President. Everyone is acting a little giddy here. It's only four days since I was standing in line at the Convention Centre for a brief audience with the Queen of England.

The Queen's visit had been well signposted, so I knew months in advance that I was one of the sportspeople chosen to meet her. It was all very formal, very proper. Maybe twenty-five groups upstairs in the Convention Centre, ten people in each. The Duke of Edinburgh coming down one side of the room, the Queen the other. I stood with Declan Kidney, Jack Charlton, Kieran Donaghy, a former British Ambassador and some others.

It was the Ambassador's job to introduce us and, as luck would have it, he wore a yellow tie with the image of a cat with a hurl and a ball. When the Queen arrived at our group her attention was, instantly, drawn to the tie. The Ambassador explained that the cat was playing hurling. So she started coming down the line and the moment he introduced me as 'a Kilkenny hurler', she interjected, 'Oh, like his tie!'

No one told us what to say and I'm not sure what came out. I was a little in awe, wondering should I bow or stand up straight and genuflect. What should I call her? Someone in the group ahead of me used 'Ma'am', so that was good enough for me.

'Nice to meet you, Ma'am . . .' Hope that's what I said.

The concert put on in her honour was extraordinary. A real celebration of Irish music and theatre, including 'The Riverdance Experience'. Sometimes you forget the breadth of entertainment talent that this country has produced, but that night was a reminder.

It had been that Thursday morning, getting ready to go meet the

Queen, that I took the call about Obama. It came from MCD, the concert promoters hired to handle the entertainment side of his visit. 'Henry, do you want to meet the President on Monday?'

I put down the phone, turned to Deirdre and said, 'Next time I'm feeling sorry for myself, giving out about rehab, just remind me of this day!'

We had to send our passports in immediately for clearance and, on the day of the visit, moving between that VIP room and the stage in College Green, you had to go through the equivalent of airport security scanners and US passport control. Six of us had been chosen from sport, myself, 'Gooch' Cooper, O'Driscoll, Harrington, Robbie Keane and Katie Taylor. The deal was, we were brought out on stage to wave to the massive crowd that had gathered in front of Trinity College. Being honest, I found that a bit uncomfortable.

The rest of it, though, I'll treasure for the rest of my life. After being presented to the crowd, we were seated in a VIP section right in front of the stage for Barack Obama's address. Then, afterwards, back into the room for what we were told would be 'a handshake and a photo opportunity'. There were maybe sixty of us there, and I think most expected maybe a little formal process that would be over in a couple of minutes.

But the President must have spent twenty minutes, charming everyone in the room, shaking hands with every single person individually, chatting warmly. The Taoiseach, Enda Kenny, introduced us all by name, and I remember at one point myself and Gooch making eye contact. I suspect we were both thinking the exact same thing: *Is this really happening?*

I greatly appreciated how courteous the Taoiseach was towards me and the complimentary things he said in his introduction. But, for the women in the room, it seemed everything revolved around Jedward.

Michelle Obama was completely distracted by (or maybe nervous of) them. And, hand on heart, they were a lot sounder than I expected. Apparently, they ran cross-country at school and they even seemed to have played a bit of Gaelic too as they were able to talk to Gooch about Kerry.

When the time came for the President to leave, I did something I wouldn't normally do. I rushed across to intercept him, making sure to shake his hand again. I just knew that this was a once-in-a-lifetime experience. 'I must look up that game,' he said with that million-dollar smile.

You know, for lads like Gooch and me, when you come from rural Ireland it's hard to get your head around spending time in that kind of privileged bubble. We were both completely spellbound. I was sent a small ocean of photographs after and, while most are still on my laptop, Deirdre has two up on the wall at home. One is of her with Brian O'Driscoll and the Heineken Cup. The other is with Jedward.

Mister President will just have to wait.

'Bullied'. That was the word Cody kept applying to our League final defeat. He'd almost wince when he used the word. It offended him.

We knew ourselves that what had gone on in that game wasn't right. It wasn't Kilkenny. I mean, if you looked around our dressing room, virtually every man there had won multiples of medals. We'd been going fine in that League too, right up to the final, then – inexplicably – lost our focus and our discipline. Something we probably hadn't done in the previous four years. But we hadn't lost our ability to hurl.

We were in Carton House the Saturday evening Dublin blew Galway off the field in Tullamore. Everything about them was progressive and self-confident. The momentum they'd taken from winning the League had carried over into two Championship victories now, giving them a place in the Leinster final.

Maybe it reflects an inherent arrogance, but we felt certain we would beat them so long as our attitude was right, so long as we hurled with our normal intensity.

I was ready to throw off the shackles too, having come through our semi-final against Wexford without mishap. I'd been extremely nervous, heading to Wexford Park that day, and I remember being a bit tentative in the warm-up. The problem with Championship hurling is you can't really simulate it on the training ground. In Kilkenny, we probably like to think we get close, but you're never quite at that level of competitive aggression.

Early in that game, I blocked a Wexford defender down right in front of the stand and a huge roar went up. It was a big moment for me, a kind of 'welcome back, Henry' sound that helped me settle into the rhythm of things. My free-taking was decent and, as we pulled away in the second half, I could feel myself almost subconsciously stepping back from things a little. Put it this way: if I was presented with a 50/50 ball in the last ten minutes, I wasn't going to contest it. I was back and I wanted to stay back.

Late in the game, I broke on to a loose ball and scored a point from play, which pretty much drew a perfect line under the day for me. I hadn't exactly been pulling up trees, but I had contributed. Sitting on the bus easing out of Wexford that evening, a voice in my head was saying, 'Let there be no more talk about that knee now . . .'

In the week before the Leinster final, Tommy Walsh decided to speak after training in Nowlan Park. I don't know what it is about Tommy, but he has a knack of hitting the perfect note in these moments. You can hear a pin drop when he speaks.

Brian had referenced the League final a few times in the build-up, but he was careful not to obsess about it. His message was, essentially, that a single game didn't make us different people. But he knew, too, that there was value to be had in mining the experience for a reaction. And he kept returning to that same word. 'Bullied'.

Tommy picked on that ball now and ran with it. He told us to take a long hard look at our body language going into that game. 'Look at us in the parade beforehand,' he said. 'Dublin are going around with their chests out, as if they're All-Ireland champions. Then look at us. We're like feckin' hunchbacks by comparison!

'Whatever happens this time, lads, we show them who we are with our body language.'

I felt that touched the perfect chord. We needed to remember the things we'd achieved in the game. If need be, even to find a little arrogance. Dublin had set down a marker in the League final; now it was our turn.

I've always felt that when Kilkenny play an Anthony Daly-managed team, myself and Tommy are targeted. Daly seems to see the two of us as lynchpins and sets people up to hit us hard and often, but fair. I've no problem with that. I actually take it as a compliment. But this time the compliment would have to be met with fireworks of our own.

And, sure enough, it was hot and heavy stuff. In the first half, I was playing down the Hogan Stand wing and their 'runner' on the sideline, Ciaran Hetherton, seemed to be in my face non-stop, mouthing at me. He was, basically, accusing me of throwing my weight around.

I certainly wasn't holding back. There was a lot of physical confrontation in the game and, if anything, I was drawn to it. Against Wexford I'd been kind of hurling in a psychological straitjacket, but now I was letting go. We all were. Dublin were beginning to believe that they could push teams around, dictate the terms of engagement. It was what they'd done to Galway, so why wouldn't they believe it? But we weren't Galway.

There was one moment in the game that probably encapsulated my mindset. I fouled Maurice O'Brien coming out with the ball and I kind of met him a second time to see if I could draw a reaction and have the decision overturned to a throw-ball. O'Brien hit me back, and then Conal Keaney came flying in, knocking me on my arse. A roar went up in the crowd and, even while I was on my way down, Tommy's words about body language came back into my head.

Instantly, I jumped straight up and went again, Tommy running past and shouting: 'That's it, Sheff, that's fucking it! Body language!'

I hadn't seen Keaney's hit coming, but I wasn't going to give him an ounce of satisfaction with my reaction. And that was our mindset from start to finish. Up you get, on your toes, chests out. Don't retreat an inch. To be fair to Dublin, they were without Tomás Brady and Ryan O'Dwyer, two of their primary ball-winners. And their centre-back, Joey Boland, went into the game with an injured shoulder, lasting little more than twenty minutes.

By then, we were pulling away from them. Richie Power gave Boland a torrid time and, although I'd been picked at full-forward, it was decided to put Eoin Larkin in instead and, typically, he scored our first goal. Colin Fennelly got our second and we were nine points clear by half-time.

Physically, we just bossed them. Noel Hickey's return to full-back helped massively and the entire Dublin full-forward line did not get a single score between them. Outside that line, Tommy out-hurled Keaney to the extent that Dublin's main ball-winning forward was moved, eventually, to midfield.

In the forty-third minute, I popped up on the right wing, TJ Reid's perfect pass setting me up for what I suppose was a match-ending goal. I was euphoric. I subsequently heard I had become the first player to score a goal in thirteen consecutive Championship seasons, but my sense of fulfilment had nothing to do with records. It was to do with having come through a hugely physical game feeling strong and a valuable part of the team again.

Nicky English named me his Man of the Match on TV3 and that meant a lot to me. You see, we'd needed to hammer into Dublin to make a statement about the future. I needed to hammer into them.

Going home on the bus that evening, I was sore all over. And loving it.

Waterford never greatly troubled us in the semi-final. They set themselves up so defensively, it would have been virtually impossible for them to win. I couldn't believe it. Couldn't understand it.

Maybe they had the '08 final in the back of their minds, but it was as if they set out with a policy of containment, never once considering the possibility of actually putting us on the back foot. Richie Hogan had a goal after only three minutes and he got a second just after David Herity saved brilliantly from John Mullane approaching half-time.

Mullane was our only problem, hurling largely at centre-forward and scoring pretty freely all day. We hurled poorly, shot an ocean of wides and still won without any drama. No one had really performed to their full potential, which suited us perfectly. It meant Brian would have something to whip us around the training pitch with now before the final.

Tipp, meanwhile, had razed Munster to the ground.

18.   Redemption

We knew what we had to do to get the McCarthy Cup back, we just didn't all agree on how to do it.

To stop Tipp, we needed to stop them scoring goals. That much was obvious. They'd scored four against us in the 2010 final, and fourteen in three Munster Championship games this season. Dublin had restricted them to one in the All-Ireland semi-final, but they'd done so playing seven men in defence. That wouldn't be Kilkenny's way.

Actually, we didn't feel we could take a great deal from their struggles against Dublin at all, beyond the fact that they clearly had not enjoyed being confronted physically. I'd been at home watching Tipp run a steam train through Waterford in the Munster final and, impressive as it looked, I was sitting there thinking, 'What are Waterford at defensively here?' When it was over, I just got up from the television and went back to helping Deirdre with the children.

So, while we needed a plan against Tipp, it had to be one that wasn't too negative, too preoccupied with containment.

And that's where I disagreed with Cody. Not overtly – not in the sense of challenging him at a team meeting. But, at our weekend away in Carton House, I expressed my reservations privately to some of the senior players. It seemed to me we were focusing too much on the danger Tipp posed to us rather than accentuating the threat we could be to them.

We did a huge amount of video analysis which, traditionally, wouldn't really have been our thing.

The analysis that weekend focused on two people: Pádraic Maher and Lar Corbett. Now, the focus on Corbett was self-explanatory. He was proving a goal-machine in the Championship, scoring seven so far, including an extraordinary 4-4 in the Munster final. Fair enough, stopping Lar was going to be pretty important.

Brian said he was thinking of going with a man-marker and, no surprise, the marker he had in mind was Jackie Tyrrell. At training the following day, John Mulhall was, basically, given free licence to run anywhere he chose, with Jackie commissioned to keep tabs on him. It made sense. If you were going to man-mark Lar, it was best to be prepared for a bit of a safari.

Training was excellent. Management focused big-time on the last twenty minutes of the Munster final and, specifically, on Waterford's defence. You could call it a tutorial in things the backs just weren't to do. A lot of people spoke well.

The implications of losing again to Tipp were grim, to say the least. It would probably signal the end for a good few of the team and, potentially, even Cody himself. It was as if we were back to '06 again. Fighting almost for our right to exist as county men.

The view was that whoever was being marked by Maher would have a big job to do. It wouldn't be enough just to hold your end up as a wing-forward. You had to curb his influence too, to stop him bursting out of defence and delivering those killer diagonal balls that had destroyed Waterford.

I'd played all the Championship matches at number 12, so I was pretty sure the job wouldn't be mine. There was speculation that Tipp might move Maher across to pick me up, but we didn't really expect that. Like ourselves, they tend to be pretty traditional in how they set themselves up and, in any event, it would be fairly widely accepted that Pádraic is happier on the left than the right.

The other bit of speculation surrounded Brendan Maher. A real stalwart of their win the previous year, he was back from a long-term injury now and pushing hard for a starting place. But they hadn't started him in the semi-final against Dublin and I couldn't really see how they could drop John O'Keeffe, who had played really well in that game.

I tried to shut out all the speculation, and focus, exclusively, on me. I was doing a bit extra at every opportunity. I'd go to the gym and do a session on my core before we'd go out on the field for training. Just back to that mindset of the more you put in, the better the chance of taking a lot out.

I only heard the Tipp team that Friday night before the final and, sure enough, they'd stayed with O'Keeffe at number 5.

Apart from the Dublin game, I'd never seen him play before. I didn't really know a thing about him. So I made a few phone calls, spoke to one or two lads who knew him from hurling Fitzgibbon with University of Limerick. I'd always do that when facing an opponent I'm not familiar with. I'd also recorded that semi-final against Dublin and would have noted a few small things about how he played. These are the kind of things I do off my own bat when it gets to that stage of the Championship. The smallest bits of information can be valuable.

Having said that, though, I didn't really care who Tipp put on me. I'd waited a year to play this game. From the moment I stood, injured, on the sideline, watching Lar Corbett sweep home his third goal of the 2010 All-Ireland final, every bead of perspiration I expended was geared for this game. For the opportunity of redemption.

Cody decided that Eddie Brennan was the man to put on Pádraic Maher, and it would prove a masterstroke. Eddie hadn't been starting games, but he was still in incredible shape and his pace alone meant that Maher couldn't really afford to let him out of his sight.

We opened like a house on fire, and the score was 0-5 to 0-0 after fifteen minutes. Tipp just couldn't win quality possession in any line, and Tommy Walsh kept raining brilliant diagonal ball down on top of me. As close as I am to Tommy, I've never actually asked him if it was something he had thought much about beforehand. But I'd swear to God he decided, 'I'm going to pepper Henry with ball today . . .'

The service he was giving me was unbelievable but, twenty-five minutes in, I was absolutely fuming with myself. By then, I'd scored just a single point from play when I should have had at least three. Watching the video afterwards, Michael Duignan says in the RTÉ commentary, 'Henry's going to be very disappointed not to have scored more at this stage . . .' He was spot on. I felt so good, so strong, I just wanted to express myself.

O'Keeffe made way for Brendan Maher before the half-hour and I wasn't terribly surprised. But the change made little difference to the overall picture. Tactically, we had our homework done. Our deliveries out of defence were much smarter than they'd been the year before. Taggy Fogarty pointed out one night in training how, the minute one of our backs got the ball in previous games against Tipp, they would just drop deep to defend their own square. Basically, they knew we were just banging ball as far down as we could. So that's where the diagonal deliveries came from. The emphasis was on much smarter use of possession. Forcing Tipp to think.

If my scoring eye had been in, I think we'd have been out the gap by half-time. It probably didn't help us either that there was a lengthy stoppage when the referee, Brian Gavin, took an accidental blow to the nose from Tommy's hurl. That incident broke our rhythm.

The Gavin incident led to an extended period of first-half injury-time, and it was just at the beginning of that when we scored a vital goal.

The score, I think, highlighted just how proactive and aware we were around the field. It came from a line cut on the Cusack Stand side. As I went over to take it, the Tipp lads would have known I wasn't going long. Eoin Larkin made a dart towards me, jabbing the ball straight back. I could easily have gone for a point, but Richie Hogan made a little sprint towards me. What followed showed just how together we were as a team.

With Danesfort, Richie's used to carrying a massive scoring burden. Basically, if he doesn't get into double figures, Danesfort generally won't win. I'd spoken to him about this, about the need to understand that hurling with Danesfort and hurling with Kilkenny were two entirely different things. With Kilkenny, he needed to lay the ball off a bit more. To realize there were others well capable of scoring.

To be fair, Richie's a quick learner, as you can see in the player he has become today. I can actually see similarities in the development of his career with that of my own.

When I rolled that line ball to him, Richie could easily have tipped it over the bar. But he had his head up. He could see Michael Fennelly coming on his shoulder. The lay-off was perfect, the power of Fennelly's burst too sudden for Tipp to readjust. GOAL. To me, that moment defined a great team performance. We were all on the same wavelength.

We went in five points clear, but it should have been double that. Jackie was following Lar everywhere and not giving him a sniff. Likewise Noel Hickey on Eoin Kelly. Tipp, having thrived on the creation of space all summer, now found themselves with barely enough room to breathe. Between them, five of their starting forwards – Corbett, Kelly, 'Bonner' Maher, Séamus Callanan and John O'Brien – would contribute a total of just 0-1 from play. That was the winning of the All-Ireland.

Eddie made a wonderful break to set up our second goal, sublimely taken by Richie Hogan in the forty-ninth minute. Although Pa Bourke quickly fired one in at the other end, we never really looked like losing it. I'm not sure I've ever been part of a more united team performance.

When Gavin finally blew for time, the relief was monumental. Just four months earlier, we'd been written off, insulted by that label, 'chokers'. Now we were heading back up the steps of the Hogan Stand again, champions for the fifth time in six years. Tommy described it later as 'the sweetest of them all'. That's how it felt.

When we finally got showered and headed to the players' lounge, I had an image of Brian Corcoran in my head. After he came out of retirement in '04 to help Cork deny us a three-in-a-row, Deirdre was sitting close to his wife afterwards in that same lounge. The first thing Corcoran did when he arrived up was to embrace his wife and say, 'We've done it!'

Much as I wished we'd beaten them that day, I always thought that was a lovely image. Because it captured how the commitment required to be an inter-county hurler in the modern age goes beyond the player. It extends to his entire family. That's what was on my mind now, walking into the players' lounge. I went straight over to Deirdre, we hugged and those words came out, as if on reflex.

'We've done it!'

19. 'Don't Do Anything Rash . . .'

In the chaos of All-Ireland-winning celebrations, little rituals bring an illusion of order.

Whether it's the almost theatrical arrival of Liam McCarthy through the doors of Citywest, the Monday morning visit to Crumlin children's hospital or the open-top bus to a civic reception at Market Yard, success now carries a sense of familiarity. I suppose we have the routine almost off by heart now.

Through all the commotion, you find yourself craving peace. While there's no better feeling than waving silverware to a black-and-amber throng, the quiet moments, the ones with fellow players, management and family, become the ones you seek.

That Monday morning, myself, Eddie Brennan, Jackie Tyrrell and Mick Fennelly took ourselves down to a small pub in Rathcoole for a few quiet pints. It was perfect: just the four of us in a corner, chatting, having the craic. At one point, the boxer Kenny Egan dropped in to say hello. I'd met Kenny at a few functions and liked him. Those pints were special because no one made a fuss of us. We were just four Joe Bloggs, enjoying one another's company.

The Sunday night in Citywest had been really civilized and, maybe because of that, all the more enjoyable. There wasn't as big a crowd there as the year before, so it was easier to chat with people and swap stories. I went over to Cody's table at one point and we laughed a lot, trawling back through the year, slagging one another about different moments.

I felt like a kid again, as if winning was a novelty. I remember looking around the function room at one point and thinking, 'This is what I hurl for!' Was it the sweetest one of all? For me, yes, definitely. I just felt so many people had been writing me off, writing us all off, I suppose. No one specific, just a general tone across the media.

I hardly ever read newspapers. But while I was struggling with my knee through the harsh winter, I knew people were wondering if they'd ever see me on a hurling field again. It was as if my obituary was being written and I used that to drive me on.

So the satisfaction of getting back to the top of the mountain was massive. I remember being at the Citywest bar with Michael Kavanagh and Tommy Walsh and thinking about the difference a year made. Around midnight, I took out my phone and rang Tadhg O'Sullivan. And I thanked him for, basically, putting me back together again.

On the post-All Ireland Tuesday, the players usually make their way from Billy Byrnes through a few pubs along John Street. (In this instance, we eventually settled up in O'Loughlin Gaels out of respect to our captain, Brian Hogan.) At some point, I like to slip away for a couple of quiet pints with Cody and Mick Dempsey. Just send them a text to find out where they are and disappear discreetly.

I love those few drinks because inhibitions have disappeared and we can slag one another without fear of any offence – on either side – being taken. Everyone's totally at ease at that moment. Usually, I end up telling Cody he got it wrong with his team selection and he'll have that grin on his face that says, 'Maybe, but did we win the cup, Henry?'

This particular time, they were in Langtons, but I didn't linger. Deirdre phoned to say Henry Junior had taken a fall off the bed and banged his head. I wanted to get home. But Cha Fitzpatrick was on my mind too because I knew he was unsettled. It was clear he'd slipped to the periphery of Brian's interest and I sensed there was a fair chance now that he'd walk away.

You see, Cha kind of got swallowed up by Tipperary in the 2010 final and I'm not sure Cody could ever get that image out of his head again. So I went to bat on his behalf as well as on behalf of TJ. A local politician, in some respects, putting his case to the Minister. Both Cha and TJ were clubmates, obviously, and neither had started the 2011 final. I felt especially for Cha here. While TJ had, at least, come on for Eddie, Cha never got a look-in.

Now I would stress this wasn't in any way a confrontational exchange with Brian. How could it be, with the cup back in Kilkenny? But, if I had a question for Brian, it was how leaving Cha on the bench squared with his mantra of always picking the team on the basis of training. Cha was training as well as anyone. The problem was that Brian seemed to have convinced himself that Cha's legs weren't up to inter-county hurling any more. He felt Kilkenny needed power around the midfield, whereas what Cha offered was intelligence and guile.

As a forward, I've never played alongside anyone with a more accurate delivery. One example. On the morning of the '07 All-Ireland final against Limerick, the two of us were driving in to Kilkenny together to join the rest of the team. I had been picked at full-forward, Cha was midfield. I said to him, 'Look, if you have the ball today and I make a little run out in front of Stephen Lucey, expect me to jink back in behind him.'

Cha knew exactly what I meant. The game was barely ten minutes old, Eddie Brennan just having got our first goal, when Cha read my movement exactly and floated this perfect ball in over Lucey's head. Nobody else could have delivered that ball the way Cha delivered it. All I had to do was step back in, flick Lucey's hurl and catch the ball behind him. Goal. It looked simple, but only because of the quality of ball delivered in.

And that's something I was endlessly stressing to Cody. That the forwards loved having Cha outside because, if you got clear of your marker, you knew he'd deliver the ball in on a plate.

But Cha was getting frustrated now. The straw that broke the camel's back, I suspect, was when he didn't get a run in the semi-final against Waterford. Michael Rice came off at half-time and, if most of us would have expected Cha to be his replacement, Brian decided to go with Paddy Hogan. I think the management view was that, physically, Cha might have found it a struggle against the Waterford midfielder, Kevin Moran.

I could see where Cha's restlessness was coming from. He'd become a big player for us since breaking on to the panel in '04. He'd been

Young Hurler of the Year in '06 and won three consecutive All-Stars
between '06 and '08, when he captained us to the three-in-a-row. To
go from that to burning a hole in the bench – it was easy to understand his frustration.

After that semi-final, I told Cha not to do anything rash. We'd
have spoken that week at club training, and my advice was to go in
and have a chat with Brian. To be up front with him and explain how
things felt from his perspective.

But I think Cha decided to just hold his counsel and train away.
Not getting a look-in against Tipp in the final then pretty much made
his mind up. We were out for a few drinks after the county final and
he told me he was packing it in with Kilkenny. What could I say?
I told him I could see why. It would have been easy for me to
start arguing about the decision being premature and how, in his
mid-twenties, he still had a huge future with the county. But how, in
conscience, could I honestly do that when – deep down – I suspected
Brian was not for turning?

So Cha announced his retirement shortly after, amidst widespread
speculation that he might transfer to Dublin (where he teaches). I
knew that wouldn't happen. To do that, Cha would have to switch
allegiance from Shamrocks to a Dublin club, and I could never see
him doing that.

Bottom line is, he's a young lad, he has no ties and he wanted to go
travelling for a summer. Was he hard done by? In one sense, yes. I
could see why he became so disillusioned. But the counter-argument
is that midfield play has become so combative that he runs the risk of
being, quite literally, overpowered. Interestingly, when he announced
his decision, Cha himself questioned whether or not he had the legs
to play the role of the dynamic, running midfielder that's now so
much in vogue. But, if midfielders were still being asked to just hang
between the two 65s, Cha Fitzpatrick would be the best in the
country.

After Cha, the retirements kept on coming. I wasn't surprised that
Michael Kavanagh called it quits. He'd been an unbelievable servant
to Kilkenny hurling over fourteen years but was no longer getting

his game, and I can only imagine how hard it must be to keep flogging yourself in that situation.

John Dalton's decision, as I said before, I considered premature. I
just couldn't understand it: a chap with everything in front of him
and a brilliant All-Ireland final against Tipp in 2010 on his CV.
Maybe it's a sign of the times, a reflection of how big the commitment required has become. John's a farmer; maybe he needed more
time for work. But I'd love to have seen him hang in there, to wait
and see how the next League went and give it another shot. Now, his
last big game for Kilkenny will always be that League final melt-
down against Dublin. I think he owed himself more than that.

And then, of course, came news of Eddie.

I was absolutely staggered by this one, never saw it coming. I had
just got a text from one of the lads when Robbie Irwin rang me from
RTÉ, looking to see if I might say a few words in tribute. My response
was, 'Look, Robbie, that's no problem but you'd want to be pretty
sure first that it's true.'

'Oh, I'm pretty sure all right,' he replied. 'Eddie's sitting opposite
me here in the studio!'

My immediate reaction was one of disappointment. Eddie proved
in the final that he still had an awful lot to offer – but then, like
Kavanagh, if you're not getting a regular start, I imagine it's much
harder to find the motivation to go again for another year.

And I will admit that, as I prepared to go on the record about one
of the greatest goal-scorers of his generation, the thought struck that
Eddie was going out on an incredible high. Maybe he'd timed it to
perfection.

Would I be able to do the same?

20. Journey to My Finest Hour

My name is Henry Shefflin and it took me thirty-three years to find out who that person is.

If this sounds melodramatic, no apologies. Because to know about my finest hour in hurling, you need to understand the wretchedness of the journey that got me there. Maybe I had to almost hate what my days had become to find a way of living again.

How can a man hate the seemingly perfect world of happy home, successful career and national celebrity? By lying to himself, that's how.

I spent so much of 2012 feeling damaged and broken down that, even now, there is a ridiculous dimension to the notion that I finished the season as Hurler of the Year. To get there required the most exhaustive of medical care from a small army of good people. But that wasn't the kernel of the story.

I'll try as best I can to explain what was.

It all started in autumn 2011 with an innocuous late hit against O'Loughlins in the county semi-final.

At the time, it seemed no big deal. Two weeks on, I even played in the county final and then the subsequent replay, albeit aware of recurring discomfort in the shoulder. I do remember the physio, Claire Lodge, suggesting that it looked like I'd 'ripped cartilage' and that surgery was a possibility. At the time, I didn't really absorb what she had said.

I was supposed to see a specialist two weeks after the county final but I rescheduled twice before presenting myself to Darragh Hynes in the Mater Private. The visit was convenient because I had work calls to make that same afternoon in Dublin. I assumed he would just recommend a course of exercises and suggest a short period of rest.

Instead he hit me with a sledgehammer.

I'm not sure I heard anything until I picked up the words '. . . after surgery, no physical contact for six months'. Darragh, a straight-talking man, later told me that he could see the colour drain from my face as he said that. As I stepped out of his surgery afterwards, I cancelled my appointments and drove straight home.

This was Groundhog Day. My arm, I was told, would be in a sling for maybe two months after surgery. Christmas was coming, and now Deirdre would have four children in her care throughout: three small ones – including our new baby daughter, Siún – and her husband.

It's funny how bad news travels. I was getting ready for work the following morning when I got a text from a local radio station, wondering would I go on air to explain my new predicament. Next thing, Des Cahill was talking about it on RTÉ; Paul Collins likewise on Today FM. The whole country, it seemed, was up to speed on news I was still struggling to digest.

I had the operation in Santry at 7 a.m. on 7 December. Emerging slowly afterwards from the general anaesthetic, I felt the pain cut through me. If asked to measure it on a scale of one to ten, I'd say nine minimum. The whole area was raw after ninety minutes of surgery, and they eventually brought me back down to the recovery ward, agreeing that I needed more morphine.

While I was there, a familiar face was wheeled in beside me. Doug Howlett, the Munster and New Zealand wing, was sleeping like a baby, having had surgery on his Achilles. God, how I envied him his peace.

I have a history of reacting badly to general anaesthetics and this one was no different. The nurses were keen to keep me in overnight but Rackard Cody, the Kilkenny kit man, had come up to drive me home and I didn't want his journey to be wasted. I tried standing up a couple of times, only to topple back down on the bed again. I was sick, in a lot of discomfort, and the room was spinning.

They let me go eventually and we had to stop at a chemist's in Thomastown to get the pain prescription. I will forever have this image in my head of two old women standing, staring at me, slumped in the one and only chair on the premises. Looking at me as if to say, 'Jesus, the state of him . . .' I must have been pale as a ghost.

The arrangement was that, in the short term, I worked from home. While doing this, I would be plugged into a 'Game Ready' icing machine, pumping freezing air and water into the padding around my shoulder. Between phone calls, I'd do some gentle exercises to avoid the joint stiffening. Pretty soon, I was fit to cry.

Christmas arrived and I felt the ultimate invalid. I'd attended Brian Hogan's wedding the week before, telling him in advance that I'd only go to the church. The one blowout I allowed myself in that time was at Tommy Walsh's wedding reception on 30 December. Soon after, Kilkenny headed to Cancún on the team holiday and I stayed home, pretty much booking myself into a private prison.

Impatience was a problem now. They told me to – at all costs – avoid jerking the shoulder, but soon I was heading down the fields with our dog, Guinness, on secret runs. I didn't even tell Deirdre what I was doing, just saying that I was 'popping out for a walk'. My knees were hurting too now but, six days a week, I made sure to get a sweat up. I was exercising maybe more for my state of mind than anything else.

On the morning of Tommy's wedding, I was down in the field with Guinness when he went over to a cattle trough to get a drink of water. The water was frozen, so I stood up on a rock to break the ice with a kick. Of course, the rock was iced up too and down I tumbled. If I hadn't got the sling on, I'd instinctively have put out my left hand to break the fall and, quite probably, burst open the stitches in my shoulder.

The incident gave me a jolt. I was basically lying to everyone around me about the kind of stuff I was doing. I'd go for physio with Kevin Curran or Robbie Lodge and they'd be manipulating the shoulder in gentle, controlled movements. The cartilage had been sewn back into place and these little anchors were holding everything down. Every visit, they'd push that little bit further. 'Now don't even think of doing this yourself,' they'd warn.

And I'm telling lies: 'Oh God I won't!'

At home, I'd started lifting Siún again with my good arm, but hurling? That seemed a million miles away.

When I think of that January, I think of sitting in my parents' house during the day, surrounded by laptop, notes, diary, a few weights thrown on the ground and a broomstick. The latter had now become another tool for exercises manipulating the shoulder. I'd discarded the sling after maybe six weeks (two earlier than advised) and, with physio cranking up, the pain was absolutely sickening.

It was all about endlessly stretching the shoulder. On top of maybe four physio sessions a week, I even took to doing exercises when driving the jeep. Brian Cody had told me I was welcome to pop in to Kilkenny training at any time, but the message with him has always been the same: 'Drive on yourself and come back when you're ready.'

That, I knew, was a long way off. I found it dispiriting watching the boys push forty-kilo weights in the gym when the maximum I was allowed was two kilos. At home, I sensed I was now starting to get on Deirdre's nerves. Once the kids were in bed, I'd lie on the living-room carpet and begin doing my stretches. After a long day at work, she'd just want to switch off and watch television. But how could she relax, listening to my grunts and groans? Soon, I moved that evening ritual to the conservatory.

My plan was to drive on so relentlessly that on the evening when I'd present myself back at Nowlan Park as a Kilkenny hurler, people would be startled by my fitness. But I came to sense trouble before they put a name on it. I suspect the physios did too. In late February, it was confirmed that I had a 'frozen shoulder' and the possibility of further surgery was first mooted. My body, it seemed, was cheating itself, the shoulder-blade flipping out to the side whenever I lifted my arm.

I tried to force it. Instead of forty-five-minute physio sessions, I doubled up by booking myself in for ninety. Trouble was, what flexibility I'd have when leaving seemed to dissipate in hours. I was getting nowhere. I spoke to Brian coming up to the opening League game against Tipperary and I sensed he was beginning to worry. 'Look, just stay at it,' he said.

Around this time, Lar Corbett had signed himself out of the Tipp squad, apparently because he felt he couldn't give the commitment. I just couldn't make sense of that in the context of my own desperation to get back.

I was operated on again in late March at the Mater Private, after which Deirdre and I went away for a couple of days' break in Cork. Yet, even here, there was no getting away from my predicament. While in Cork, I had to go in to Euromedics to get a couple of scans on the shoulder. Over the next few weeks, I sensed improvement and began, again, to push.

And that was when the story lurched towards black comedy.

Having upped the weights I was pushing, I started to get severe pain in the shoulder again, as if someone was pushing broken glass into the muscle. Even playing with the kids at home, it would come at me without warning. Claire Lodge made the diagnosis on Easter Saturday: I now had a trapped nerve in my neck. Straight away I was thinking how Brian O'Driscoll had needed surgery for something similar. I was in despair.

A diet of anti-inflammatories and paracetamol followed, but I was going nowhere. I went in to Kilkenny training at Nowlan Park one evening, tried hitting the ball and – three minutes in – had to stop. Another chorus of sympathy: 'Just give it a couple of days . . .'

By the week of the League final, I was finally training fully, but still a long way from contention for a place in the squad. That Tuesday night, I marked John Tennyson in training. 'You're moving well,' Mick Dempsey said after. But, twenty-four hours later, crisis again. Pushing weights in the Nowlan Park gym, I had to abort. I knew Eoin Larkin and Jackie Tyrrell were watching me as I walked around, hoping the pain would subside. Then I went to the changing room, thinking for a second I'd have to get one of the boys to help me put my shirt on. It was now as if a knife was plunging into my shoulder. Had I ripped the stitching?

'Jesus, Henry,' one of the lads joked, 'it's not a company car you need, it's an ambulance!'

That evening I was fighting back tears as Kevin Curran sent me home in a sling. I couldn't function now, couldn't really speak. Just got in the door, went upstairs and lay on the bed. In the space of an hour, I must have taken six Panadol. I was so fed up. Fed up of scans, fed up of physio, fed up of pain. Fed up even of talking. My career was over.

That Sunday, Kilkenny blew Cork off the field in Thurles. Eleven minutes in, they were eleven points ahead. In the stand, all the old invalids of the dressing room – me, Richie Power, Michael Rice, Taggy Fogarty and Noel Hickey – comforted ourselves with gallows humour: 'Jaysus, Power, they always play well when you're in the stand . . .'

Sitting there laughing, I remember thinking I'd never been less relevant to the Kilkenny hurling team.

'Henry, when you're done here, will you come up to my office?'

The GAA President, Christy Cooney, wants to see me. I am in Croke Park for the launch of a Centra summer camp and, when I go upstairs, he comes straight to the point. The Olympic torch would be coming to Croke Park and the Association needed someone to represent them. A hurler, preferably.

'We see you as a brilliant role-model and we'd be delighted if you'd do it,' says Christy.

I am speechless. If my career is, as it seems right now, tapering to an inauspicious end, this feels like glorious consolation. Last year, I met the Queen of England and the US President. Now this. I'm told to keep it a secret, and I keep that side of the bargain. Apart from telling Deirdre and my parents, of course.

The week before it happens, I'm brought up for a dry run. They're making sure that I've a head for heights as I'll basically be carrying the torch on the stadium rooftop tour. No fears there, although an invitation to stand on the Perspex ledge jutting out from the roof does induce gentle nausea.

The Olympic uniform arrives via courier and we decide that Sadhbh and Henry will come to Dublin with us for an overnight. They're restless in the hotel room the night before, so sleep proves fitful. I need to be up at 6 a.m. in any case and I end up lying there with one eye on the clock. That morning, as I put my top on, I get a short, sharp rebuke from my shoulder: *Remember me?*

Later, as I make my way around the stadium roof, photographers asking me to wave to the watching world, I change hands because of fatigue. I am over the Hogan Stand when they want a great, warm swing of my free arm. Just one problem. The torch is in my right hand now and, well, my left arm is not for lifting. I'm really squirming as I force it higher than it wants to go.

'Smile, Henry!' they tell me. Through clenched teeth, I manage to oblige.

It proves the only wrinkle in a beautiful experience. Cameras follow me every step of my route around the roof. Seb Coe is always near by, next to the Olympic Council of Ireland President, Pat Hickey.

There is one moment, just over the Nally Stand I think, that makes me quite emotional. I'm standing there, slightly separated from everyone else, looking down across Croke Park. I think of Deirdre and the kids below, looking up at me perched, quite literally, on the top of the world. That's when the symbolism hits home. Just one GAA person had been asked to carry the torch here. Out of a vast community, awash with incredible people, I am the one chosen. Standing here feels unbelievably special.

We go back to the Mansion House for lunch afterwards, where I meet Kenny Egan, Ruby Walsh and, to my delight, an idol of my childhood. They say it's best not to meet your heroes, but Paul McGrath's easy grace and courtesy disprove it.

It's been the perfect day.

The road to redemption began with twenty minutes against Dunnamaggin in Hugginstown, Brian Cody in the crowd.

The following week, another run against Muckalee. Then a training weekend with Kilkenny in Fota Island and Cody's words echoing in my head: 'You want to up it a little now, Henry!' I marked Richie Doyle in a practice match, happy afterwards that I had answered that instruction.

But the Monday evening before we played Dublin, I was pucking a ball against the gable wall of my parents' house when this pinching pain returned at the top of my shoulder. One minute in, I had to stop. Drove home in absolute disgust.

Phone calls to the physio, to the team doctor: 'This is fucking crazy!' The advice was more anti-inflammatories, more painkillers, more time. We were five days out from a Leinster semi-final against Dublin and this had taken over my life. The one person I didn't ring was Cody. That call I just couldn't afford.

I went in to training the following evening without either gear or a hurl. It wasn't unusual for me to opt out of the physical stuff on the week of a big game. 'You taking it handy tonight?' Brian asked. I had to be truthful, and his response was unsurprising. 'Ah Jaysus, this is not on. What if this happens again on Saturday morning?'

Kevin Curran batted for me, trying to reassure Brian that all would settle again within a couple of days. He would have known about the statistic of me starting every Championship game of the Cody era and probably understood how much I wanted to sustain that record.

I trained as normal that Thursday. No sharp pain, no great interrogation afterwards from the manager. Just a simple 'How are you now?'

'Grand, not a bother,' I replied. And that was it. I was named in the team.

That day in Portlaoise, I went out just to survive. It was a dirty, miserable Saturday evening and I was unnaturally nervous beforehand.

Dublin had annihilated us in the previous year's League final and they were expected to present a pretty ferocious physical challenge. But, this time, they were stuck to the ground and we beat them easily. It was a massive relief to come through it, but the shoulder just wasn't right. I was still getting these sudden shocks.

That Monday, I met Darragh Hynes and he proposed another MRI scan. The scan was performed on the Thursday. A week later, Tadhg Crowley came over to me at training in Nowlan Park. 'By the way,' he said, 'that scan showed up nothing!' I didn't know whether to laugh or cry.

In my time with Kilkenny, we'd never experienced anything like what Galway were about to inflict upon us in the Leinster final. I can't say I saw it coming. Looking back, I do remember taking it upon myself to talk at team meetings in the build-up, but I was talking for the sake of talking. It was just self-serving stuff, trying to get myself going as much as the team.

All along, we were feigning stomach for battle, and the media — blinded by the ease of our victory over Dublin — bought into the idea again of us being some kind of unstoppable force.

Hindsight makes it all seem so obvious now. Everything we believed we stood for that day was missing. Galway were out the gate and gone within twenty minutes, around which time we finally registered our opening score. If there was an image that caught our condition in microcosm, it was probably Tommy Walsh fluffing two line cuts in quick succession. That wasn't Tommy, that wasn't us.

Galway led by 2-12 to 0-4 at half-time. In the dressing room, Brian tried to rouse us. 'This isn't over,' he said. I can only imagine what he made of the expressions on the faces looking back at him. He talked of Michael Rice, who had barely trained for two months, being our best player while so many other fellas seemed to be lying down.

People often ask me, was he in a rage. But rage isn't a setting Cody needs.

He knew that we understood the implications of what was happening. I certainly didn't need anything in writing. I'd spent the half under Kevin Hynes's thumb, watching Galway shirts swarm upon any ball that came towards the Hill-end goal. Unless I got my act together, I could be finished as an inter-county hurler.

It's probably a measure of how low I found myself that a little scoring burst of 1-1 from play in the second half would mean so much to me. Psychologically, the goal was a big thing especially. It was the first moment all year I felt, 'Yeah, there is still something there . . .' Selfish thoughts, admittedly, but, at that moment, it felt like every man for himself.

Otherwise, the game was an awful shock to the system. We went back to the Crowne Plaza hotel in Santry for a meal after, and it was as if people were just walking around in a trance. I spoke to Brian and he made clear his concern about where we stood as a group now. We'd won the League at such a canter and, maybe, bought into our own publicity.

Now we were deep in crisis. The vibe at home seemed one of gentle requiem. A kind of 'sure ye owe us nothing' tune, as if the season was already over. In the eyes of our own people, some of the players were now unofficially finished.

No question, Henry Shefflin among them.

The night after the defeat to Galway, I found myself in Callan, opening my heart to a stranger.

The first thing I came to realize about Brother Damien Brennan is that he'd be no sycophant. Humouring people just isn't his thing. 'What marks out of ten would you have given yourself for the Dublin game?' he asked me.

'Em, maybe five?'

'I'd have said three!' he shrugged.

This was new. I was so accustomed to people tiptoeing around me, filling my head with cotton-wool kindness, his words landed like an uppercut. So I'm lying on this bed in a school classroom, the students' chairs stacked up on the tables around me, and this man has begun all but waging war on my precious ego.

'I saw something in that Dublin match I never saw before from you,' he said flatly. 'I saw a man just playing for himself!'

I'd phoned him that morning when taking the kids for a swim in Mount Juliet. He was, I'd heard, 'gifted' with his hands. My shoulder was still bugging me despite all the conventional care and, maybe, I just yearned for some kind of break in the repetition of physio.

Who was he?

I knew little beyond the odd anecdote from other players. He comes from Arles in County Laois, football country, and he spent time teaching in Dublin before moving to Callan CBS. Today he is the last remaining Christian Brother teaching in an Irish secondary school. He coached Callan to an All-Ireland Colleges 'B' title as well as a famous Leinster Colleges victory over St Kieran's. He then guided Kilkenny minors to two All-Irelands. I'd heard that he had some kind of background in counselling and physio, but the word – above all – was that he could fix things. Other players swore by his ability to get them right for games.

Before visiting him, I'd gone in to a Kilkenny team meeting in Nowlan Park. There was a sense that, as a group, we'd been deluding ourselves. We'd been fooled into believing that we were up for it, then suffered the consequences. Cody alone spoke that evening. 'We've dropped our standards,' he said. 'Everyone in this room, players, selectors, me.

'We're gone soft and I'm telling you that's going to end here!'

I squirm now when I think of my morning phone call to Bro. Damien. 'Look,' I said coyly, 'can we keep this on the QT?' He would have been entitled to hang up there and then because, if anyone's privacy needed protecting here, it was his.

I had never used a sports psychologist in my life and, being honest, I still don't believe I have to this day. Brother Damien's approach seems completely instinctive. He is quiet-spoken, with steady, challenging eyes and an understanding of the power of silence. Going to him that Monday night would be the turning point of so much more than my season.

To begin with, though, I couldn't see that. He had me doing various stretching exercises, not just with my shoulder, but my groins, my knees, my hamstrings, even the soles of my feet. He seemed startled by the amount of tension in my body, and concluded that I was flat-footed. I didn't know this man from Adam and, after six months of almost daily physio care, I had the feeling that I'd jumped from the devil I knew to one that I didn't.

So I can't say the penny dropped straight away. That first night, he worked with me for about an hour, then said it was up to me if I wanted to see him again.

'Is that it?' I asked.

'That's it!' he said. Maybe he could detect some disappointment in my expression. He just looked me straight in the eye and told me that I wasn't doing myself justice, that if I wanted to go on a journey with him, so be it. If not, I need never contact him again.

There were, he said, some things he would ask of me if we were to work together. Three things, in fact: honesty, trust, courage. We shook hands and I drove home, thinking to myself, 'Jesus, that was mad!' But I suspect I already knew deep down that I couldn't leave it there.

I don't want to paint Bro. Damien as any kind of psychiatrist or mind guru. He's neither of those things. But he is one of the most deeply intelligent people I've ever spoken to. He has this gift of simplifying things, of cutting through bullshit. I'd gone to him looking for help with my shoulder but, almost unknown to me, his best work would be in ridding the clutter from my mind.

Until then, I'd been internalizing everything, pressuring myself endlessly to meet others' expectations. On one of my first nights with him, I was talking about an upcoming club match against Tullaroan. 'I need a big one against them,' I said.

'Why?' he asked. 'Why not just go out and play?'

I didn't realize at first the value of what he was doing. But the more I relaxed in his company, the more I opened up. I'd had this need to be Henry Shefflin rather than just Henry. In my life generally, I was rushing around the place, constantly stressed. The shoulder had been a nightmare to rehabilitate, and that was impacting on everything else.

I felt under pressure with work and I was coming home cranky to Deirdre and the kids. I had become regimented in everything I did, believing that life was just pulling against me. Up at 6.30 a.m. for a half-hour minimum of stretching the shoulder with a makeshift pulley, same thing again that evening before going to bed. In between, a blizzard of work, physio, training and – it seemed – recurring setbacks.

I was so caught up in myself that I wasn't enjoying my hurling life. I had become preoccupied with what other people thought of me. Deirdre, Brian Cody, team-mates, media, everyone. This hadn't always been the way, it was just something that had built up over maybe the last two seasons. Even training with the club, I had come to crave reassurance.

Tommy, my brother, was Shamrocks manager that year. I'd be on the phone to him after training: 'Well, how did you think I was moving?'

Psychologically, I had hit a brick wall and that's one of the first things that Bro. Damien identified. 'Whatever's outside now, leave it outside,' he said that first night. 'There are four walls here and it's just you and me inside them. You just be Henry now!'

When he watched me hurling, he said he could see someone playing with a sense of desperation.

'You're more concerned with what other people are thinking than what you yourself are feeling,' he said. The Dublin game had shocked him. He'd seen only self-absorption and panic in my body language that evening, as if the pursuit of a record ninth All-Ireland medal had short-circuited something precious in my brain. I was playing only for myself, he reckoned. For the protection of an image. The way he puts it, he'd never seen somebody 'try so hard to prove that he was finished'.

When I thought about it, he was a hundred per cent right. In opening my eyes to those things, Bro. Damien would become indispensable.

I can say with absolute certainty that, without him, my year would never have transformed as spectacularly as it did.

So Bro. Damien turned my season around, but it didn't happen overnight. Looking back, the journey wasn't just difficult, it was borderline ridiculous.

For the quarter-final against Limerick, Brian had decided to relieve me of the free-taking duties. While I said nothing at the time, the decision left me reeling. It was as if I was being systematically down-graded in the hierarchy of the dressing room now. *Next spot for me is in the stand*, I remember thinking.

Then, running out the tunnel in Thurles, I felt my hamstring sud-denly tighten. As I pucked the ball over and back to Tom Breen, one of the subs, I was racking my brain about what to do. If I held my hand up, Cody's patience might finally snap. I seemed to be hitting trouble at every turn now, and he might reasonably conclude I was no longer worth the bother. My head was putty.

Robbie Lodge was doing physio that day and I got him to stretch me out a bit. But when we did a few sprints, the leg clearly wasn't right. In my head, people were looking in at me now, watching an old man struggle. An old man trying to keep a secret.

I probably should have declared myself unfit, but I bottled it. As the game started, my ears were ringing with a sense of guilt. Then, maybe five minutes in, the equivalent of a scratch-card win: Tommy Walsh drilled a ball towards my corner and Eoin Larkin and Richie McCarthy between them inadvertently shielded my marker from attacking it. I'd made a hesitant run and the ball fell really kindly in front of me. A point.

The first score of the game and, arguably, the most critical one of my entire year.

Minutes later I got a second, and then their keeper, Nicky Quaid, fumbled for me to score a simple goal. Next thing, Colin Fennelly came through, gave me an off-load that floated a little high and Quaid was out to meet me. I was near the end-line, hitting off my left side and, in anticipation of being hooked, just flicked the ball. It spun up in a loop, settling in the Limerick net.

This was all in the first twenty minutes of a game that, deep down, I knew I shouldn't have started. I had 2-2 from play. Then Richie Power got knocked out and I was back taking the frees as well, a sta-tus I would retain for the remainder of the year. Crazy.

At half-time, I went straight to the physio and Robbie had me hopping in pain on the bed. The twinge I'd felt was a bleed in the hamstring that had now travelled down my whole leg, which was excruciating to the touch.

Brian came over. 'Are you all right?' I wasn't, but a herd of elephants wouldn't stop me going back out.

The game was still level after forty-two minutes, everything about our performance marked with the same strange lethargy that had weighed upon us in the Leinster final. It was as if there was no anger in us, no backlash. Kilkenny looked gone.

But it all turned in twelve minutes when we scored an unanswered 2-5. What changed? Maybe something as simple and unromantic as work rate. The backs certainly improved. In the forwards, Taggy and Larkin and Colin Fennelly were all excellent.

Then there was the story of TJ, replacing Power and having a stormer. In the very same week he'd tried to pack it in! Now, I'd be close to TJ. When I was a young hurler, starting out with Kilkenny and practising frees down the field in Ballyhale, TJ would come in off the school bus from Kieran's to collect the balls for me. Our families are friends and I'd like to think he regards me as someone who looks out for him.

When the team for the Limerick game was announced, he wasn't in it. TJ went straight home after training, texting me as I arrived in Langtons: 'Any chance of a chat?'

We met up at his house and he was unequivocal. He'd hurled his last game for Kilkenny. TJ had just started a new job and was also busy making hurls. 'I'm giving it up,' he said. 'I'm fucking finished with this.'

I was adamant that he shouldn't, that he should buy himself time to calm down. 'Just think about this,' I said. 'I know you feel hard done by, but you're only after starting a new job. What happens if we lose on Sunday and you've just pulled off the panel? It doesn't look good . . .'

After our conversation, I put his anger out of my head. Just texted him encouragement that Saturday without knowing if he'd taken it any further. (Martin Fogarty subsequently told me he'd taken a fairly frank phone call.) Anyway, TJ would come off the bench against

Limerick, effectively controlling the game with an unbelievable second-half performance.

And he would end the year with an All-Star.

In our history with Tipperary, the 2012 All-Ireland semi-final has an oddly eccentric status.

We won comfortably in the end, but that wasn't the headline story. The game is best remembered for a sense of pantomime, specifically Lar Corbett's peculiar marking job on Tommy Walsh, a half-forward chasing a half-back around the field. I wasn't really aware of it at the time, but you could hear roars erupt around them when the ball was at the other end of the field. Something was clearly entertaining the crowd.

Tipp actually led by a point at half-time and, bizarrely, the game had restarted by the time Lar came running back out the tunnel. I was actually standing over a free as he arrived, the din now a real distraction.

My main memory of that half-time break is of a tearful Michael Rice in the dressing room. He'd suffered a horrendous hand injury from a reckless pull by Pádraic Maher, just in front of the Hogan Stand. That hand was now heavily bandaged, but blood still seeped freely from it. Ricey didn't know it at the time, but he'd be out of the game for a year.

In the dressing room, he was shaking that bandage at people, driving them on, telling them that he had every intention of being back for the final. Brian and the selectors were angry over the incident. It had happened straight in front of them and, later, Maher was probably fortunate to stay on the field after a ridiculous challenge on TJ.

That challenge pretty much signified how Tipp had given up the ghost. We won the second half 3-15 to 0-5, beating a mere skeleton of our greatest modern enemy. I was elated because, for maybe the first time since doing my second cruciate, I felt I was truly running freely again. In the first half, I'd spun Conor O'Brien with a perfect first touch to put TJ in for a goal with a thirty-yard hand-pass.

I'd reclaimed the confidence to float out the field. I was catching puck-outs again. I was starting to reacquaint myself with that lovely sense of lightness in my feet.

On the Monday, I went for a swim in the Hotel Kilkenny pool. Tommy turned up too and was typically deadpan about the circus with Corbett. 'Sure 'twas unusual, I suppose . . .' Next thing, Noel Skehan arrived in, hungry for hurling talk. Tommy and I were of the view that the real Tipp hadn't shown up. That we'd just beaten some kind of ghost.

But Skehan wouldn't hear of it. To his generation, there could be no such thing as an equivocal Championship win over Tipp. 'God, no,' he laughed. 'Yesterday was mighty!'

Two weeks before the All-Ireland final, we went to Carton House, where we spent quite an amount of time talking about tactics.

This was unusual. Ordinarily, you arrive into September just going through the rituals of reinforcement. If you've got that far, chances are the team is settled and the hurling feels uncomplicated. But Galway troubled us. The roving movement of their forwards had caused chaos in the Leinster final and, I suppose, posed questions about the rigidity of our shape.

We were nervous and uncertain now, the Leinster final having blown a big hole in our confidence. Should we trust in that shape or adopt some kind of man-marking strategy?

We decided to go with the latter. Joe Canning, Damien Hayes and David Burke were identified as the men who needed constant policing. This was tricky. In the previous year's final, we'd settled on a specific man-marking plan for Lar Corbett. Extending that plan to three players meant we ran the risk of corrupting our entire defensive structure.

For the media, the possibility of me winning a record ninth All-Ireland medal became an obvious point of focus. I decided to embrace it, going to our press night and choosing not to duck any of the questions. 'Yes,' I agreed, 'if it happens, it would be a massive honour.'

Walking out to collect my record tenth All-Star Award at the National Convention Centre, November 2011 (*Brendan Moran/Sportsfile*).

With Sadhbh and the Olympic Torch in Croke Park, June 2012. Being asked to carry the torch was one of the biggest highlights of my career (*Brendan Moran/Sportsfile*).

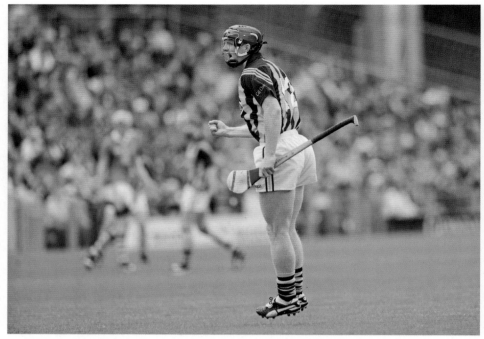

Celebrating my first point of the 2012 All-Ireland quarter-final against Limerick. I was struggling to find form after a shoulder injury, and Brian Cody had relieved me of free-taking duties, but my first scoring chance fell nicely for me that day, and from then on it was a magical summer (*Brian Lawless/Sportsfile*).

Winning a high ball, despite the close attention of Galway's Kevin Hynes, in our drawn All-Ireland final. In the second half of that match I played with a freedom I had never known before (*Brendan Moran/Sportsfile*).

Celebrating a point that levelled the scores in the 2012 replay against Galway (*Brendan Moran/Sportsfile*).

I had a huge battle that summer, physically and mentally. In the end we won the All-Ireland and I was named Hurler of the Year, but only my family and close friends knew how hard it had been (*Stephen McCarthy/Sportsfile*).

With Sadhbh, Deirdre, Henry Junior and Siún after a victory for Shamrocks over Dicksboro, November 2012 (*John McIlwaine*).

Coming back from a stress fracture in my foot, I came on for the last six minutes of our All-Ireland qualifier against Tipp at Nowlan Park in 2013. The atmosphere in the ground that day was one of the best I've ever experienced (*Ray McManus/Sportsfile*).

When Barry Kelly flashed the second yellow card, and then the red, in our All-Ireland quarter-final against Cork, I didn't protest. But I felt the first yellow had been harsh and it was subsequently rescinded (*Ray McManus/Sportsfile*).

Arriving with Aidan Fogarty for my first inter-county match since the red card – our Walsh Cup semi-final against Galway in January 2014 (*Ray McManus/Sportsfile*).

Getting ready to go on in the 2014 All-Ireland final replay against Tipperary (*Pat Murphy/Sportsfile*).

Tenth time around with Liam MacCarthy, it was great to share the moment with Sadhbh and Henry Junior (*Ray McManus/Sportsfile*).

Savouring the moment with Henry Junior, long after the crowd had gone (*Piaras Ó Mídheach/Sportsfile*).

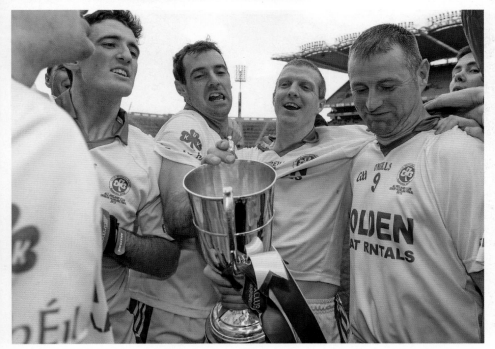

It was great to celebrate my last match, and my last trophy, flanked by old friends like Aidan Cummins and Bob Aylward, with whom I started school in Ballyhale all those years ago (*Ray McManus/Sportsfile*).

Deirdre and the kids – Freddie, Siún, Henry Junior and Sadhbh – and a mess of trophies: the Allianz National Hurling League trophy, the Irish Press Cup (for the All-Ireland minor champions) the Liam MacCarthy Cup (for the senior All-Ireland champions), and the Bob O'Keeffe Cup (for the Leinster champions).

The end of the road: announcing my retirement in Langtons, Kilkenny, on 25 March 2015 (*John McIlwaine*).

Was it playing on my mind? I'd be a liar if I denied it. When you think of how the names Christy Ring and John Doyle reverberate through GAA history, the notion of passing them out for Celtic Crosses won now seemed mildly crazy.

Just for the record, it wasn't my own call that finally set me free in Croke Park, it was Brian Cody's.

Legend has it that I decided to take charge of business maybe twenty minutes into the first All-Ireland final, moving myself to the '40'. I didn't. Mick Dempsey came running in with the instruction and, suddenly, I was at the pitch of the action, feeling empowered to make things happen.

What followed wasn't a million miles from an out-of-body experience. All of the trophies and awards that would follow, I don't doubt, came framed in the context of that single game.

Yes, I was aggressive. Yes – as Joe Canning would later point out – I was argumentative. I just felt so totally free, I wanted to meet everything at full pelt. There was a moment in the first half when the ball spilled out over the Hogan Stand sideline; on the video you can see me sprinting after it like a giddy ball-boy.

I was incredibly clear in my emotions. The more I got on the ball, the more exhilarated I felt. It wasn't one of those days when possession seemed to follow me and I was racking up easy scores. This was totally different. It may sound daft, but even the mistakes I was making felt like perfect mistakes.

The most satisfying thing was that I knew I was now performing on the biggest stage in Kilkenny's hour of greatest need. I was leading. And I had this subliminal sense of the crowd reacting to what I was doing. I knew that something special was happening. When you look back on any player's career, that – to me – is the ultimate accolade. To be remembered as a great team-player.

The game was nearly over and the scores level when we were awarded a penalty. I thought about it for maybe three or four seconds and decided going for goal was simply too risky. That was my immediate instinct. On another day, I'd have gone for it, but there was too much at stake here. I couldn't afford to risk having my shot saved and giving Galway the chance to break away for a winning score. My mind was crystal clear about what to do.

I looked over to Brian, but he didn't give me any pointers. He never does. Then I tried killing a little time. There were sixty-eight minutes gone on the clock and if I could use up maybe thirty seconds here . . .

After as much foostering as I could get away with, I took the point.

Next thing I remember is Joe Canning lining up that injury-time free under the Hogan Stand. He was just after missing one from a similar position, and I felt oddly torn watching him. If he missed, we were champions. People might find this hard to believe, but I didn't think it fair that he might go down in history as the man whose miss had got us there.

Don't get me wrong. Given a choice at that moment, I wanted the ball waved wide. But when the Galway roar erupted, part of me was relieved for Joe. Relieved that history wouldn't identify him as some kind of fall guy.

I was driving to Dublin a few days after the drawn game when a voice came on the RTÉ *News at One*, mentioning my name in the headlines. Didn't quite get the gist of it, so I pulled in, took out the iPhone and tried to get the item up. Next thing, the phone rang. It was JJ Delaney.

It turned out that Joe had done an interview in Thurles at a media event previewing the All-Ireland under-21 final in which he'd branded me 'unsporting'. He picked specifically on one incident in the match when I'd run 'thirty or forty yards' to remonstrate with referee Barry Kelly over the awarding of a Galway free.

I remembered that incident clearly and, having seen the replay, knew I had been wrong. I thought at the time that Damien Hayes had taken a dive, but the replay showed it had been a foul. If the way I'd argued the call offended certain sensitivities, maybe I was guilty as charged.

Joe also reckoned that my decision to take the point from the late penalty had disappointed some of my team-mates. 'JJ wasn't too impressed anyway behind me,' said Joe to the journalists.

I couldn't quite believe that his comments were deemed worthy of inclusion in the *News at One* headlines. And now I had a worried JJ on the line. 'Jesus, JJ, would you cop yourself on,' I said. 'Even if you said it, I wouldn't have an issue. There's absolutely no hassle.'

And there wasn't.

There was a view among some within the Kilkenny camp that Joe's comments had been no accident, that they had been a carefully chosen tactic on Galway's behalf to create discord. To this day, I don't pretend to know the truth. Joe apologized to me after the replay. By then it hardly mattered — and we'd have a good laugh when we found ourselves seated beside each other at the All-Star function — but I will admit that when I heard the story at first, it knocked me for six. I'm probably well known for giving out to referees, but as one of the more experienced players on the team I would have felt it was natural that I should be the one fighting our cause. And I was particularly angry about what Joe had said about JJ, apparently trying to create some tension between team-mates. My initial reaction was, 'I'll shove those words down Galway throats the next day!'

But then I spoke to the people I trust, and the consensus seemed to be that there was nothing much in the story, that maybe it had all been blown out of proportion. It seemed pointless to be second-guessing in any event, stressing myself out over something I couldn't change.

It might seem strange when people hear this, but the story never became an issue in the Kilkenny dressing room. Richie Hogan did mention it once at a team meeting, but it never got much traction. The consensus view, rightly, seemed to be that it could only be a distraction.

At some point in the three-week gap between the drawn game and the replay, Kilkenny remembered who we were.

We were, I'll admit, cutting it fine. It was not until the Friday night before the replay that we finally decided to shelve our preoccupation with what Galway might do to us. I was one of those who spoke against further man-marking. At one juncture during the drawn game, Galway's movement dictated that Tommy Walsh ended up playing full-back. It didn't feel right.

I felt it was time for us to go back to being ourselves.

Brian had, largely, held his counsel, leaving us to assume the tactics would stay unchanged. It has always been one of the things, I think, that make him such a special manager: that ability to read a situation and just time his input to perfection. That Friday, he said we were now going to hurl with the freedom of old, trusting ourselves to set the tempo. I was thrilled. I knew we had the forwards to hurt them, we just needed to hurl with more self-belief.

I'd got an inkling that Tuesday that young Walter Walsh might start. Brian hadn't been happy with the forwards and admitted to me that he had some 'hard decisions' to make. Those decisions would be the omission of Taggy Fogarty and Colin Fennelly from our starting fifteen. I was really disappointed for them both, but there's very little you can say to players who hear they're being left out for an All-Ireland final.

I made a point too of leaving Walter alone until maybe an hour before throw-in. I could see lads literally lining up in the dressing room to give him advice and I was hoping that wouldn't over-complicate things in his mind. 'Look,' I said, 'forget anything you've been hearing, and just go out to play your own game.'

When I thought about it after, this was probably precisely what everyone else had told him.

Of course, it turned out that Walter didn't need our guidance, ending the day as RTÉ's Man of the Match, striking a personal tally of 1-3. He proved a revelation, but he was getting exactly the kind of ball that had been denied to Taggy and Colin three weeks earlier.

I suppose the call to pick him had been typical Cody. A bit like picking Eddie Brennan and TJ the year before. It takes a lot of nerve to make those calls, but that's why he's the best manager hurling has ever seen.

As a team, we hurled with more freedom that day. David Burke scored two quick-fire goals for Galway but, each time, we responded with an immediate score of our own. After Burke's second, we won the next quarter 1-7 to no score. At one point, Canning had a terrific shot rebound off the butt of an upright and that was the end of Galway.

While the presentation was being made, it wasn't Eoin Larkin I was looking up at in the Hogan Stand. It was Deirdre and Sadhbh. That ninth medal was mine, but only family and close friends really understood just how hard that journey had been.

In a sense, for me the year could basically have been distilled down into the second half of the drawn final. That was it, the perfect feeling. From my whole career, that thirty-five minutes would rank as my absolute favourite.

And it came just as I had begun to wonder if I was finally a beaten docket.

21. Seeing Red

It's a Wednesday morning in the Blackrock Clinic and a run of pretty lousy luck brings two old crocks together on the fifth floor.

Brian Cody and I stop just short of laughing at one another. It's as if we've become the punchline in someone else's joke. Less than an hour from now, I'll check myself in upstairs for surgery on my foot but, at this moment in time, that seems a minor inconvenience.

Brian's wife, Elsie, has left the room to let us talk. I'm looking across this hospital room at one of the most influential people in my life, who sits in a chair and describes his heart surgery as if it was a tooth filling. Brian shows me the scar, but he seems more interested in discussing me. Specifically my latest sorry injury drama.

'So what's the story with that foot?'

I'm here to get a couple of broken pins removed, one more brush with a general anaesthetic that I could certainly do without. But even speaking about it makes me feel privileged now. Brian's heart surgery is the talk of the GAA, though you can take it there'll be no newspaper exclusives down the line, no *Late Late Show* appearance to feed the public's appetite for gory detail.

He is one of the most private people I know and one of the least self-absorbed.

I feel real warmth between us as we talk. He looks well, all things considered, but his voice is very weak. He wants to know about a Monday-night fitness test held in his absence at John's Park. He is hungry for snippets from the dressing room. He is still talking and planning like a man with big hopes for the year.

People who don't know us have probably come to see Brian and me as two constants of a GAA summer. Imagine if they could see us now! Me on these crutches; him with that scar. Two of the big powerhouses of Kilkenny hurling, weakened.

I stay for maybe half an hour, all apprehension about my looming anaesthetic completely flushed away by Brian's calm. I'm struck only by the loyalty I feel. My language is often blue with hostility towards him on those evenings when the whistle gets swallowed at training and the back-men know they can lower their blades without fear of prosecution. Yet, more than anyone, Brian Cody made me the hurler I am.

It strikes me that fame in a small place is a condition full of tiny assumptions about friendship. In Kilkenny, hurling does its best to impose that condition on personalities who aren't always warm to the intrusion. It's a complication of winning All-Irelands. People prefer you to throw open all doors when, quite often, there's little or nothing you want to do less.

The broad perception of Cody seems to be of some kind of fearsome enigma you wouldn't wisely cross. He has a name for being unemotional and ruthless and, I suspect, is perfectly happy to allow that image to pass as his personality. No question, he doesn't suffer fools and there is a side to him that endlessly reminds players that his priority as Kilkenny manager is not the accumulation of friends.

I'm seen to be closer to Brian than most others, given the simple longevity of our relationship as manager and player. There is, I will admit, a massive bond of trust between us. But we've never lived in one another's pockets and, when it came to hearing of his heart surgery, I didn't – as many might assume – get the news any quicker than my team-mates.

Martin Fogarty delivered the bombshell in a generic text sent to the whole squad, just a matter-of-fact, deadpan announcement that Brian had gone in for 'a procedure' and that we could expect the release of a statement to that effect from the county board.

I couldn't believe what I was reading. Apart from natural concern for his well-being, part of me responded a little selfishly. What if he didn't come back? What if the surgery was the prelude to his retirement as Kilkenny manager?

He'd known about the surgery for a couple of weeks, apparently, but kept the news to himself. For the first few days after, we all seemed to exist in a blur of recycled stories about other people we knew who'd had similar procedures.

I was due in Dublin the following week for another operation on my foot, and it was only then that the penny suddenly dropped. I'd be having my operation in the Blackrock Clinic, where Brian was now recuperating. Mick Dempsey said he'd ask if it was OK for me to pop in. Speaking to Elsie later, I was keen to emphasize that I really didn't want to intrude.

'Look, if he's too weak or whatever, I'll leave him be . . .'

'No,' she said. 'He'd like to see you!'

'You've probably never heard of it,' I'm saying to Damien Duff. I start telling him about the problem with my foot: it's called a Lisfranc injury.

Duffer wheels away, his laughter whistling like a kettle coming to the boil. 'Never heard of it?' he shrieks. 'Oh, Jesus, I've heard of it all right. Nine months it took me to get over it!'

We've been introduced in London's Grosvenor Hotel, the two of us dressed in black tie for Brian O'Driscoll's testimonial dinner. Someone just happened to mention how I was injured again. Big mistake. My default setting now is to slip into lecture mode about the uniqueness of my latest problem.

'It's when the metatarsals . . .'

Though I can't claim to know him well, I feel a strange connection to O'Driscoll. We were born ten days apart and, somehow, I've come to align the longevity of my own career with his. Just two months have passed now from one of my blackest days, and even that seemed to find a certain reference point in O'Driscoll.

In February, I was diagnosed with pneumonia. After trying to chase the symptoms away with paracetamol and Lemsip, I ended up spending five days in St Luke's, wired up to an IV drip. The Saturday I went in, I felt sick beyond words. Sitting in the A&E, I remember thinking, 'There's not a chance of me hurling this year. I'm definitely finished!' One thing to be losing ground on your team-mates through injury, but the pneumonia left me with barely enough strength to walk in from the car park.

There was a TV set on in the waiting area and I was semi-aware of a rugby game on the screen. Ireland against Wales in the Six Nations. It would end with the image of a smiling O'Driscoll being named Man of the Match and, sitting there in St Luke's, every breath a chore, that image gently cheered me.

If he could still do it at thirty-four . . .

The invitation to London was flattering and completely unexpected. Apart from encountering one another at end-of-year awards functions and, of course, the Obama visit to College Green, we didn't really know one another. But O'Driscoll had been quoted in lovely, complimentary terms about my achievements of 2012, and I'd always found him open and exceptionally down-to-earth to meet.

In this instance, his timing couldn't have been better. I had become a virtual invalid with the foot. After ten weeks on crutches, I had moved to a protective boot with the absolute instruction not to put any weight on it.

So the BOD testimonial was virtually the first time since Christmas I actually wore a shoe. Had to buy an extra-large pair to accommodate the orthotics and, even then, Deirdre needed to go down to reception for a pair of scissors beforehand so that I could cut the foot some slack. In a shoe, it felt hopelessly imprisoned.

At the table, I soon bowed to the inevitable, ending up sitting amongst the great and the good of international sport with my left foot in just a sock.

Fast-forward then, maybe to around 4 a.m. in the residents' bar, and I'm chatting now with Johnny Sexton. He's injured and frustrated. I ask him what the problem is, and it's as if he's rehearsed his answer.

'Not really sure yet,' he says. 'But they think it might be a Lisfranc . . .'

I'd had the operation on St Stephen's Day, which meant Christmas passing without the consumption of even a single glass of beer.

For a month I'd essentially been walking around on a broken foot. The injury happened in late November, just another 'nothing' incident with brutal ramifications. A Leinster Club Championship game against Oulart in Wexford Park, and in shielding the ball from Paul Roche I suddenly got this odd sensation as my foot jarred into the ground.

Initial X-rays showed up nothing, and maybe that emboldened me. Without any mention of surgery, what could possibly go wrong? We did the Christmas shopping, taking the kids to see Santa, and all the time I knew that something wasn't quite right. Then a scan revealed the bad news.

So surgery in the Beacon Hospital and an instruction to keep my foot off the ground for ten weeks. I'd broken the mid-foot and needed four pins inserted, fixing bone to ligament. Maybe one week later, I hobbled into the Hotel Kilkenny gym, taking matters into my own hands. There's this little hand-cycle inside, like Mark Rohan used in the Paralympics, and I lashed away on it. Did some chest presses, too. The inner lunatic had cut loose again, drawing curious stares as I struggled to the showers after.

When the stitches came out, it was discovered I had an infection. Everyone was telling me to take things easy now – the surgeon, Alan Laing; the physios; Brian Cody. And all I could think was that this could be my last year in the big time. I had to push. Had to cut corners. In the middle of it all, I got a Saturday-night text that just reinforced my sense of urgency: Noel Hickey telling me he was about to announce his retirement.

I didn't actually get talking to him until they ran a little tribute programme on local radio the following Monday. But his retirement genuinely saddened me. We'd been good friends, soldiering together since the '97 minors. Regular room-mates on weekends away with Kilkenny too. I knew I'd miss him.

Maybe I brought the pneumonia on myself then. I certainly brought on the complications with my foot, discarding the crutches around St Patrick's Day. Even Brother Damien had taken to warning me about doing stuff on my own. By early April, I was back running when the foot began to get really sore again. Couldn't even put a runner on it.

Alan Laing sent me for X-ray, and that's when they discovered the broken pins. His physio in the Beacon told me later that, in all his years of practice, he'd never seen anyone break them. What in God's name had I been doing?

And that's when they booked me into the Blackrock Clinic.

When you're in the latter stages of your career, and injured, the sympathy of strangers has a way of morphing into something else.

Old men especially would see me in the protective boot and tell me to catch myself on: 'Ah, give it up, Henry!' Either that or 'Take your time, sure, so long as you're ready by August . . .' As if they imagined rehab to be no more complex than the flicking of a switch. Worse, they seemed to regard Kilkenny's capacity to stay in contention as somehow bombproof.

We played Tipp in the League final and, being honest, I felt a bit of an intruder in the dressing room. With Brian absent, I made a point of saying a few words. Just felt it was the right time to do it, albeit with a voice in my head recognizing how the players would be entitled to think, *Jaysus, Henry hasn't hit a ball this year, what's he on about?*

I got a rub on my calf too, and the thought struck that people might be staring as I left the dressing room. Looking at me, wondering how was the invalid walking now? In that scenario, I want nothing more than to be invisible. All was fine until I heard applause start to ripple down out of the new stand. I was maybe thirty yards behind Power and Tennyson, watching them dip in through the wire, and instinctively I broke into a jog behind them.

The kindness of the handclaps made me cringe. Here was Old Henry again, still dragging his broken body along the ground.

Kilkenny won a tough game and I'd say I was in Langtons within ten minutes of the final whistle. Deirdre had been waiting, with the engine running. We were in a quiet corner of the restaurant having some food when the team arrived. Instinctively, everyone got to their feet and started to applaud.

And, in a surreal moment, I realized that the only respectful thing for me to do was to join in. The League champions had arrived. I wasn't one of them.

By now, Brother Damien had devised specific drills to help me recuperate. I was leaning on him more heavily than seemed reasonable. During the pneumonia, he'd taken to driving down from Callan between classes just to keep my spirits up. Sometimes just chatting to him made me feel better.

I knew I had a friend for life.

At one point, the foot became so fragile, even physio was being discouraged. He'd massage it and, instantly, I could feel the heat dissipate, the swelling go down. I hadn't told Cody anything about Bro. Damien because I didn't see the need. This was a private arrangement that had become indispensable in my life. The more I worked with him, the more he was getting into the psychology of my predicament. Challenging me.

By the end of 2012, I'd taken to meeting up with him the Saturday before every match. He'd get me to hit frees, challenging me to score 1-9 from ten balls. Always I seemed to get to 1-7 or 1-8, then a miss. Every new night, I'd arrive declaring that this one would be different.

Basically, he helped me do the work I would otherwise have had to do alone. I'd meet him on the nights between Kilkenny sessions, often arriving frazzled and fatigued. Work, I might complain, was dragging me left, right and centre. 'Today I had to . . .'

He'd stop me in mid-sentence. 'Did you never hear of delegating, Henry?' he'd say with a smile. I had begun actively building a persecution complex through nobody's fault but my own.

My record of starting every Championship game of the Cody regime formally came to an end when the surgeon confirmed my latest mishap. An MRI identified the stress fracture.

There were just three weeks to the Offaly game in Tullamore and my deadline for re-engaging with club activity had arrived. Shamrocks were due to play Clara in the third round of the local league. That had been my long-term target, a target I would now miss.

The problem had arisen after a session of fifteen 100-metre sprints during Shamrocks training. The initial sensation was that of having a stone trapped in my shoe, just under the toes. Alan Laing confirmed I would have to go back in the protective boot for 'four to six weeks'. Devastation.

It wasn't the loss of the record that killed me, just the sense of getting nowhere. Ordinarily, I'd never miss a club match, but I just didn't have the heart to go in to the Clara game. Psychologically, this was a new low. With the two cruciates and the shoulder, I'd always met the deadline of returning for Shamrocks by the third round of the local league.

Now that deadline had passed me by.

While it was good, having our manager back for the Championship, there was also a faint sense of chasing our tails. We duly beat Offaly in Tullamore, but conceded four goals in the process.

The two games against Dublin captured the lack of flow in our play, the sense of group anxiety. Their physicality seemed to tie us up and, when we lost the replay, I had every reason to wonder if my days as a Kilkenny hurler were coming to an end. Defeat now pitched us into the All-Ireland qualifiers and a straight knockout against our old friends from Tipperary.

I walked alone out of O'Moore Park that evening, strolling down the town to the Heritage Hotel for our meal. There was the odd unsympathetic roar from a car window, delighted Dubs feeling no pain now as the traffic crawled at snail's pace towards the freedom of the N7. There had been no question of me playing either game against them and now, I knew, my year was really spiralling out of control.

We had a week to plan for Tipp and I had a hell of a lot to consider.

That Monday at training, the players not used heavily against Dublin had a game of backs against forwards. I was one of them. It was the first night I'd put on a pair of boots to hurl and, maybe, it was pure adrenalin, but I felt surprisingly good. Now I'll admit it wasn't the tightest of marking or the heaviest of hitting but, for me, this was the first glimpse of blue sky.

The following day I met Alan Laing. He'd told me not to do anything for six weeks and now that time frame was about to end. He could see what I was thinking.

'Henry, when I said nothing for six weeks, I meant you might resume training after. But only training!'

He made clear his view that any involvement against Tipp would be premature, that I couldn't possibly be ready. But I suppose he could see that desperation in my eyes too. His parting words were, 'Look, ultimately it's your decision . . .'

That was enough. I told Brian that, if needed, I'd be ready. To be fair, I did so with the stated proviso that no offence would be taken either way. But after six months of unrelenting hardship, I reckoned this could be my one and only shot for the year. 'I feel grand,' I told him. When you have those conversations, you're never quite sure which way he's thinking.

That Thursday night, he broke the suspense. 'OK, Henry, you're togging as a sub!'

Even now I get goosebumps thinking of the occasion that followed. The atmosphere in Nowlan Park was unique, a real heavyweight contest in our own backyard without the lure of titles or silverware. Just bragging rights on the line and a shot at survival.

The hairs stood up on the back of my neck when, with six minutes to go, I got the signal to come on. But those six minutes fooled me, maybe fooled us all. We edged an epic contest that had our people utterly euphoric at the end and we'd leave the field afterwards to the kind of ovation that, ordinarily, only accompanies an All-Ireland win.

When we trained the following Monday, I was flying. I almost convinced myself that I didn't need match practice to be up to speed. I felt I could operate to different rules. During my six-minute cameo against Tipp, I'd helped set up a point. Afterwards had been all back-slaps and declarations that I'd 'made a difference'.

And I swallowed every single compliment going. I embraced the lie.

One week later, Waterford's Kevin Moran exposed it. Cody sent me on early in the second half, my head still light from the noise of Nowlan Park.

To say it didn't go well would be an understatement. I was awful. Moran just had me in his pocket from the moment I arrived and, with the game then on a knife-edge, I almost threw it away for Kilkenny. I had, at that point, been moved out of harm's way to full-forward when Matthew Ruth came running through with the ball. As he fed me a pass, I could see Taggy steaming through the middle. Instead of catching, I went to flick the ball into Taggy's path, making only minimal contact. Juvenile error.

It was intercepted and, a couple of plays later, Moran delivered the monster score that sent the game to extra time.

In the dressing room, Brian asked me if I was OK. 'Grand,' I lied.

The selectors went out for a chat, came back in and said they were making one change. 'Walter, you're going back in for Henry!'

There could be no hiding from the truth now. I went back out, took my place in the dugout and just prayed that Kilkenny would get through. They did too, but this time with none of the great, boisterous back-slaps of Nowlan Park.

This time we could see through the noise.

I am told there were gasps in Thurles when Barry Kelly produced the red card to send me off against Cork, but I heard nothing. Honestly. Not a sound.

People ask me why I didn't even argue my case, but what was the point? I was on the ground as I saw him coming with the second yellow. So I just picked myself up, unclipped the helmet and walked to the stand, determined to avoid eye contact with Brian Cody.

Why? Guilt, most probably. There was a voice in my head wondering, 'Jesus, have I let the team down?'

I'm pretty sure lads were offering consoling words as I sat into the dugout, but I can't remember anything. All I recall is wanting to get myself out of general sight. To be invisible. If the ground could have opened up and swallowed me at that moment, I'd have taken it.

Had Barry been harsh?

Well, the first yellow was subsequently rescinded, so I suppose you could say yes. I suspect he was fooled by a noise more than anything he actually saw. The ball broke from a ruck of players and I tried to flick it away with my hurl. Unknown to me, Lorcan McLoughlin had come up alongside, his momentum leaving me a little flat-footed.

He went to rise the ball and my flick caught his hurl. Now hurls hit off hurls all day in a game but, I suspect, Barry reckoned I had made contact with Lorcan's hand. I hadn't.

The second yellow?

This was where my lack of match practice told against me. I was clumsy. I'd run back about thirty yards to cover a loose Cork midfielder and, suddenly, found myself unintentionally on a collision course with Jamie Coughlan.

Instinctively I put out my hands but, through that lack of game-time, they were slightly higher than they should have been. Coughlan's a good bit smaller than me and, well, I could hear Jackie Tyrrell's voice behind him, shouting, 'Don't foul, don't foul!'

Too late. We collided and I remember thinking I needed to avoid falling on top of him as that would probably look bad. Trouble was, my feet were gone. I fell on top of him.

Cork's appetite devoured us and, maybe, exposed how we'd been papering over cracks from the very start of the year. We'd battled well in the second half without ever quite looking like we might find enough.

In the dressing room afterwards, I just sat there in a world of my own. Brian spoke beautifully to the group, something along the lines of lads holding their heads high and being in little doubt that Kilkenny would rise again.

At some point, he came over and asked about the two yellows, and I just told him what I thought. There was no great forensic inquiry.

Bruce Springsteen was on in Nowlan Park that evening and, like everyone else, I had tickets. But Deirdre collected me from the bus and we drove straight home. I had no appetite for beer that night, no appetite for the Boss, no appetite for picking the sores of a brutal season. Maybe the starkest image I have in my head is of sitting on the tractor mower at six o'clock that July evening, cutting the grass with the children around me. That will always stay with me. Because coming home from Kilkenny that evening, all the lads hanging around in town for the Bruce Springsteen concert, I remember thinking that I could quite easily break down crying. I just wanted to disappear.

The day of the Cork v. Dublin All-Ireland semi-final, I took the kids swimming in Mount Juliet. When I rang Deirdre afterwards to say we were on the way home, her voice was full of excitement: 'God, this match is brilliant . . .'

I got in to see maybe the last fifteen minutes of a game I just didn't want to see, my head still all over the place. When I looked back on the year, it seemed a jumble of bad luck, one setback piled on top of the other. The injuries, the pneumonia, the sending-off . . . I suppose I felt hard done by.

I hold no grudge against Barry Kelly, incidentally, but I firmly believe he got things wrong that day. I discovered subsequently that he was miked up for a TV documentary that has since been broadcast. I didn't actually see *Men in Black*, but I heard about his comments in it, something along the lines of 'he knew himself' and 'the man he was, he didn't say a word'.

If Barry reckoned my acceptance of the decision represented some kind of acknowledgement that I deserved to walk, he was mistaken. I was taken aback to hear afterwards that he'd been miked up and I couldn't help wonder if he'd felt under any extra pressure to make an impression.

It was at Brian's insistence that we appealed the red card. He was right about that, and we got it overturned, but I felt no satisfaction when the decision came in. Maybe I still felt a little guilt about the whole thing. I'd left the team in the difficult situation of playing with fourteen men for maybe the last forty minutes. That still niggled at me. I'd been on the team to provide scores and leadership but, that day, produced neither.

On the morning of the first All-Ireland final between Cork and Clare, I played a club match against Castlecomer in Ballycallan.

It was odd to feel so distant from the occasion. I got home for the second half of the minor game, then settled down to watch the hurling equivalent of *Rocky*. Clare and Cork hurled at such a furious pace, I remember thinking to myself that it was all a little crazy.

And I commented to Deirdre about how young the players were. Everything about the game just felt unnerving.

In my entire career with Kilkenny, this was only the second year we hadn't made it to Croke Park in September. Henry Junior had started school that week and I'd been bringing him in, something I'd never normally have done in All-Ireland final week.

Life had begun changing now in so many ways. The future was a mystery.

22.   The Myth

When we collect up the dead and place unidentified body parts in a black bag, we like to round off Kilkenny training with cold showers and big plates of bat stew . . .

There's an impression out there that, come summer, Nowlan Park is home to scenes taken straight from the Battle of Gallipoli. We occupy a strange place in the imaginations of those who see our hurling as all heat and no light. I've actually read the description 'lawless' used to describe a typical Kilkenny training match. The wonder is any of us have fingers left with which to hold a hurl.

Maybe that's what happens with successful teams, a little mythology gets written into the story. I mean, I've always believed that some of the stuff put out about Clare in the 1990s didn't exactly ring true. Do you honestly think if lads were getting lumps taken out of one another every night they went training, they'd have much of an appetite to keep going in?

Now it's not kindergarten in there, I'll give you that. Brian Cody encourages self-sufficiency in his players. Always has done. Sometimes it's as if he's swallowed the whistle and I'll admit there were nights that wrecked my head. When there was a blatant foul and I felt I'd been hard done by, I'd occasionally let out a roar, or mumble under my breath. Either way, I'd let him know what I thought of it.

I went through a spell in my career when I was constantly getting on to referees, but I calmed down a little in recent years. And I think that came from Brian's training. He tells you straight out he's not going to blow everything and that calls for a careful balancing act. You have to be sure that fellas don't slip into the habit of fouling and end up paying for that when they play a proper game.

But people miss the point of what Cody is trying to achieve. He's not trying to build some kind of ruthless hitting machine that gives and takes punishment without quibble. Speed is his priority. I think he wants everything to keep flowing without stoppage so that the players become accustomed to hurling (and thinking) at that high intensity. Awarding frees slows down a practice game. It breaks momentum.

What Cody wants is quickness, quickness, quickness. It's not about fellas belting each other so they'll be able to handle it in a match. What good would that be if it meant being constantly blown up by the referee? That's the equivalent of self-harm.

When you think about the time lost for a fella jogging over to line up a free, it really serves no purpose in training. Free-takers practise in their own time. The key to a decent training game is having a real and constant flow.

We often had our differences on it. Sometimes I'd be in full-forward, being marked by Noel Hickey, and Noel was blind as a bat under a dropping ball (mind you, he'd argue I was never entirely blameless either). He'd be hanging out of me to make sure I didn't make the catch, and the one thing I knew for certain was that Cody wouldn't blow the whistle.

And for all the years that this was the norm, I still couldn't help myself but, occasionally, to complain. I never completely lost it in training, never actually felt that a situation was slipping out of control. The point is that, generally, Cody just doesn't tolerate any real stupidity. If you pull a bad blow, he picks you up on it.

When Eddie Brennan was with us, he certainly had the occasional scrap with Jackie Tyrrell. It's not exactly a state secret that Jackie takes no prisoners. He's one of the strongest, fittest lads in the panel and he trains exactly as he plays. It was one of the funnier images that came back from the 2011 All-Star tour to San Francisco that, in the exhibition game, Jackie was – apparently – terrorizing a few fellow tourists! That wouldn't have been an act. It's just how Jackie hurls.

When, sometimes, himself and Eddie would square up in training, Cody had his own way of dealing with it. He's a clubmate of Jackie's but, if he thought he was out of order, he'd let him know it in no uncertain terms. Brian would walk straight over to Jackie's corner and say what needed to be said. To be fair, the players themselves wouldn't tolerate any stupid stuff either. If a fella gives a bad blow, he's picked up on it by the group. He knows he'll probably get one directly back anyway.

You'll get the odd eruption within any group, but the important thing is that it doesn't carry over into a second night. Fellas are no use to a squad when their heads are turned by personal vendettas.

If anything has stood to Cody's teams over the years, it's probably that unity of purpose. Club hurling in Kilkenny is high intensity too, a lot of teams now following the county template. You can't be precious about how a fella marks you. You've got to just be a man. Stand up for yourself and hurl.

Under Brian, every single season with Kilkenny would start with the same instruction. 'Forget about your All-Star awards,' he'd say. 'We're working off a blank sheet of paper again and, if you don't shape up, you'll be out.'

He's a good reader of things and of people. He knows it can't all be head-down, foot-to-the-floor seriousness. There has to be fun too. People seem to imagine that Brian manages on the basis of fear. That's not how it works at all. If anything, I think he's drawn to the lads who are good craic, the fellas who carry a bit of mischief.

Now, he hates messing before a match. That's when he has his game-face on and he doesn't much appreciate anyone acting the clown. But he nearly gravitates towards the funny lads once a game is over. He loves the quick one-liners, the fellas who can bury you with a single sentence.

True, 2001 changed him in terms of socializing with us. He took a step backwards from the players. A little barrier went up that year which essentially told people he wasn't in the job to be their friend. And that barrier never came back down. There was a job to be done, and keeping that sense of distance would help him do it.

If this created an impression that our dressing room was some kind of grim interrogation camp, nothing could have been further from the truth. Every team needs characters. Cha was always one of the best of them, sitting down the back of the bus with Tommy and

Tennyson and Richie Power. They'd be the fellas you didn't want to engage with in a slagging match.

If I have a memory from the day of the 2012 League final, for example, it's of Cody's booming laugh as he sat listening to Tennyson telling jokes. Or of one of the lads taking Richie Hogan's phone on the way home and texting Cody from it: 'Brian, why am I not taking the frees?' I don't suppose you'd be doing that in an environment of fear.

I was once one of the lads sitting at the back, with fellas like Aidan Cummins and John Hoyne. But age kind of brings you forward in the bus. The seating arrangements change as lads move in and out. Over the years, I'd have had Michael Kavanagh, Derek Lyng or PJ Ryan for company. As they drifted away, it was kind of a question of whoever became available. Someone joked in the dressing room a couple of years back, 'Jesus, Henry, any of the lads that sat next to you seem to be dropping like flies!'

They were, too. Kav, Lyng, PJ, Richie Mullally, Martin Comerford, Pat O'Neill, Philly Larkin . . .

I remember the first time Richie Hogan came into the old Nowlan Park dressing rooms for training and dropped his bag down in the general vicinity of where Kav and I liked to sit. We didn't spare him.

'Richie, you're in next door with the minors. Now take that bag with you like a good lad!'

It's funny, looking at the youngsters now, their heads stuck in iPhones and iPads. Paddy Hogan was the first to turn up with those big headphones the size of saucers that you see on professional rugby players. It all seems so far removed from the old routines, the games of cards down the back.

Fellas like Brian Hogan and Jackie could actually sleep on the way to a game. It used to drive Noel Skehan mad when he was a selector. He'd be looking at them with their eyes closed and ask, 'How in the name of Jaysus can fellas sleep on their way to a Championship match?'

Each to his own, I suppose.

I always liked to take a bit of time to myself. I was never into music or books or computer games. A good few years ago, Brian banned newspapers. I liked to get up and move my legs as often as possible, maybe go over to where the toilet was and get a good stretch. I might chat to some of the lads of my own vintage. But, by and large, I had no ritual. Often I was quite happy just to stare out the window and slip into a private world. Then, when we'd get close to the stadium, I'd keep my head down. Even when lads might bang on the side of the bus, I'd pretend I heard nothing. Just stare into a private place.

In the dressing room, different people need different things. Jackie was always so neat and tidy, his clothes nicely folded, everything in place as if ready for a shop window. Hickey was the polar opposite, so laid back he could pull two left boots from his bag. Cha could have produced anything, garden shears, homework copybooks, anything. Some lads took longer to get ready than a beauty queen. Others would be ready for road in ninety seconds.

I'll miss that, the diversity of the room, the unity of those who shared it, the sense of everyone literally striving to be the best that they could be.

Looking back over my shoulder now, I couldn't imagine a better place in the world.

23. Struggles and Celebrations

Paul Murphy peered across at me through the gloom of a January night in Thomastown, playing the comedian: 'Jaysus, Henry, the last time you played Walsh Cup, was Noel Skehan in goal?'

The lads were welcoming me back into hurling's hard-hat brigade. I'd been picked to play against Galway this coming Sunday in Fresh-ford, and the prospect made me giddy.

My heart had been thumping the moment Brian Cody angled his walk towards me as we were doing the warm-down.

'How are you keeping?'

'Fine, Brian, perfect!'

'You'll be starting on Sunday, you OK with that?'

'Yeah, not a bother!'

Why was I so happy? Because I knew that I couldn't let 2013 be the final act of my time in a Kilkenny jersey. The red card Barry Kelly flourished in Thurles last July was rescinded within weeks, but the stigma stayed with me for a lot longer than that. Dealing with it was hard. To begin with, maybe I buried my head in the sand a bit, immersed myself in other things. To some degree, I hid.

It hadn't been old age or loss of pace that brought me down in 2013. To my mind, it was rotten luck.

That said, driving to the game on my own that January morning, all kinds of little worries began crowding in on me. The day was bit-terly cold, the fields flooded from a night of heavy sleet and rain. I didn't know Brian's exact plans. Would I be taking frees? Would I be given the whole hour?

As I drove into the village, the sight of two newspaper journalists sitting in a car reminded me that this might be a minor media event now. Then, as I walked in from my car, the 'click, click, click' of Ray

McManus's camera followed me to the dressing room. An unfamiliar sound in January.

I'd got a text from Martin Fogarty that morning . . . 'Great to see you back, but it's a long year, don't go too hell-for-leather!' A lovely touch, I thought.

I had no real apprehensiveness togging out now. I wanted to be there, wanted to get involved, wanted to take a few hits without getting into anything stupid. The first few frees were into the breeze, but they flew over. Good. It struck me that this was my first time hurling in daylight since last year! Despite the biting cold, I was happy.

Brian left me on for the whole game, we won and there was that surreal sound of that camera again as I stood on the field afterwards, signing autographs. The journalists were hoping to have a word with me, but all I wanted now was to shower and get back to Langtons for the food. To feel as if this was normal again.

To still be a Kilkenny hurler.

If I'd carried any frustration into the New Year, it was probably more to do with Shamrocks not winning another county title than anything specific to my own story.

We'd been good enough to beat Carrickshock in the semi-final, so I came away pretty frustrated that we'd lost. My consolation was that I was walking into the winter break free of injury now, a rare enough situation for me. That winter I never seriously entertained the notion of retiring as a county player. The only question was whether my services would be required.

Almost immediately after the Carrickshock defeat, I threw myself into gym work, determined to be ready for any pre-season fitness test. In the winter break, Brian had added Derek Lyng and James McGarry to his management team, Martin Fogarty stepping away.

Funny, the day I went to Croke Park for that hearing about the red card, we'd sat outside one of those premium-level suites, just Brian, Ned Quinn and me, shooting the breeze, hopping balls.

'Ah, I think I'll give it up now,' Cody said, 'they're fed up listening to me!'

'Would you go away out of that, the boys are mad for you to stay . . .'

A question came up in the conversation about who might train the county's under-21s next and Brian actually asked me if I thought anyone specific might be suited to a selector's role. He seemed to be thinking long term, almost to succession. I remember saying to Deirdre that night how I found the conversation a little strange. At the time, I'd no idea that Martin was leaving.

Soon after the announcement, Derek was on the phone to me, sounding me out. We'd be good friends and I told him I just wanted to see how things finished out with the club. In truth, I was bluffing. I knew I wanted to go back.

On a Thursday evening towards the end of October, I was up in Armagh, getting ready to present medals, when Brian rang out of the blue. Just general chit-chat to begin with.

How's the body?

Disappointed with the club?

All good with the family?

Then: 'Look, we're meeting up with some of the older members of the squad to get a feel for what they want to do. Just getting them to come in and give us their thoughts . . .'

I started laughing. 'So ye're wheeling in us older lads to tell us that we're finished?'

He was completely deadpan with his answer. 'Yeah, well everyone's in the same boat, you know that yourself, Henry!' Cody's style.

So the following Monday I presented myself at Hotel Kilkenny to meet the new management team, feeling a bit awkward. Sat down at a table facing Brian, Mick Dempsey, James and Derek, as if for a job interview. I knew Tommy Walsh and Jackie Tyrell were due in after me.

I can't remember anyone specifically asking me if I was staying on. It was similar in tone to previous pre-season meetings. They wanted to know if people were up for the challenge. The group would be back training in November, but management wouldn't be looking for some of the older brigade to resume that soon. I interjected, 'Well,

I wouldn't mind going straight back in because I've missed a lot of the winter training in recent years. Even for the camaraderie, if nothing else.'

Dempsey disagreed. 'No, Henry, we feel you might be better off just doing an individual programme for now.'

Coming away, I certainly had no sense they thought I should be considering retirement. I'd told them I considered it a massive year for me personally, given it was probably my last, and that I'd be doing everything possible to get myself right.

The fitness tests were held in Carlow IT over two nights, groups of maybe twenty each night, on the second week of November. For all the misery of 2013, the only one missing from that group was Paddy Hogan. The average score in a bleep test for that time of year is eighteen or nineteen, but I scored twenty-one, putting me in the top ten per cent. That felt good.

For the first time in years, I thoroughly enjoyed Christmas. It had been unusual for Kilkenny players not to be required at any of the end-of-season functions, and I found it almost liberating to watch them from the comfort of my own home without the need for a sling, a crutch or some kind of special boot. In a twenty-day stretch through the Christmas period, I reckon I trained on seventeen.

I was excited for the year ahead. Deirdre was expecting our fourth child and my only real feeling about 2013 was a determination to put it behind me.

Something Tommy had said to me, maybe on the Wednesday after the Cork defeat, was ringing in my head too. 'Jesus, Sheff, wouldn't it be brilliant to come back from this to win it next year?'

We went back training as a complete group in Thomastown on 6 January. Just a few drills, then a 1,500-metre run to check our levels of fitness. Some of the lads were mildly entertained by my presence, given how little winter training I'd been present for in recent years. 'Slow down, Henry, it isn't 2002 any more!'

People maybe imagine Cody would be on some kind of war footing, those first nights back. He isn't. He's very much of a mind that people just get back to basics in January. There are no big speeches. The time for talking is well down the line.

The National League had become a foreign country to me, so I warmed to the idea of reacquaintance.

Tradition holds that the All-Ireland champions are given a glamour opening to the competition, and we've become accustomed to welcoming some of our biggest rivals to Nowlan Park in February. This time, though, we were the support act. Clare would play host to us in Ennis and, while I wasn't looking to start every game in the League, this was one I desperately wanted a run in. If I performed well against the All-Ireland champions, I would see that as having put a marker down. A way of saying, 'I haven't gone away, you know!' In the dressing room before that game, I felt like one of the new lads almost, a kid just starting out.

Brendan Bugler, the All-Star number five, was my marker and, when he caught the first ball over my head, the crowd went ballistic.

But I got into the flow of things, we had a right battle and, though Clare won, I went home thrilled to feel relevant again. I'd had a very decent first half and, though my legs tired in the second, I was delighted to be going home sore, with a few marks on the body. It was what I would call a healthy soreness.

We could tell from the start that Cody wanted to win the League, and there was a great atmosphere in Nowlan Park when we managed a sixteen-point turnaround to beat Tipperary. Tipp led by ten points in that game, Séamus Callanan absolutely rampant. But Colin Fennelly was having a huge game for us, and a goal I scored approaching half-time was important to keep us in touch as it brought the margin down to seven. It would be very much in the back of our minds that the more we could mess with Tipp's heads, the better. We would also have felt that backs like JJ, Tommy, Jackie and Brian Hogan wouldn't countenance letting Tipp or anyone else back into a game in the same circumstances. The roars as we came off the field that evening carried a specific edge.

Our priority from the start of the year was to rebuild the aura that once had opponents thinking, 'Jesus, we can't break these lads . . .' remember actually saying as much that January afternoon against Galway in the Walsh Cup final: 'We need to get these lads fearing us again!' That aura had been lost in 2013.

In a comfortable win over Waterford, I was disappointed to miss three frees in a row. I remember a former selector, Johnny Walsh, saying to me once that I had a tendency to miss my first free of a match. And during the course of a game I might, sometimes, miss a second. But I had become pretty good at limiting it to those kind of statistics. To miss three was poor. Three in a row was downright foolish.

I remember the body feeling sore that day, a sign maybe that I was doing too much in the gym. And I was conscious of ironic roars from the Waterford crowd as those frees drifted wide. That said, I still played myself into the game, got a couple of points from play and was happy with my performance.

After that? I got just eight minutes in the quarter-final against Wexford and began to wonder was I drifting to the periphery of a team that could win games comfortably without me. Shamrocks were playing the county champions, Clara, in the first round of the club championship after that, and I felt I put down a bit of a marker in it, moving well and scoring freely.

Our fourth child, Freddie, came into the world on 10 April, returning the Shefflin household to a routine of nappies and whispered conversation. It made life extremely busy again for Deirdre particularly, because, while I'd be very hands-on as a father, we both knew that this might be my last throw of the dice with Kilkenny. The focus was very much on getting me right.

What I couldn't legislate for was how other people would interpret my condition or my form.

On 20 April we beat Galway in a tough, low-scoring National League semi-final in which my 0-4 from play pretty much made the difference, and I was named Man of the Match. It felt as if I had made a big statement, and that was very much the vibe I got from people afterwards. We were closing in on the Championship now and I looked to be back as a key player.

But two weeks later, our final against Tipperary went to extra-time in Thurles and I didn't get a score off their young corner-back, Cathal Barrett. Just never really got into the flow of the game. Cody took me off in the first period of added time and, suddenly, my status in the changing room began to alter more fundamentally than – at the time – I fully understood.

We won the title, and I felt I had plenty of hurling in the tank. But I had just started my last game for Kilkenny.

Maybe management had already made a decision about me.

I look back now and recognize little signs that they no longer saw me as a seventy-minute player and, accordingly, stopped factoring me into their thinking as a core leader.

I remember a meeting the week after the win over Tipp and just sensing a subtle change in the message management was sending me. James McGarry said something along the lines of 'Henry, you've always been strong mentally, but you're going to need to be even stronger mentally this year than ever before . . .'

And I remember Brian saying to me quite early in the year that the main reason older players struggle is that their confidence goes. Looking back, they might seem prophetic words, but I was determined that that would not happen to me.

As ever, I probably did not help myself. My compulsion to train hard kept putting my body under pressure and, on the Tuesday after that League final, I was driving home from a meeting in Dublin when a familiar ache returned to my foot. I took the shoe off in the car, yet still went training with the club that night.

When I got home after training, the dog had escaped down to my parents' house, so I went to retrieve him, running back up through the fields, the foot feeling increasingly uncomfortable along the way. The following morning, walking Sadhbh out to the school bus, I knew within half a dozen steps that the stress fracture had returned.

By that Friday, I was back in a protective boot and slipping out of contention for our opening Leinster Championship game against Offaly.

We went to Carton House the weekend before that game and, for all the advice given to me not to force things, I was determined to do as much as humanly possible. The advice of Alan Laing was that I could slip on the runners, but I was not to engage in anything too strenuous. While the lads trained that Friday, I made a point of doing my own work on the side of the pitch, making myself as visible as possible.

Afterwards I went straight to the gym, and the next morning took myself out to the National Aquatic Centre to do some aqua jogging, followed by more gym work. I look back at this now and realize I was stretching a thirty-five-year-old body to its limit. When Laing confirmed the stress fracture, a setback that would rule me out of the Offaly match, I knew I had work to do to get back to my best.

Was that the injury that sealed my fate? Was that the moment Brian Cody decided my place for Kilkenny now was on the bench?

The work I have done with Brother Damien gives me a great sense of perspective on life generally, but I'm not sure anyone could subdue my inner compulsion to over-train. I was rooming with Brian Hogan in Carton House. Having lost his place during the course of the League, he was feeling frustrated too. It might sound selfish, but you just don't really go there in conversation. You have a kind of tunnel vision about what's brewing now, a preoccupation with just getting yourself back into the picture.

I was back doing a bit of running by the time we played Offaly and, when Mick Dempsey told me he was meeting Richie Power (who was also injured) for a running session that morning in St Kieran's, I insisted on joining them. Mick protested that I'd be better advised relaxing, but I was having none of it.

In my career, I never lost a Championship game to Offaly and, despite Richie, Brian, Tommy Walsh and myself sitting in the stand now, there was never much danger of it happening this time. It was flagged as a big occasion, given the presence in Nowlan Park of Sky Sports' cameras and a space-age construction at the corner of the Ted Carroll Stand housing their studio. But Sky's hurling debut just brought another Offaly slaughter.

The general atmosphere was encapsulated when Tommy went on as a forward in the second half, the crowd desperate to see him score. Three times he shot for the posts, three times the ball just tailed away wide. In the stand, we joined in the general merriment. It didn't feel real. If I'm honest, it didn't feel like Championship.

That could never be the case against Galway and, two weeks before our Leinster semi-final meeting, I immersed myself fully in Kilkenny training. I played two practice matches, feeling pretty good. It was obvious I wouldn't be starting, given how well the forwards had gone the previous day, but I was now an option from the bench again.

I think we were nine points up in Tullamore when Brian finally sent me on. 'Just stay in around full-forward and keep the shape,' he said. I was going in essentially just to see out time. Kilkenny had just scored an unanswered 1-7 in less than ten minutes. The game looked over.

What followed was a bit of a blur. Suddenly Galway started to open huge channels down the spine of our defence and goals were flying in. Conor Cooney got two, and then Joe Canning converted his second penalty of the day in the seventieth minute. You could sense panic seeping through the team as, with a minute of normal time remaining, the sides were level.

Eager for the ball now, I moved out to centre-forward. A puck-out was drilled down on top of TJ and, sensing it would break between the two of us, I made a run. Taggy got the ball in his hand and I was straight at his shoulder near the corner now, screaming.

I didn't quite realize how close I was to the end-line, but I managed to hit this looping shot that, somehow, found its way over from the tightest of angles. Elation just flooded my body as the roar erupted. After all I'd been through in 2013, this was the chance I'd been waiting for, a moment of redemption.

It was a glorious few seconds, but then Colm Callanan took the puck-out so quickly that, almost instantly, the ball materialized in Canning's hand out on the left wing. Joe was maybe the last man we wanted to see in that position, and he nailed the equalizer.

People probably imagined I was gutted at that moment, but I wasn't. I left Tullamore with my chest out that evening. I reckoned I'd maybe given Brian and the management team something to consider for his next team selection.

That said, the message didn't seem to register too loudly. Brian didn't talk to me over the next week, which I found disappointing. On the Wednesday night, I watched him go to different individuals for one-to-one conversations, but I seemed to be invisible. They made two changes for the replay, and I wasn't one of them. Maybe I'd been naive to think I might come into their thinking for a start.

This was when I first began to realize that the dynamic between Brian and me had changed. I was now a squad member essentially, going through something that other players probably endured throughout their entire careers. Trouble was, I still saw myself as a key player for Kilkenny.

In sport, your mind is so important. And mine was now struggling to recalibrate to a new set of circumstances in which I was, for the first time since my debut season, trying to second-guess the manager. To some degree, I began over-analysing stuff.

John Power was the first forward sub used in the replay and I sat there thinking about where that decision left me in the general pecking order. I got about eight minutes in the end and, despite our win, I left the field wondering where I now stood in the plans of the management team. I was just thinking, 'Jesus, this is going nowhere for me . . .'

Brian finally spoke to me the week of the Leinster final and said something along the lines that I was moving well, but had few enough games under my belt. I was, he said, just to keep myself right and be ready if needed. I told him of my frustration at the lack of communication the previous week, and he said he'd been trying to get different players involved and just didn't happen to get around to me.

It's remarkable how much weight I could place on a few encouraging words from that man. I felt happier that the lines of communication were open again, but I knew I wouldn't be considered for a start against Dublin. I look back at my career now and feel only absolute respect for those who managed to drive themselves relentlessly despite rarely getting into the starting fifteen.

I felt really good when I got on against the Dubs, and to finish with 0-3 from play changed my mindset again. Taggy had made a big difference off the bench too, and I sensed that both of us had now given the selectors something to think about for the All-Ireland semi-final. As we stretched away to win pulling up, I felt full of confidence. Brian offered congratulations on the field afterwards, but only in the general context of having won another Leinster title. I now had five weeks to try to reclaim his attention, albeit I knew things were different now. I might have had nine All-Irelands and eleven All-Stars, but I felt I was going to have to prove myself at every single session between now and our game with Limerick.

I'm not sure I have greater respect for another man alive than I have for Brian Cody, and there is no doubting his utterly pivotal role in my hurling career. Do I consider him a friend? Yes. But will we ever be buddy-buddy types, on the phone every second evening, chatting away for hours? No. That's not him and it's certainly not me.

After a while, not making Kilkenny's first fifteen became less of a problem in my own mind than simply not knowing where I stood. I felt communication could have been better and I told him that. Eventually.

There were certainly fewer chats between us as the dynamic of the relationship shifted. Previously, it had been relatively simple in the sense that I was always going to be selected. Now that that was no longer the case, I suppose both of us were less comfortable.

And so the mental challenge became the hardest part of 2014 for me. If anything, maybe I had become too comfortable in my relationship with management throughout my hurling career. I had had a connection with Brian that, if I'm honest, the other players didn't really have. Suddenly, that was gone and it left me feeling a strange disconnect that was new to me.

But Tommy Walsh was going through much the same thing that season, and I never heard a word of complaint from Tommy. And I've often marvelled at Aidan Fogarty, one of the most resilient characters I know. Taggy's an unbelievable fella, a terrific hurler who was Man of the Match in an All-Ireland final, was dropped for others, but dealt with it all in the most amazing way.

My career was spent largely oblivious to the frustrations of those working every bit as hard as me, but getting only snatched little pockets of game-time off the bench. In 2014, I came to understand just how psychologically difficult that role can be. I kept hoping, of course, kept driving forward, kept believing that I could break back in.

Before the All-Ireland semi-final, I'd gone well against Muckalee in the local championship and I was moving strongly at Kilkenny training. When we went away for a weekend in Carton House, I suppose the picture became clearer.

It was the morning of an A v. B game and Mick Dempsey called me in to see management. Eoin Larkin had been summoned before me. It's a funny kind of dynamic, stepping into a room with the entire management team sitting facing you at a table. Brian did all the talking.

'Look, Henry,' he said, 'we know you like to have clarity about where you stand and it's different for you this year. You've had your injuries, you've missed a lot of training. Do we still see a role for you with Kilkenny? Very much so. You still have a big role to play with this.'

This was precisely the reassurance I craved. But he continued . . .

'Look, you're not thirty any more, you've had massive injuries, it's a testament to you that you're still here sitting in front of us. But we can't guarantee anything. Today we're playing that A v. B game, you'll be in the Bs . . .'

He explained that being on the Bs didn't necessarily mean I wouldn't be starting against Limerick in the All-Ireland semi-final. He told me I was moving well and to keep it going. 'You'll be marking Brian Hogan today . . .'

None of the other lads spoke. 'Have you anything to say?' I was asked. I hadn't.

This was maybe half eleven in the morning, training was at one. I walked outside, my head a bit frazzled now. I'd been really positive for the previous few weeks but, deep down, I knew now I wouldn't be starting against Limerick.

I went out into the grounds of Carton House and just walked around for a while. When I went back in, the banter in the group was going full pelt, everyone buzzing, laughing and joking. I felt a bit of a zombie in their company, but there was a training match to play and I needed to get my head clear now.

I needed to hurl.

The A v. B match that day was a cracking game, everything Brian could have asked for: Tommy roaring and shouting, Mick Fennelly with us on the Bs, everyone just hammering into it. The Bs almost beat the As in the end and I hurled well enough, scoring three or four points. But, for some reason, I went home feeling bruised.

The Saturday week before we played Limerick, I was on the Bs again in our last proper training game and did not hurl to my usual standard. It was a dirty day in Kilkenny and, much as it pains me to admit it, my heart just wasn't in it. My overriding emotion at that time was one of growing disappointment. One moment I was thinking, 'I'm surely good enough to be starting!' The next, wondering, 'Jesus, am I?'

I rang Brian the following Monday. Maybe I was forcing the issue now, maybe it wasn't the wisest course of action to take, but I felt I had to do something.

Brian told me: 'Look, just say what you have to say now . . .' I was delighted to hear him say that. I had so much stuff I needed to get off my chest and I knew I needed to do it one-to-one. That call settled me a little. It gave me, at least, a sense of where he saw me.

The tone of the conversation was different from the one at Carton House, less formal, I suppose. Brian talked about another reason I wasn't starting: he worried about the possible implications of having to bring in a sub for me. My profile meant that taking me off in a big game would probably trigger a burst of energy from our opponents, not to mention their supporters.

'On the other hand,' he said, 'if you come on with half an hour to go, I know I can trust you to react in a positive way, to have an influence.'

I could see the logic. Our chat essentially confirmed that my days of starting for Kilkenny were at an end. Still, you keep looking for the fairy tale, don't you?

I would come on in the middle of a monsoon against Limerick and be met straight away by a welcoming shoulder. I've always hated the bullshit of a sub being hit straight away by a defender's shot when he goes in but, to be fair, there wasn't much in what Gavin O'Mahony did that day. It was just his way of saying, 'We're the big boys here today, be a good chap now and keep out of the way!'

There's an absolute compulsion to respond in these situations and I think I gave him three dunts in return. The crowd loved it and I felt, as a team, we maybe took some energy from that moment. But the first ball I got then, I was knocked backwards on to my arse, Limerick being awarded a free. There were defenders swarming all around me, roaring. Nothing especially personal, just a few letting me know they believed they had my measure.

The game had a huge intensity and, shortly after Richie Power and I came on, Limerick scored their fifth consecutive point to take a two-point lead. But from the moment Richie got us a goal, I always believed we were going to win. I hit the top of a post with a shot when Richie had been unmarked inside but, because of the conditions, I just felt I couldn't trust a fifteen-yard hand-pass off my left side. It would have been lovely to get a score in the circumstances, but there seemed a consensus afterwards that Kilkenny had taken vital energy from Power and myself coming in.

We now had four weeks to the All-Ireland final. A month to get our heads right for Tipperary.

There's no point pretending that my tenth All-Ireland medal came in the fashion I would have chosen. I wanted to be starting.

It was not what I dreamed of, and all the way through the season I put a fierce amount of pressure on myself. But I can honestly say that the vibe in the Kilkenny squad, the chemistry between young and old, was as good as I could ever remember it. So, yes, I became a bit player in the end, but I could still embrace that special sense of a group working to be the absolute best that it could be.

No question, the personal unease never fully lifted. For the drawn final, I was called down out of the stand three times before being eventually put on. Taggy had been the first forward sub in after maybe fifty minutes and, shortly afterwards, I got the signal to get ready.

I spent about five minutes warming up on the line before James McGarry told me to go back up into the stand. Soon after, another signal to get ready and – this time – maybe ten minutes spent stretching and waiting. Brian was just a few yards away, totally consumed by the game.

What could I do? Tap him on the shoulder? Start tugging at his sleeve like I used do as a child with Joe Dunphy in Ballyhale National School?

You feel as if the whole stadium is looking at you when, in reality, everyone is completely spellbound by an extraordinary game. Maybe the only people who could see me were family.

In retrospect, I could have no issue with Brian. The game was crazy, just charging along independent of logic, pattern or form-line. In those circumstances, a manager is only human if he keeps changing his mind. A forward might be having a nightmare, but just one little touch wins a stay of execution.

'Jesus, we can't take him off, he's coming into this . . .'

But there are 82,000 people in Croke Park, and you're standing there, conscious only of your own predicament. I felt almost like an old man in the end, flicking out his leg just for want of something better to do. Eventually, I made the decision myself, turned away and climbed back up into the stand.

When the third call came, there was probably a bit of impatience visible in my body language. I went down and put my helmet straight on, as if to say, 'Am I goin' on or not?'

Finally, with three minutes to go, I was sent in to full-forward with instructions to try to hold the ball up there. We were three points up as I was going in, then BANG, BANG, BANG, Tipp got three scores to draw level.

Suddenly, we were deep in crisis mode, similar to the drawn game with Galway in Leinster. I drifted out to centre-forward, desperate to get the ball in my hand. I almost did, too, but Mickey Cahill just flicked it away and in a matter of seconds 'Bubbles' O'Dwyer was lining up that monster free into the Canal-End goal.

I fully expected him to score and was just desperate to get myself into the general vicinity where Eoin Murphy's puck-out would be landing. They had to go to Hawk-Eye to establish that Bubbles's shot was fractions wide.

The final whistle, initially, left me with entirely selfish thoughts. When we'd drawn the 2012 final, I departed the field, completely pumped by the performance I'd just given. Now I was, it seemed, a three-minute man.

To be fair to the players and management, Tipp would have beaten any other team that day quite comfortably. They'd hurled out of their skin, but our lads refused to buckle. They just hung in there, kept trusting one another and, in the end, probably should have won.

Afterwards, maybe mindful of my place now, I joined the other subs – lads like Ricey, Joe Brennan and Joe Lyng – in the warm-up area, where we just pucked around, killing time. I remember Brian speaking exceptionally well in the dressing room, basically making the point that we would drive on and make sure to finish the job in the replay.

Before going home, we slipped into the Citywest Hotel in our tracksuits for dinner, a big crowd already gathered there, having bought tickets for what they hoped would be a coronation. But with a replay to prepare for, there was minimal interaction between players and supporters now. The priority was just getting fed and getting home.

Inevitably, I wondered if there might be an opening for me now. Some of the forwards hadn't gone great and the general view seemed to be that Kilkenny would have to make changes. I trained on the As the next Friday and was feeling good, but returned to the Bs the following Wednesday.

In any event, management had other priorities now. The concession of 1-28 in the drawn game pointed to big defensive fault-lines, and the backs were held back after training one night to have a meeting among themselves. I think the general consensus among them was that, because of Tipp's brilliant forward movement, no one had been entirely sure just who was marking who. That wouldn't happen again.

It was in our interests to keep things tighter and, to that end, Joey Holden and Brian Hogan made way for Pádraig Walsh and Kieran Joyce. In the forwards, John Power was coming in for Walter Walsh. I was told a week beforehand that, in the event of a change being needed, I'd be the first man in this time. This was music to my ears.

The game proved much tighter than its predecessor, and I took it upon myself to say a few words at half-time, as did Brian Hogan. I just mentioned how it reminded me of the '02 All-Ireland semi-final against Tipp with its sense that the game was there for us if we just upped things slightly.

The fact that both Hogie and I were comfortable speaking reflected just how tight the group had become. I can honestly say I don't remember a more united group hurling for Kilkenny in my time. The bond between young and old was really strong. I think it's what got us over the line.

I got on for Richie Hogan in the fifty-eighth minute and didn't manage to decorate those last twelve minutes of my inter-county career with anything especially epochal. But I did feel involved again, I did feel part of the story. Richie Power got a critical goal shortly after my introduction and, almost instantly, his younger brother, John, drilled home another.

I basically went in to centre-forward, haring around the place, just trying to make my presence felt. My final act was to set up Colin Fennelly for the last score of the game, a beautiful feeling.

At the final whistle, all the emotional uncertainty I had experienced through the year just washed away. Standing there, as the first man to win ten All-Irelands, I was struck by the scale of the journey I had travelled from those childhood nights with my brother Paul, imagining All-Irelands in the squash court at home. Those seconds, immediately after the final whistle, I will cherish for the rest of my days.

I lived the dream.

Brian Cody was a huge part of that dream. As Deirdre put it, the man 'moulded' me into the player I became. I absolutely agree with that. And his track record brooks no argument.

Look at the big calls made. In 2012, he threw Walter Walsh into an All-Ireland final replay for his Championship debut. Result? Walter wins Man of the Match. In 2014, he turned to Kieran Joyce, someone who must have been wondering if he'd ever get a start for Kilkenny again. Result? Joyce wins Man of the Match.

As we were going up the steps of the Hogan Stand to collect Liam McCarthy, I could see Deirdre behind the Ard Comhairle with Sadhbh and Henry Junior. She handed them down to me, which meant they were both with me as I lifted the cup. A perfect moment.

Down on the field after, Sadhbh became a little upset, but Henry was just lapping it all up. And there was one lovely picture taken. Tadhg Crowley's son, Tadhg Junior, had been running around with this black-and-amber dragon hat on and, in his excitement, left it on the ground.

I picked it up and put it on Henry's head. It was a beautiful moment.

Up in the players' bar afterwards, I had a beer with Eoin Kelly, who was in two minds now whether he'd be back with Tipp again. Eoin's of much as the same vintage as me, and hadn't been used this time as much he'd hoped to be. I knew exactly where he was coming from but – at that moment – our emotions were on different galaxies.

The guessing-game about my future as an inter-county hurler started with that final whistle, continuing all the way to a Wednesday in March. I wasn't an enthusiastic participant and, at times, it made me feel deeply uncomfortable.

But the truth was, I couldn't decide. I said I'd wait until Shamrocks' season was over and, of course, that ran all the way to St Patrick's Day. On one level, this proved a godsend. It kept the decision at arm's length and, meanwhile, allowed me get in some proper game-time.

But it also meant the question kept getting asked, and I had to keep dodging a path around it.

Maybe people imagined that, through this time, there was a constant line of communication between Brian and me. But that's not how things work. Brian's style in these circumstances is to give players space, to allow them to focus fully on their clubs.

The day after Shamrocks' Leinster club final win against Kilcormac-Killoughey, I travelled to Dublin for the Irish Youth Foundation Sports Awards in what used to be the Burlington Hotel. Brian and his wife, Elsie, were guests at the same event and we chatted beforehand about pretty much everything bar hurling.

When I was called up to receive an award, what do you imagine the Master of Ceremonies, Shane O'Donoghue, asked me about? Retirement, naturally. As I scrambled for a diplomatic answer, my eyes briefly caught Brian sitting at the table, rubbing his chin in amusement.

I'm sure he was thinking, 'Well, Henry, what are you going to say here?'

Standing there on stage, a microphone in hand, completely tongue-tied, I delivered the blandest response I could summon, only to be asked twice more what my intentions were. Brian and I had discussed nothing. The crowd was giggling, the Cody chin was being rubbed and I was willing the ground to swallow me whole.

It was a winter of retirements. Tommy Walsh had told me of his intentions before the All-Ireland final replay, but when his message landed on WhatsApp, I felt quite emotional. He'd been the heart and soul of the group for so long, a status that I think was reflected in the decision of the whole panel to take a bus out to his house the Tuesday after the replay.

Brian Hogan was gone, Taggy was gone, David Herity was gone.

Then a 7 a.m. message from JJ Delaney one day: 'JJ has left the group.' That one I never saw coming. No one did, I suspect.

When did I decide to join the ranks of the retired? Well, I'd already set up a WhatsApp group for 'The Old Lads', hoping we'd maybe be able to get together for a drink over Christmas. They were quick to remind me that, not having retired yet myself, I didn't qualify to meet them.

Would it shock you to know that, right down to 5.30 p.m. on the Monday when I rang Brian to say I was going, there were still little doubts in my head? My time with Kilkenny had meant more to me than I will ever really be able to express, and it felt a little scary after sixteen seasons to be pulling the shutters down on a way of life.

I'd gone to Brian's house the previous Friday morning for a conversation we both knew we needed to have. We'd had a really warm chat about anything and everything.

No question, he has a ruthless streak, he has all those characteristics that I found really difficult to deal with in my last year. But you know, that's the peculiar beauty of it. The very qualities that I struggled with in 2014 were the qualities that made me.

I believe that his greatness as a manager comes from an ability to always create the right environment. He had tough calls to make with me at the end, and I can see now that it would have been a betrayal of everything he stood for if he hadn't made them. Bottom line, I'm massively indebted to him for my success as a hurler just as, I imagine, he feels on some level indebted to me for his success as a manager.

That Friday morning, he essentially suggested that I reflect upon my decision over the weekend but, deep down, I suppose I knew there was only one wise way to go here.

So it didn't feel strange making that call in the end. I was comfortable with it – albeit I knew my life would never be the same again. 'Right, Brian, I've come to my decision,' I said. 'I'm going to retire.'

And it felt as if I'd just launched myself off a diving board a mile high in the sky.

★

I suppose a GAA life almost always begins and ends with the club, and mine will be no different.

Approaching Christmas of 2013, Shamrocks were on the lookout for a new manager, my brother Tommy having decided not to continue. We'd won a county title during his first year in charge but had gone out at the semi-final stage during his second, and he just felt a new voice would be no harm. A committee was set up to identify Tommy's successor.

As much as possible, I try to stay out of the politics of running the club, but I knew that we were struggling to get the right person and I wanted to help. I made a few phone calls to different people, just testing the water to see who might be available. One of those I rang was Tomás Mullally, who had just guided Mount Leinster Rangers of Carlow to an unlikely Leinster club title.

I knew he wouldn't be in a position to make any immediate commitment, given that they had an All-Ireland semi-final looming; but if there was a possibility of him coming on board by the end of March, it seemed a call worth making.

Tomás, understandably, felt he couldn't do it, and about a month into the process we were still struggling to find the right man. For all our honours won as a team, I think there was a sense in Kilkenny that our best days were now behind us. To put it bluntly, Shamrocks were seen as a team that had gone soft.

Then I heard that my old Fitzgibbon Cup sparring partner, Andy Maloney, might be leaving Ballygunner and I decided to put in a call. There was talk of Andy being keen to link up with Colm Bonnar, so I became a kind of middleman, tipping the committee off that he might be available, then ringing Andy himself to tell him he could be getting a phone call.

Discussions went well, and by the middle of January Andy and Colm were confirmed as our new management team. I was delighted. I knew they'd be very professional and that Andy wouldn't be over-playing our personal friendship in the dressing room. We needed someone to push us hard now, me included.

That sense of us as a group in decline became a source of motivation now. On a personal level, I can't deny I felt I had my own point to prove. By the time we would come to the business end of the county championship, I was incredibly hungry for game-time.

About three weeks after the All-Ireland final replay, we played an internal match and I was marking Mick Fennelly. Now I should say that Mick had been hurt in the replay against Tipp and didn't train for those three weeks, but that evening I scored eight or nine points from play at centre-forward. I was flying.

The following week, we played Danesfort and I got 0-6 from play, some of the scores off my county colleague, Paul Murphy. I felt there was a freedom to my hurling now, as if stepping out of the pressure cooker of county had given me a new lease of life.

Maybe my poorest game of the campaign would be the county final against defending champions Clara. It didn't matter, though. TJ shot the lights out with 0-10 to give us our sixth title in nine years, our fifteenth in total, and it was wonderful to see the emotion on some of the club's old-stagers that evening in Nowlan Park.

But there's always a sting in the tail to winning a Kilkenny county medal in November, and this time it came in the form of a Leinster semi-final against Kilmacud Crokes at Parnell Park the following Sunday. These games always make me nervous. They mean you don't really get the opportunity to savour a county win, although some of the younger lads especially had done their best, spending two or three nights on the beer.

We came through that, and next up was Kilcormac-Killoughey in the Leinster final, a game played on one of the worst days of the year. It went to extra time and I took a lot of pleasure from the fact that, even approaching thirty-six, I got stronger the longer the game went on.

The big thing was that I was injury-free now, hurling without physical or psychological discomfort. It seemed everyone kept asking me about Kilkenny, but our victory over the Offaly champions effectively bought me the space I needed to postpone any decision about my inter-county future. Shamrocks would now be hurling into February at least.

That presented its difficulties too, mind. The Galway champion-ship had been delayed and it was a week after our Leinster win that Gort emerged as our All-Ireland semi-final opponents. By that stage I was trying to take a little step back from hurling and, though I taped Gort's victory over Portumna, I just watched the start and finish.

We took a little break from training through Christmas, then set-tled into a few challenge games. One of those was against Cork at WIT and, though I tweaked a hamstring after about twenty min-utes, we played exceptionally well as a team against the likes of Mark Ellis, Aidan Walsh, Séamus Harnedy, Pat Horgan and Paudie O'Sullivan.

By now I was back in that bubble of feeling anything was possible again and, sure enough, I scored 0-5 from play as we beat the Galway champions comfortably.

This, I will admit, gave me cause to wonder if maybe I might just have another year in me with Kilkenny. Just one problem. In the Gort game, I took a heavy knock to the shoulder that – it would later emerge – ripped tendons. The diagnosis was late, essentially because I didn't want the scan taken. I knew there was something wrong but didn't want anything jeopardizing what, most probably, would be my final game in Croke Park.

In the dream, I would have a stormer against Kilmallock, then ride off into the sunset in whatever direction I chose. That just wasn't to be, though. I can't say the shoulder restricted me in the final, but it impeded my preparation and, at that level, you have to be a hundred per cent.

The sound of the final whistle brought that beautiful realization that Ballyhale were top of the mountain again and that we had crossed it with the likes of Aidan Cummins and myself, kindergarten partners thirty years earlier, still wearing the colours.

Our celebration dinner that night was in Carrolls of Knocktopher, and we brought the whole family down with us. It was lovely, seeing all the familiar faces beaming with a realization that our tiny village was back, top of the pile again. The 'soft' boys of South Kilkenny.

Deirdre and I found a little snug and just settled there, taking the moment in, reflecting upon what had been achieved at the end of a remarkable season.

Acknowledgements

A GAA life is probably unique in the degree of celebrity it confers on people who live otherwise normal existences.

Hurling has, I suppose, given me that status in Ireland even if I've always guarded my privacy pretty carefully. By and large, there's a lovely, respectful way to how Irish people interact with publicly known figures.

Writing this book was a project I pursued with some deliberation because I wanted the end product to be true to me and my experiences, not simply some kind of cut-and-paste regurgitation of details already known.

I've been blessed in so many ways both inside and outside the game, and I hope those responsible are given due credit between the covers of my story now.

There are so many people I need to thank, not least my own family: my parents, Henry and Mai; my sisters, Aileen, Helena and Cecilia; and my brothers, Tommy, John and Paul.

A word too for Deirdre's parents, Michael and Mary, and all the extended O'Sullivan family.

It goes without saying that I owe a massive debt to Brian Cody, not to mention all of the management teams that have worked alongside him since '99. The same goes for every last Kilkenny player with whom I've shared dressing rooms and wonderful memories in that time. Thank you too to the backroom staff, especially the physios and Dr Tadhg Crowley, whose workload must have lightened considerably on my retirement!

Thanks to the surgeons whose talents always got me back on a hurling field, no matter the odds presented by an assortment of serious injuries.

My greatest childhood dream was always to hurl with Ballyhale

Shamrocks in Croke Park, and it was wonderful to achieve that again so memorably last March. Sincere thanks then to all the Ballyhale hurlers (those retired and those I continue to hurl with) for memories that will never be lost, and to the various management teams that helped us accumulate them.

Thanks to the real founder of the faith in my case, the former principal of Ballyhale National School, Joe Dunphy.

Thanks to Brother Damien Brennan, a truly inspiring man whose influence in the latter stages of my county career will be apparent to anyone who has read this book.

Thanks to my employers, Bank of Ireland, particularly the colleagues who have been so supportive of me through the days when juggling work and hurling became challenging.

Sincere thanks to Vincent Hogan for helping tease out the different threads to my story and putting them into a coherent shape. He is a remarkable sportswriter, and I'm grateful to him for his hard work and patience over the years of this project. Thanks also to Vincent's wife, Geraldine, and his family.

Thanks to Ray McManus, of Sportsfile, and to John McIlwaine, for their brilliant photographs.

Thanks to Michael McLoughlin and all at Penguin Ireland for the high-quality production of my autobiography that, I hope, will add to the readers' enjoyment.

And, finally, thanks to hurling people everywhere for the respect you've always shown me through my career. I hope you know that it was reciprocated.

Henry Shefflin
July 2015

Index